NEW NEW MEDIA

PENGUIN ACADEMICS

NEW NEW MEDIA

PAUL LEVINSON
Fordham University

Allyn & Bacon

Boston Columbus Indianapolis New York San Francisco Upper Saddle River
Amsterdam Cape Town Dubai London Madrid Milan Munich Paris Montreal Toronto
Delhi Mexico City Sao Paulo Sydney Hong Kong Seoul Singapore Taipei Tokyo

Acquisitions Editor: Jeanne Zalesky
Assistant Editor: Megan Lentz
Marketing Manager: Wendy Gordon
Production Editor: Pat Torelli
Manufacturing Buyer: Debbie Rossi
Editorial Production and Composition Services: Elm Street Publishing Services/Integra Software
    Services Pvt. Ltd.
Cover Designer: Kristina Mose-Libon

Library of Congress Cataloging-in-Publication Data

Levinson, Paul.
    New new media / Paul Levinson.
        p. cm.
    Includes bibliographical references and index.
    ISBN 978-0-205-67330-8
    1. Social media.   2. Computer network resources.   3. User-generated content.   I. Title.
    ZA4150.L48 2009
    302.23'1—dc22

                                                                                    2009017972

10 9 8 7 6 5 4 3 2   RRD-VA 13 12 11 10 09

Allyn & Bacon
is an imprint of

www.pearsonhighered.com

ISBN-10:   0-205-67330-9
ISBN-13: 978-0-205-67330-8

To Tina, Simon, and Molly, always new to me.

contents

CHAPTER 3 YOUTUBE 58

CHAPTER 4   WIKIPEDIA   84

preface and acknowledgments

A new book is sometimes an expression of ideas that its author has been thinking about, researching and developing for decades. Other books are just the opposite—an embodiment of insights that came to the author just before writing the book and drove the writing of every page. Given that some of the media considered in "New New Media"—such as YouTube and Twitter—did not even exist in 2004, this book is clearly a recent inspiration. But the themes addressed in "New New Media"—most importantly, the impact of media that make all of us producers as well as consumers of news, opinion and entertainment—also draw upon fundamentals of human communication that have been with us for millennia.

The notion of new new media first occurred to me late in the summer of 2007. In those days, I was Chair of the Department of Communication and Media Studies at Fordham University, where I still enjoy being a professor, and Lance Strate was my Associate Chair for graduate studies. Lance and I were discussing why our department's courses in "new media" were suffering from low enrollments, and it dawned on me that these courses, despite their appellation, were focused on topics that were old: how to use HTML, the general impact of the Web and email and so forth. These subjects were "new" in the mid-1990s. In contrast, in the summer of 2007, students and people at large were eager to talk about blogging, Facebook and YouTube, and we had noticed many a student logging on to a social medium during classes in the prior spring and fall semesters. I said to Lance that we should begin offering courses in *new* new media. The following spring I taught a graduate course that examined how the 2008 presidential campaign in America was being fueled by blogging, Facebook and YouTube.

Lance Strate played another formative role in this book. In the fall of 2007, he gave my name to Aron Keesbury, an acquisitions editor who was looking for new books for CQ Press. I pitched several books to Aron, and he seized upon "New New Media." I sent him a provisional table of contents, and, although we were not able to come to mutually agreeable contractual terms, Aron deserves credit for seeing the need for this book and thanks for providing stimulating conversation about its topics.

In the same week that I met Aron, Charles Sterin came to Fordham University to videotape me, all day, for the "Mass Media for the Digital Millennium" multimedia textbook he was writing and producing for Pearson books. Several months later, Chuck suggested that his editor, Jeanne Zalesky, might be interested in "New New Media."

Jeanne has been an ideal editor. An author writes a book, and an editor commends it to a publisher and in turn guides the publisher in commending the book to the world. Jeanne's spirited and savvy championing of "New New Media" has been invaluable in the publication of this book. Thanks as well to Danielle Urban of Elm Street Publishing Services for fine project management.

In my dual capacity as author and professor, every book that I write—even my science fiction—is to some degree indebted to the inspiration of my students, now and over the years, to the questions they asked and the stimulus they provided. But "New New Media" is especially a product of the undergraduate classes I taught at Fairleigh Dickinson University in the 1970s and 1980s, the graduate classes I taught at the New School for Social Research and for the Connected Education Online Program in the 1980s and 1990s and, most significantly, the undergraduate and graduate courses I have been teaching at Fordham University the past decade. I cannot possibly thank every student by name. But two, in particular—Mike Plugh and Yulia Golobokova—made contributions so valuable that their names appear not only here in my acknowledgments but in the pages of this book.

Thanks, as well, to several practitioners of new new media who provided valuable insights and information—Barna Donovan, Emon Hassan, Ken Hudson and Mark Molaro.

One of the themes of "New New Media" that I have been exploring for years is how digital and mobile communication have been blending business and personal, family life. My wife, Tina Vozick, has been an indispensable discussant and reader of this book prior to publication—in fact, the only reader of the complete book prior to its reaching my editor's desk—and her work on Wikipedia was especially helpful to me in the writing of that chapter. Our children, Simon and Molly, now adults, have also been a continuing resource. Simon introduced me to Facebook in 2004, and Molly was the one who first alerted me to the degree to which people her age, in their early 20s, watch television online.

That was several years ago, and "New New Media" is a snapshot and analysis of the extraordinary revolution in communication, and thus our lives, that has occurred since then and is still occurring almost daily. Consider, for example, that just about a month ago the first tweet was sent from an astronaut in outer space....

PAUL LEVINSON
NEW YORK CITY
JULY 2009

CHAPTER 1

Why "New New" Media?

"NEW NEW MEDIA" IS ABOUT THE ADVENT AND IMPACT OF MEDIA newer than "new" media—as different from the classic new media of email and Web sites as those new media are different from old media such as newspapers and television. New new media are so new that few of them had a major place in our world five years ago. Several did not exist four years ago. Students are conversant and expert in most of them, because they use them all the time. Students look at YouTube videos and send and receive twitters or tweets on iPhones and BlackBerrys while teachers are lecturing. But few of these new new media are discussed in classrooms or at any length or detail in textbooks nor in many other kinds of books, either. "New New Media" seeks to remedy that understandable omission.

And what, exactly, do I mean by "new new media"? The current roster is listed in the chapter titles of this book: blogging, YouTube, Wikipedia, Digg, MySpace, Facebook, Twitter, Second Life and podcasts. But what are the distinguishing characteristics of these media, behind their names, that lead to a designation of them as "new new media," as distinct from just "new" media?

Blogs are the oldest form of new new media and embody their defining principles most clearly. These include:

Every Consumer Is a Producer: Anyone reading a blog can start a blog nearly instantly. A blog on MSNBC.com or on NYTimes.com is an example not of new new media but of new media. Those blogs are on the Web, which makes them new media. But their readers at most have a secondary, indirect impact on the words in the blog—they may be able to comment on the blog, but they cannot write directly to it or create a new blog post. In contrast, a blog created by a reader, in which the reader has total control, is one of the hallmarks of new new media, in which readers become writers and viewers become producers.

You Can't Fake Being Nonprofessional: Blogs in the new new media world can be written anytime, night or day, at the drop of a hat or an event. Although money can be made from these blogs, earning an income is usually not their main purpose, and they gain authenticity in significant part because their authors are not working for a newspaper or broadcast medium (old media) or even an online component of a newspaper or broadcast medium (new media).

Choose Your Medium: People have a diversity of talent, not equally distributed. An unclear writer will not make a very good blogger. But he or she may have a perfect voice for podcasting. Another person may have superior editing in contrast to writing skills. Wikipedia would be a new medium better suited for people with such editing skills. Other people may excel at short bursts of text rather than longer disquisitions. Twitter would be their medium. From the point of view of the creator, the world of new new media offers a menu of media avenues. You can walk down however many you like and stay with the ones that work best for you.

You Get What You Don't Pay For: New new media are always free to the consumer and sometimes to the producer. Amazon and iTunes therefore would be examples not of new new media but new media, because the books and other items on Amazon, and the songs on iTunes, are for sale. In contrast, a video with a song on the new new medium YouTube is free. Blog host sites such as Blogspot and Wordpress are free to the blogs' producers. Typepad charges them a fee; Movable Type and Live Journal offer both options. Libsyn charges for its podcast hosting; Mevio and Talkshoe are free. But all of these blog and podcast sites are free to readers and listeners. Note, however, that being free to the consumer does not mean the creator cannot earn income from the new new medium through placement of ads on blogs, podcasts and via other modes of monetization. And note, also, that free new new media proprietary systems make money—sometimes not enough money—in different ways. Wikipedia relies on funding drives (much like the Public Broadcasting Service); Twitter on venture capital; Digg, MySpace and Facebook earn money from advertising. YouTube runs ads, but as of April 2009 was reported losing $1.65 million a day (Silversmith, 2009), fortunately not that large an amount to its owner, Google, which saw revenue of nearly $22 billion in 2008.

Competitive and Mutually Catalytic: As I detailed in "Human Replay: A Theory of the Evolution of Media" (1979; see also "The Soft Edge," 1997), media compete with one another for our time and patronage and live or die much as living organisms in the Darwinian biological world. But as in the natural world, where organisms live in symbiotic relationships—bees feed on plants and pollinate them, and we enjoy the honey—media in general, and new new media in particular, not only compete with one another but work to each other's benefit. A post on my blog with an embedded YouTube video is automatically sent to Twitter, which generates a one-line message with the blog's title, first line and link, which in turn shows up on widgets or special applications I may place on Facebook and MySpace. Each of these new new media supports the others, even as they compete for our attention. Further, new new media are similarly competitive and synergistic with older media. Bloggers take readers away from books and viewers away from television but then write books and appear on television themselves.

More Than Search Engines and Email: Google and Yahoo are the nervous systems of the Web, the online equivalents of Microsoft Explorer, Firefox and other systems on our computers that we use to traverse the Internet. Email and searching are essential to new new media, but they are not new new media themselves. Web-based money systems such as PayPal also can be crucial to new new media but similarly work as their service systems rather than as new new media in their own right. Although Google, Yahoo and PayPal are free—and users can customize the operation of their email, searching and, in the case of PayPal, banking procedures—these systems cannot be fundamentally created by their users in the way that readers can be writers and editors of Wikipedia or can choose what to put on the front page of Digg. In the same way, although group members can write to Yahoo message boards, the moderators of these groups have complete, old-media control over the discussions, with the power to remove any given message. Applications such as Google's AdSense can play specific supporting roles for new new media—in the case of AdSense, earning money from blogs—and we will examine the value and impact of those applications for the new new media they support.

New new media do require underlying platforms beyond the control of their consumer-producers—whether blogging systems, YouTube formats, Wikipedia editing procedures, etc.—but the ratio of user input to a fixed system is much more in favor of the user in new new media than in infrastructures such as Google and Yahoo.

We will look, in this book, at how these principles guide and animate new new media.

New New Media Encompass Prior New Media Principles

One of the defining characteristics of new media—clear since they arose over a decade ago in the mid-1990s—is that people can use, enjoy and benefit from them on the user's rather than the medium's timetable, once the content has been posted online. This offered and still offers a big advantage over having to wait for the delivery of your morning newspaper, for a radio station to play your favorite song or for the weekly broadcast of a series you like on television. Those "media by appointment" were and are characteristic of all old media, and the freeing of users from some of this appointment bondage by TiVo and DVR represents an evolution of television from old to new medium.

New new media give its users the same control of when and where to get text, sound and audio-visual content as provided by new media. Indeed, new new media package all the advantages that new media provide over old media. But new new media do more. Thus, unlike with new media, where the user has to wait for the content to be produced by someone else—whether a book to be ordered on Amazon or a song to be downloaded on iTunes—the true or fully empowered new new media user also has the option of producing content and consuming content produced by hundreds of millions of other new new media consumer-producers.

Why "New New" Rather Than Social Media, Screen Arts, or Web 2.0 or 3.0?

New new media are intrinsically social, and, indeed, whether the readers and commenters on a blog, the reader/editors on Wikipedia or the activist groups on Facebook, the social element is not only indispensable to new new media but provides the human dynamic that makes all new new media tick.

But older, just plain new and old media had significant social components as well—ranging from group emails to online bulletin boards and forums. Indeed, what is a bookstore reading group if not a social medium, and books—not to mention in-person meetings—are the oldest social media of all.

So the social aspect of new new media, though crucial, is not unique enough to new new media to warrant our use of the terms interchangeably. In addition, other primary elements of new new media—such as the consumer becoming a producer—can be easily practiced individually, not socially, as in writing a blog post or recording a podcast.

The University of Michigan offers undergraduate and graduate programs in Screen Arts and Cultures, which examine media that flourish on movie, television and computer screens. Blogging, YouTube and most new new media are found on screens, so would "digital screen arts" be an adequate name for the media we will consider in this book? The following problems would make it not very useful: (1) no distinction between "new" and "new new" digital screen arts; (2) although blogging, YouTube and even Wikipedia editing and writing might be considered "art" forms, the designation does not fit as well for Facebook and MySpace (unless we want to consider online relationships an interactive "art"); and (3) most important, podcasting and purely audio new new media usually come to us via earbuds not screens.

What about Web 2.0? The new new media we will examine in this book are certainly part of a Web that goes beyond its initial mass breakthrough in the mid-1990s and would no doubt fit better in a Web 2.0 rather than just Web or Web 1.0 designation. But why not Web 2.5 or Web 3.0, names for new versions of Web life and business that have also become common? John Markoff of The New York Times used the term "Web 3.0" in 2006, and Wikipedia lists, among its defining characteristics, "mobile Internet access and mobile devices"—after indicating that the definition of "Web 3.0 is highly speculative" and "yet to be fully realized." But Internet access from mobile devices has been commonplace since the introduction of the iPhone in the summer of 2007. So when we log on to MySpace or watch a YouTube video via our iPhones, are we in Web 2.0 or 3.0?

And that's precisely the problem with numbers: Unlike words, they have no semantic content and therefore convey no meaning, other than a comparison with something before or after but with no clear indication of the basis for that comparison. In contrast, new new media tell us the following: Just as the term "new media" described life and work on the Web very different from traditional or old media (the difference between email and mailing a letter or reading anything online versus in a book or newspaper), so too does the term "new new media" describe life and work on the Web very different from "new media" (the difference between reading an article on Wikipedia, which you can easily edit, versus reading an essay on CNN's public Web page).

And the use of "new new" is not without precedent. William Greider titled his September 16, 2005, post-Katrina article in The Nation "A New New Deal," and Time magazine picked up this appellation to describe Barack Obama's plans for America in economic crisis on its November 24, 2008, cover (the Time cover, just for the record, appeared after I had almost finished writing this book).

Categories of New New Media

New new media come in a plethora of names—just look at the names for blog host sites in the preceding section "You Get What You Don't Pay For"—as well as in more general categories such as "social media." Let's try to clarify this a bit and see the ways in which new new media relate to one another, based on the services they provide and the way they provide them:

Print, Audio, Audio-Visual, Photographic: The written word plays a role in all new new media, if only in the form of captions and titles for photographs and videos. But written words are the primary mode of communication in blogging, Wikipedia, Digg, MySpace, Facebook and Twitter. (These new new media of course also may have images, audio tracks and videos.) Audio-visual media in the form of videos characterize YouTube and, in a very different sense, Second Life, which consists of moving, virtual avatars through which users can speak. Podcasting is purely audio (in contrast to vidcasting, which is audio-visual), and Flickr and Photobucket store photographs and other images.

News: News pertains to the purpose, not the media form, of the new new medium. Although most new new media have some sort of news content, Wikipedia, Digg and blogging in general would be the leading examples of new new media whose primary purpose is to inform. YouTube contains many newsworthy videos and indeed has become a vibrant, alternate form of news—as in Obama's Presidential YouTube chats. Facebook and MySpace convey news, among many other things, and the same is the case for Twitter.

Social Media: All new new media are inherently social—commenting on a blog or about a video is a social activity—but several new new media are primarily social in that their main purpose is to connect people. Facebook and MySpace are the leading examples, along with Twitter, where short, one-line posts encourage people to tell their friends what they are doing at any given time.

General vs. Specific Systems: Blogging, podcasting, vidcasting and social media are examples of general new new media applications, which can and do exist or "live" on sites devoted solely or completely to the blogging or podcasting application, or on specific proprietary sites such as MySpace, which provide blogging, social media and other new new media opportunities. Specific systems such as YouTube, Wikipedia and Digg are primarily devoted to just one application: videos (YouTube), encyclopedic information (Wikipedia), and news headlines and links (Digg).

Politics and Entertainment: Given the democratization of new new media production, which enables any consumer to become a producer, it is not surprising that new new media are devoted to food preferences, gardening, pets, self-help, finances—to even more subjects than can be found on a newsstand in a big city or a magazine rack in a big bookstore. Indeed, the "even more" is a distinguishing feature of new new media, since, as we saw previously, production is almost as easy as reading and viewing in new new media and often just as free. To keep this book to manageable length, however, we will look at two dominant subjects of new new media—subjects addressed daily, hourly or even more often in social media discussions, in news media, and in print, audio and audio-visual venues. First, given the election of Barack Obama as president in 2008 and his campaign's reliance on new new media ranging from blogging to Facebook, Digg and YouTube, we could not consider the advent of new new media without considering its political impact and implications. Indeed, as I often point out, Obama likely will be known not only as the author of the "New New Deal" in economics but the deft applier of new new media in his politics (see my blog post "Not Just New New Deal, New New Media," 2008). The other focus of new new media, which is unavoidable and therefore will be a mainstay of this book, is their impact on the presentation and appreciation of entertainment, more specifically, television. As the Writers Guild of America's strike in 2007–2008 made clear, the Internet in general has become a key venue for the public's viewing of television. (My daughter Molly, in her early twenties, watches far more television on the Web than on her television set.) Blogs and social media have also become prime vehicles of media criticism and reviews of what we see on television, as well as places in which viewers can easily discuss what they just or recently saw. In so doing, these new new media have changed the nature of television, just as they did the nature of politics in the 2008 presidential campaign.

New New Media and Governmental Control: One problem that new new, new, and old media share is how to operate without government censorship or at least a minimum amount of governmental control. The old media of the press struggled to break free of the royal printer model, in which the monarch owned the press. Here in the United States, the First Amendment was an attempt to make sure that control was not reasserted in our new democracy. But broadcast media have repeatedly come into conflict with the Federal Communications Commission in the United States, and the Communications Decency Act of 1996 was an unsuccessful attempt to exert some of this control on the Web (see Levinson, "The Flouting of the First Amendment," 2005, and Levinson, 1997, for details). It was hoped that new new media might be free of the worst of these constraints, as the Internet is not a "public airwave." But as we will see in this book, bloggers have been denied First Amendment rights accorded to print and broadcast journalists in the United States, YouTube was shut down for two hours in Pakistan by its government (Malkin, 2008), and Wikipedia was temporarily banned in the United Kingdom over concern about an album cover displayed on the online encyclopedia deemed to be child pornography (Kirk, 2008; Raphael, 2008). Pakistan was a dictatorship at the time of its banning of YouTube, but the United States and the United Kingdom are democracies, which indicates that the problem of censorship of new new media is by no means limited to nondemocratic countries. New new media may be democratizing agents of change, but that does not mean that democratic societies are always their friends.

Microblogging and Blogging: As an example of a significant categorization that might seem inconsequential but is not, consider the difference between the short microblogs on Twitter or status reports on Facebook and MySpace—which consist of just a handful of words—and blogs of "normal" length, which usually are posted in one or more paragraphs. This difference in length turns out to be important and even profound, because the short bursts make for much more personal communications. And, indeed, length is an important factor in new new media such as YouTube, which generally limits its videos to not more than 10 minutes, and on Wikipedia, where debates about what is the proper length for an article and what is a "stub" rage every day among the reader/editors.

Hardware vs. Software—iPhone, BlackBerry, Laptop: As a last example, for now, about how new new media can be characterized, we will consider in this book the hardware that brings new new media to us—are we reading a blog, watching a YouTube video, or looking up a famous or not-so-famous person on Wikipedia on an iPhone, a laptop or a desktop? Mobile media especially cater to social media such as Twitter and Facebook and their appetite for updates sent over their systems on a moment's notice, at any time.

The upshot of all of this categorization or taxonomy—its use to us as students of new new media—is that we can learn a lot about a new new medium by noting the categories in which it fits. Facebook, for example, is a primarily print and social medium, which traffics in entertainment, politics and news in primarily microblogging-length posts, and works on both mobile and desktop hardware. In contrast, Wikipedia, though also primarily print, is not primarily social—meaning its main purpose is not to meet and interact with other people but to write and edit the encyclopedia. It deals mostly with news and facts, has little to do with microblogging, and, given the seriousness and attention needed to write and edit its articles, is most likely addressed by people in homes and offices rather than on the road.

Speed in New New Media Evolution Not Only in Software but Hardware

The speed with which the above new new media systems have become available has been matched—and indeed propelled and made possible—by equivalent leaps in hardware, or the equipment on which new new media live in the hands of consumers. The advent of the iPhone in July 2007, a cellphone that connects fully and easily to the Web, is the hardware event that most marks and typifies the new new media revolution. But there are many other markers.

Consider, for example, the different cellphones that James Bond uses in "Casino Royale," from late in 2006, and "Quantum of Solace," in late 2008. Wikipedia ("List of James Bond gadgets," 2009) describes Bond's Sony Ericsson K800 in the 2006 movie as a "cellphone with sophisticated GPS." It also had a powerful megapixel digital camera. In contrast, Bond wields a Sony Ericsson C902 in the 2008 movie. The 102-point jump in the serial number gives 007 "a built-in identification imager, capable of compiling a composite facial image of a potential suspect even when the person being photographed is looking to the side" and the capacity to "receive information immediately regarding the suspect as it is also tied into the MI6 data mainframe." That last phrase is key to a new new media world, in which mobile devices, whether iPhones, BlackBerrys or similar devices, are appendages and controllers of the vast array of images, videos, text and all information stored, manipulated and transmitted on the Web.

The Prime Methodology: Learning by Doing

Most of the sources cited in this book are articles on the Web, for the simple reason that most current books that seek to address new new media, by whatever name, are out of date—even if published in 2008. "Mousepads, Shoe Leather, and Hope: Lessons from the Howard Dean Campaign for the Future of Internet Politics" (Teachout & Streeter, et al., 2008), for example, has no listing in its index for Wikipedia, Twitter or Digg; Facebook gets mentioned on just one page; YouTube on one page; and MySpace on three. But email is discussed on more than 35 pages. The book, in other words, is more interested in new media (email) than new new media (Wikipedia, etc.). Many of the new new media we will consider in the following pages did not exist at the time of Howard Dean's unsuccessful campaign for the 2004 Democratic nomination for president. Wikipedia did exist but in a much younger, untested form. But understandably and most likely, the authors of the essays in "Mousepads," writing in 2006 and 2007, had little reason to think that new new media would be important enough in the 2008 election to extensively discuss them—unlike the new media at Howard Dean's disposal in 2004.

"Millennial Makeover" (Winograd & Hais, 2008)—as we would expect based upon its subtitle, "MySpace, YouTube, and the Future of American Politics"—does have extensive treatments of MySpace and YouTube, as well as Facebook. Wikipedia is also mentioned but not Digg or Twitter. Barack Obama is discussed on 15 of 267 pages (he appears on just one page in "Mousepads"), but Ron Paul, who ran unsuccessfully for the Republican presidential nomination but had more stories than did Obama on Digg's front pages for months in late 2007 to early 2008, has no mention in "Millennial Makeover." Of course not—the author's preface is dated August 2007, which is more than a decade ago, in terms of the pace and impact of new new media evolution, from January 2009, the time I am writing this.

"The Huffington Post Complete Guide to Blogging" was published in December 2008, and its examples of blog posts by Gary Hart, Alec Baldwin, Arianna Huffington herself and other notables are as recent as August 2008. The book provides excellent, brief introductions to blog platforms, how to keep track of the number of readers of a blog, how to make money from blogs and many of the subjects covered in more depth in Chapter 2 of "New New Media." But in addition to being a handbook rather than a sustained analysis, the "Complete Guide to Blogging" offers no discussion of Wikipedia, MySpace or indeed, apropos the title, of any new new media other than blogging, and no consideration of the crucial role of blogging and the online world in the final months of the 2008 presidential campaign or the time between Barack Obama's election and his inauguration as president on January 20, 2009.

Fortunately, all media on the Web—even old-fashioned, editorially driven articles—can instantly report and analyze new developments, in any area, including politics and new new media. But beyond the use of the Web rather than books as a primary resource, the "research" conducted for this book is consistent with the reader becoming a producer in new new media, and with the American pragmatic philosopher John Dewey's principle (e.g., Dewey, 1925) that we learn best by practicing, working in or doing the activity that we study. For, indeed, the prime source of much of the information in this book will be what I have learned in my excursions—my work as a writer, producer and publicist—in all the new new media we will consider here. There is, of course, always the possibility that my, or any individual researcher's, experience as a practitioner may not be representative of the world's at large. Where relevant, I have thus noted where my status as an already well-published author and professor may have colored my experiences as a new new media practitioner and what I learned from those experiences. And the citations from other sources about the subjects considered in this book will also serve as a check on the veracity of my own program of researching this book by "doing" the new new media.

Here is a brief list of initiations of my new new media experiences:

I joined Facebook in the fall of 2004 on the advice of my son, Simon, who was a student at Harvard (where Facebook began), and on the strength of my .edu account at Fordham University, where I was and still am a professor. In those days, only people with .edu email addresses could join Facebook.

Facebook has long since changed that requirement, and, indeed, one of the hallmarks of all new new media is that anyone can join, play or work on them. I joined MySpace in May 2005 but did not start participating there until the publication of my most recent science fiction novel, "The Plot to Save Socrates," in February 2006. I put up my first blog post on MySpace that month. I had two reasons for participating on MySpace: researching for the purpose of writing about it and promoting my novel. This dual purpose points to one of the other characteristics of new new media: their speed, and our ability to go from one system to another, allows and even encourages multitasking. As William James (1890, p. 462), another pragmatic American philosopher and psychologist, noted back in the 19th century, our brains are wired to make sense out of the "great blooming, buzzing confusion" of the world.

I've been appearing on the old medium of national cable and network television since my appearance on Jesse Ventura's short-lived program on MSNBC in October 2003, and I began uploading video segments of my various appearances to YouTube in August 2006. I also discovered, that month, that articles had been posted about me and "The Plot to Save Socrates" on Wikipedia, and that led me to join it. I soon wrote Wikipedia articles on subjects and people ranging from Village Voice reporter and Pulitzer Prize winner Teresa Carpenter to Paul Feiner, town supervisor of Greenburgh, New York, and got involved in a heated debate about whether the podcast Jawbone Radio deserved to have an article. (I thought it should but lost that debate. But I soon after won a debate to retain an article about Podcast Pickle, a podcast-hosting service and message board.)

I had begun my own, first podcast—Light On Light Through, about popular culture, television, politics, "the works," as my blurb for it says—in October 2006. A month later I added Levinson News Clips for tv reviews, and by the end of that year I had a third podcast, Ask Lev, which offers tips to new writers.

I began Infinite Regress, my first and still primary independent blog—not associated with MySpace, Salon, etc.—in November 2006. By January 2009, I had posted more than 1,000 entries on Infinite Regress, which attracted more than 500,000 readers. One of the ways of attracting readers is to post links and brief summaries of your blog posts on Digg, which I joined in December 2006. Twitter is another way, and I joined in the summer of 2007. Applications—"apps" or special programs—can be employed to send titles and links of your blog posts, podcasts, etc. directly to Twitter and other sites, which in turn can be automatically relayed to sites such as Facebook.

In November 2007, I was invited by Ken Hudson to give a lecture about new new media in Second Life. I joined and discovered that I had to outfit my avatar with hair, body type, gender and clothes, as well as make sure my microphone was working. Second Life is the last of the major new new media I joined and learned how to use.

I continue to maintain accounts on all of these systems, not only because I intend to draw upon them for updates to this book, but because I enjoy and otherwise profit from my work and experiences on them.

The Order and Content of the Chapters

I could have presented the chapters in this book in groupings of similar new new media—primarily print (blogging, Wikipedia, Twitter), social (MySpace, Facebook, Twitter), etc.—but as this example and the preceding discussion of categories indicates, these groupings are highly overlapping, to say the least.

Another approach would have been to present the chapters in order of the initial creation or birth of the new new medium. The order of the chapters in that case would have been Blogging (1997), Wikipedia (January 2001), Second Life (June 2003), MySpace (August 2003), Facebook (February 2004), Podcasting (2004), Digg (December 2004), YouTube (February 2005) and Twitter (March 2006). But this would have placed YouTube and Twitter at the end, which would have been inconsistent with their extraordinary role in politics and news in 2008–2009. Even in 2006, Time magazine significantly highlighted YouTube with Wikipedia, MySpace, Facebook, Second Life and podcasting as media that empowered consumer-producers, when Time made "You"—or what we will refer to in this book as the new new media practitioner—its "Person of the Year" (Grossman, 2006).

An alternative to media birthdates would have been to present the chapters in descending order of the number of users attracted to the new new medium, links to the site and other measures of the new new medium's significance at the end of 2008. This approach would have left out blogging (Technorati tracks more than 130 million blogs, with 1.5 million active weekly) and podcasting (podcasts have received millions of downloads), because they are general applications of new new media, not specific sites with trackable numbers of visitors and links on other sites. Alexa ranks specific online media with an algorithm that takes into account number of visitors, links on other Web sites, etc., and had the following ranking in December 2008 for new new media examined in this book: YouTube 3, Facebook 5, MySpace 7, Wikipedia 8, Digg 294, Twitter 669 and Second Life 3354 (Yahoo was ranked 1, and Google 2). This chapter order works better than the historical approach. But, given the role that Wikipedia and Digg played in the 2008 presidential election in the United States and their exemplification, more than MySpace and Facebook, of the prime new new media principle of consumers becoming producers, I decided that their chapters needed to appear earlier in this book.

The chapters in this book are thus presented roughly in order of the importance of the new new media in the 2008–2009 world, followed by several chapters that address across-the-board issues pertinent to all new new media ("The Dark Side of New New Media," "New New Media and the Election of 2008," etc.). But several points need to be made about my criterion of "importance." First, although I take such objective factors as Alexa ranking into account and consult and cite media coverage and analysis of new new media (in the press, on television, in newspapers and online) throughout this book, the ultimate designation and comparison of the importance of new new media also encompasses factors such as how clearly the media demonstrate new new media principles, as indicated by the placement of the Wikipedia and Digg chapters before the chapters about MySpace and Facebook. But I always provide my reasons, and readers are free to disagree.

The second point is that new new media appear and evolve so quickly that their relative importance can change quickly, too. When I first started drafting this book, in the spring of 2008, the chapter on Twitter was near the end of the book. In November 2008, I decided to move that chapter forward. The December 25, 2008, issue of the Globe and Mail in Toronto carried a story by Ivor Tossell, titled "Teeny-tiny Twitter was the Year's Big Story," and noted that "it was somewhere around the middle of 2008" that Twitter hit big. By the time you are reading this, it may be crystal clear to everyone that specific new new media examined in this book have become more or less important than indicated here—in addition to the possibility that new new media that do not currently exist may be playing major roles. (And the reverse can happen: Pownce, a Twitter-like system, shut down because of the enormous success of Twitter, in December 2008. A very early draft of this book had a chapter titled "Twitter and Pownce," which Aron Keesbury, an editor at Congressional Quarterly Press at the time, told me sounded like a chapter about a cat.)

"New, New Media" thus starts with a chapter about blogging, the oldest and easiest to use of new new media. Unlike Wikipedia, Facebook and the other specific, proprietary new new media systems we will consider in this book, blogging is a general, new new media application of the Web and best exemplifies the guiding principles of new new media. A blog can be written on a moment's notice, can be amended indefinitely and can last forever. Anyone, including any reader, can become a blogger. Consumers of other new new media daily become producers of new new media in this way. Readers can also contribute to the narrative of the blog by writing comments. Major blog platforms are totally free, but bloggers can earn money through a variety of advertising options. You do not need a degree or a job or a contract to blog. The lingua franca of blogs is the written word, but they can be enhanced with images, audio and videos. Blogs can also be enhanced with "widgets," or complex linking programs that pull text, images, etc. into the blog from other places on the Web. The subjects of blogs range from the most arcane, little-known subjects to politics and entertainment of interest to millions of readers.

Until very recently, videos and any media of sound and/or images were far more difficult to produce than anything written on computers or online. Many of the most important clips on YouTube come from old media—clips from network and cable television, ranging from "Saturday Night Live" to presidential press conferences— but videos from new new media "amateur" or "nonprofessional" sources can receive millions of views, such as the "Leave Britney Alone" video in 2007–2008. One advantage of these "people-produced" videos is that neither the producer nor YouTube need worry about violating the copyright of the network or whoever controls the copyright of a professionally produced television clip. As we will see, traditional copyright is not always compatible with the dissemination of new new media, and this is especially the case for video clips on YouTube and music in podcasts, when the music is created by someone other than the podcaster.

Webcams, digital cameras and camera phones have made creation of videos far more easy, but it is still the case that uploading videos to YouTube or another video host is a little more difficult than posting a blog. Certainly, the time between the writing and posting of a blog is instant and therefore much shorter than the creation and appearance online of a video. But the video has also always been easier on the human intellect to see than any printed text is to read—watching takes less attention than reading—and that gives YouTube a unique appeal, along with the power of real, moving images to inform, entertain and persuade, which we have witnessed since the invention of motion pictures near the end of the 19th century. YouTube has therefore had a revolutionary impact both on entertainment and the democratic process, which was first seen in the election of Barack Obama to the presidency in 2008. The number of network television viewers continues to decline, but, as the success and impact of YouTube demonstrates, this is not because people have lost their taste for audio-visual entertainment and news. Rather, they are enjoying the new new media power of watching a video when and where they choose—especially if they have an iPhone—rather than on the fixed schedule of television, which has been loosened considerably by TiVo and DVRs but still lacks the flexibility of YouTube and indeed anything on the Web.

Wikipedia opened online shop in January 2001, which makes it the oldest specific new new medium we will consider in this book. The roots of general blogging go back further, at least as far as 1997 and the unrelated online postings of Dave Winer, Jorn Barger and Justin Hall (see McCullagh & Broache, 2007), and Wikipedia notes that blogging about specific news events harkens back to August 1998, when "Jonathan Dube of The Charlotte Observer published [a blog] chronicling Hurricane Bonnie." (Computer conferencing in the 1980s would be a far earlier online precursor – see Levinson, 1997, pp. 130 ff., and Levinson, 1985.) But Wikipedia is unique in ways that reach beyond its age: (1) First, although blogging competes with older media such as newspapers, and YouTube with television, the new new medium of Wikipedia is, in effect, a head-on challenge to one of the most venerable media in the past few hundred years: the encyclopedia. As a repository of authoritative information, encyclopedias such as the Britannica operate as the epitome of expert-driven, top-down, vetted media systems. In contrast, Wikipedia is literally written by its readers. (2) This points to a second, related way in which Wikipedia differs from most other new new media: its production, or writing, is, for the most part, editing. Although Wikipedia's readers daily initiate new articles on a wide variety of topics, most of the writing on Wikipedia is editing—correcting, expanding, tightening—of previously written articles. This vetting by the world-at-large is another one of the prime principles of new new media. (3) Wikipedia is also the most consistent in its denial of the old-media, professionally produced method of generating articles. Although reader/editors work in a hierarchy, with some editors having more power than others, there are no articles on Wikipedia in which even the newest reader/editor has no input. In contrast, many of the videos on YouTube are professionally produced, and venerable press media such as The

New York Times and the cable news media CNN, Fox News and MSNBC publish daily and more frequent blogs.

Digg is much lower in its Alexa ranking (294) than are Facebook (5) and MySpace (7), but the Digg chapter belongs right after Wikipedia, because Digg is the most like Wikipedia in being a source of news and information that operates in accordance with the new new media principle of readers becoming editors, or, in the case of Digg, deciders via "Digging" and "Burying" about which stories get on the front page. This makes Digg as different from the old medium of The New York Times as Wikipedia is to the Encyclopedia Britannica.

Wikipedia and Digg are not without gatekeeping—Wikipedia has "administrators" with powers superior to those of the editor/readers, and Digg has behind-the-scenes programmers—but these two new new media operations nonetheless bring an unprecedented amount of democratic, nonauthoritarian decision-making about content to encyclopedias (Wikipedia) and newspapers (Digg). Unsurprisingly, this opening of the gates is not without controversy, sometimes veering toward anarchy, as partisans of various people and causes fight over what should and should not be included in Wikipedia and the Digg front page of popular stories. "New New Media" will carefully examine and assess these dynamics (see Levinson, 1997, pp. 132-135, for a history of gatekeeping in media).

MySpace and Facebook are two huge peas in the social media pod. MySpace (August 2003) is six months older than Facebook (February 2004) and claimed more than 300 million accounts in contrast to Facebook's more than 140 million "active" accounts at the end of 2008. But Facebook "took over the global lead among social networking sites in April 2008," according to Comscore's well-known report (2008), which also indicated some 132 million unique total visitors to Facebook in June 2008, in contrast to 117 million on MySpace. Because users can easily create more than one account—by linking to a different email—the number of "unique visitors" is a better measure of a social medium's popularity than the number of accounts. The two sites are thus more or less equivalent in age, size and function. I could have examined both in a single chapter titled "Social Media," or put the chapter on Facebook before the chapter on MySpace, but we will consider Facebook after MySpace in this book because I decided in their largely equivalent cases to go with chronology.

Unlike blogging, YouTube, Wikipedia and Digg, which are about content in one form or another, social new new media such as MySpace and Facebook are about people—or, in the terminology of social media, "Friends," around which all the many other functions and applications of social media revolve. Social online friendships certainly play a major role, below the surface, in the operation of Wikipedia, as editors try to get support for what they think should be included in articles, and Digg has formal "Friends," which allow mutual tracking of posted links. But "Friends" are elevated to a primary, predominating status on MySpace and Facebook, where the main measure of the success of any member is how many "Friends" he or she has attained. This requires us, in this book, to consider the nature of online friends and how they compare with our friends and our notions of friendship in the in-person, offline world. One activity in which both kinds of friends partake is the formation of groups relating to common interests. Both MySpace and Facebook have such groups, but if Facebook has one significant difference from MySpace, it is the use of groups on Facebook to mobilize for political and other social causes.

The ease of setting up and maintaining accounts on these systems, as well as furnishing them with your work and imbuing them with your interests, make them unprecedented as vehicles for pursuit of personal and professional satisfaction and success. But their very openness also can make them dangerous, and we will examine some of the abuses of social networking—such as cyberbullying—especially found on MySpace and Facebook, with a later chapter devoted completely to these and other facets of "The Dark Side of New New Media."

Twitter is also a social medium but one that injects content first and foremost back into the equation. Friends "follow" each other's twitters, or tweets, which are one-line blurbs that range from eyewitness news reports to disclosing what a friend is doing ("I'm eating pizza") to providing links to a new blog post or YouTube video. The blurbs, or "microblogs," are limited to 140 characters—thus providing a good, ongoing test of whether brevity is the soul of wit—and can be seen on computers and, even more conveniently, on cellphones.

Completing our tour of specific, proprietary new new media in this book, we pay a visit to Second Life—another kind of social realm, in which our avatars chat, listen to music, walk through ancient or alien streets, look at the night sky, do all kinds of business, make virtual love, get married and buy and sell property. With just 15 million avatar accounts as of September 2008, some inactive, many by single users with multiple emails, Second Life is a tiny social medium in comparison to MySpace and Facebook. But its total immersion in a virtual life puts it in a social medium class of its own and warrants our examination, whether or not its alternative to Facebook/MySpace text-based social media represents the future way of social media.

We next return to a new new media general application, podcasting, which in effect is an audio kind of blogging. Speaking may have come before writing in our evolution as a species, but the spoken words of podcasts arose after the written content of blogs. Podcasts are at once more intimate than blogs—words in your ear have more visceral impact than words on a screen—but the podcast is more difficult to produce and in that sense puts a greater distance between podcaster and audience than between blogger and reader. But because there are no network executives, producers or engineers, other than the podcaster, to come between podcaster and audience, the podcast also offers a more personal, direct communication than anything anyone is likely to hear on professionally produced radio. But, as with radio, you can listen to a podcast when driving a car or doing something else, unlike when you are reading, and this makes the podcast more accessible to its potential audience. A podcast with a video component is a "vidcast" and can be uploaded to YouTube or another online host, or situated on its own blog page, the same as a podcast. But unlike the purely audio podcast, the video requires our visual attention and cannot be multitasked like the podcast. Watching a YouTube video while driving is no better than watching television behind the wheel; in either case, and unlike listening to an audio program, the driver's eyes are on a screen and off the road. The world of new new media is all about trade-offs, or pros and cons.

We conclude with three chapters that address elements and issues common to all new new media. The general position of this book is that new new media provide significant, often revolutionary, benefits to we who employ these media for work, play and education. But new new media, like all human tools, can be put to personally and socially destructive purposes, including criminal and lethal actions, and we explore some of these, as well as possible remedies that arise from new new media, in "The Dark Side of New New Media."

This book was conceived in the fall of 2007, when the campaign that elected Barack Obama as president of the United States was already under way. Obama has been called the first "cybergenic" president (Saffo, 2008; but see Levinson, quoted in Zurawik, 2008, for why I think this is a bit of an oversimplification)—or someone who made good on the political promise of the Internet initiated, unsuccessfully, by Howard Dean in 2004—and we look in the chapter on "New New Media and the Election of Barack Obama in 2008" not only to understand what helped elect Obama in 2008 but what will certainly play a significant role in his presidency.

A consideration of the hardware through which new new media operate—how the world at large tweets, reads and writes blogs, watches YouTube and visits MySpace and Facebook—serves as the departing anchor of this book. All media, old and new, are really media within media. We read an article (medium of writing) published in a magazine (medium of the press) that we buy on a newsstand (medium of the newsstand). Similarly, we read or write a blog post (medium of writing) published on a blog (medium of blogging) that we obtain on our laptop or whatever kind of computer (medium of personal computer). Hardware is usually the outermost vehicle, shell or packaging of the communication process—the physical device that we must hold, touch, see, hear or otherwise interact with in order to receive and sometimes send the media of information within (see Levinson, "Digital McLuhan", 1999, for more on media within media).

The iPhone most typifies the new hardware of new new media—a cellphone that provides easy access to all of the Web—but BlackBerrys and other mobile media are doing similar work. I expect that "New New Media" and its updates will be available not only on printed paper but in various forms on the Web, which means that many of you, perhaps most of you, who are now reading these words are doing so through your laptops, Kindles, iPhones and BlackBerrys. (I'm tempted to say "raise your hand now" if that is true.) I certainly hope this book generates discussion on Facebook, Twitter, perhaps Wikipedia…and blogs, which we consider in more detail in the next chapter.

CHAPTER 2

Blogging

Bloggers are often referred to as "citizen journalists," to underline the fact that a blogger need not be a professional journalist to write and publish about the news. But the adjective "citizen" is still insufficient to convey the scope of liberation that blogging—and all new new media—has bestowed upon us. The truth is that one need not be a citizen of this or any particular country, one need not be an adult, one need not have any attribute other than being able to read and write in order to blog. Consider, for example, the following, and bear in mind that, although I am a professor of communication and media studies, I have no professional expertise in politics. I am just a citizen. But, even if I were not...

It was past one in the morning on May 7, 2008. Ninety-nine percent of the vote had finally come in from the Democratic presidential primary in Indiana. Hillary Clinton had won by just 2 percent. A few hours earlier, Barack Obama had won big in North Carolina. I wrote a blog post saying Barack Obama would be the Democratic nominee for president.

I posted it not only on InfiniteRegress.tv—my television review and politics blog—but on my MySpace blog as well. I put up links to it on Facebook, Digg, Fark and Buzzflash. My blog on Amazon automatically posted it via a "feed." A link to my post also automatically appeared on Twitter.

My various "stat counters" reported that thousands of people had read my blog within an hour of its posting.

Just a few years ago, the only possible recipient of my thoughts about such a decisive political development, moments after it had occurred in the middle of the night, would have been my wife. We could have talked about the results in Indiana. I also could have written about them and sent this to any number of online magazines, but my words would not have been automatically posted. Gatekeepers—otherwise known as editors, likely not at work until the next morning—would have needed to approve them.

From its outset, from the very first time that two people spoke, speech has been as easy to produce as to consume. We switch effortlessly from hearing to talking. But speech lacked permanence, and we invented writing to safeguard what our memories might lose. The written word was also almost as easy to produce as to consume—writing well is more difficult than being able to read, but to be literate was and is to be able to write as well as read. As long as the written words remained personal, individual and not mass-produced, the process of writing was as widespread as reading.

The printing press changed all of that. It opened many doors. It made Bibles, reports of Columbus's voyages and scientific treatises readily available to millions of readers. But it ended the equality of consumers and producers, and radically altered the one-to-one ratio in which every reader was also a writer. A sliver of the population contributes what goes into books, newspapers and magazines.

And now blogging has in turn changed and reversed all of that. Although there are still more readers than writers of blogs, any reader can become a writer, either by commenting on someone else's blog or, with just a little more effort, by starting a blog of one's own. Technorati tracked more than 112 million blogs in December 2007.

Although speaking is easier than writing, publishing of writing in digital form—online—requires much less production than online publishing of audio or audio-visual clips of spoken words. In fact, publication of a written blog requires no production at all beyond the writing and initial posting of the writing. Blogging, which has been known by that name, or "weblogging," since 1997 (McCullagh & Broache, 2007) and has roots in the digital age in "computer conferencing" and message boards that go back at least 15 years prior (Levinson, 1997), thus became the first big player in the new new media revolution.

A Thumbnail History of Electronic Writing

Writing always had some advantages over speaking as a mode of human expression. Not only was writing permanent, in contrast to the instantly fleeting quality of speech, but writing also allowed for greater control of the message by the sender. An angry, very happy or extremely sad speaker can find disguising those emotions difficult in speech. But the same emotions can make no appearance at all in a written document, unless the writer chooses to make those feelings plain. This is one reason why texting surpassed speaking on cellphones in the hands of people under 45 around the world (Nielsen Mobile report, discussed in Technology Expert, 2008).

But after the enormous boost given to the dissemination of the written word by the printing press, the progress of writing in the evolution of media was slow. The telegraph in the 1830s gave the written word the capacity to be sent anywhere in the world—or anywhere connected by wires and cables—instantly. But the requirement of a telegraph operator to make this happen, as well as someone to deliver the telegram, not only worked against the immediacy of this electronic communication but also made it far more impersonal than written letters. It was one thing writing to your lover in a letter and quite another to utter those words to a telegraph operator.

The telegraph, however, revolutionized news delivery by allowing reporters to file stories instantly with their newspapers. Baron Julius von Reuter started his news service with carrier pigeons, which could convey news more quickly across the English Channel than via boats and rails. The baron's news agency soon came to rely on the telegraph. Its successful descendant was bought by the Thomson Company for $15.8 billion in 2008 (Associated Press, 2008).

Blogging takes the dissemination of news and opinion one big step beyond the telegraph by allowing "reporters"—that is, people, everyone—to file their stories instantly not with their newspapers but on their blogs and, therein, with the world at large. And because blogs are under the personal editorship of the writer, they can be about anything the writer pleases—unlike the newspaper or magazine.

This personalization or "de-professionalization" of communication is one of the signal characteristics of new new media. It was not until the deployment of the fax in the 1980s, and the advent of email around the same time, that the writer finally reclaimed privacy and control over the written word. But the fax was primarily for one-to-one communication—much like the telegraph. And even emails sent to groups were less than a drop in the bucket in the reach of mass media such as newspapers, radio and television. Blogging combines the best of both—the personal control of email and the long and wide reach of mass media.

Blogging About Anything, Forever

The personal control that the writer has over his or her blog means that the blog can be about any subject, not just news. On the evening of May 29, 2008, my blog received 20,000 "hits" on a page (views of the page) I had written the year before, about the previous season's finale of "Lost" (Season 3 finale: "Through the Looking Glass"). This development, something that happens on blogs all the time, highlights two significant characteristics of blogging, in particular, and new new media, in general. The first is that anyone can blog about anything—I'm a professor and an author, not a professional television critic. The second is that the impact of a blog post, including when it will have its maximum impact, is unpredictable. My blog post about "Lost" received thousands of online visits shortly after it was written in 2007, but these were less than half of the visits or hits it received on that one day a year later in 2008.

Permanence is one of the most revolutionary aspects of new new media and underlies all new new media—from YouTube to MySpace—as well as blogging. One of the prime characteristics of old electronic media, such as radio and television, was their fleeting quality. Like the in-person spoken word, the word on radio and television was gone the instant after it was spoken. This evanescence led Lewis Mumford (1970, p. 294) to critique the viewers of television as in a "state of mass psychosis" in which "man" is confined to a "present time-cage that cuts him off from both his past and his future." Mumford apparently was not aware of the professional video recorders and "portapak" video cameras which were already giving television some permanence in 1970 (see Levinson, 1997, for more of my critique of Mumford), but he was certainly not wrong that the electronic media of his day offered information that was far less permanent than that conveyed by print. The first wave of new, digital media—the Web of the mid-1990s—began to invest its communications with more permanence. But until the use of "permalinks" became widespread, a development that awaited the rise of blogging in the first years of the 21st century, items on the Web lacked what I call the "reliable locatability" of words on pages of books on shelves (see Levinson, 1998; Levinson, "Cellphone," 2004 and Levinson, "The Secret Riches," 2007, for more).

Blog pages still lack the complete reliable locatability of books—after all, a blogger can remove a post or his or her entire blog—but their instant availability to anyone, anywhere with a connection to the Internet may give them a greater net durability (pun intended), or durability to more people, than any book. In other words, if a text is available online for 10 years to millions of people, is it more or less durable to the culture than a thousand books available for a hundred years on library shelves? Indeed, it may well be that the ease of making permalinks, along with the sheer number of people who can easily access them, will make the contents of blogs more permanent, in the long run, than books.

The blog post is thus not only immediate and universally accessible, but it can last forever. Indeed, whether photograph, video or text, once it is committed to the Web, it is in principle impossible to completely delete. This is because anyone can make a copy and post it to his or her blog or Web page. The immediacy of new new media can disguise this permanence or make users think that anything posted on the Web is easy come, easy go. But in fact the indelibility of anything posted online may be, literally, its most enduring characteristic.

We might also say that the sovereignty that the blogger has over his or her blog—the freedom from foreign gatekeepers ("foreign" being anyone other than the blogger)—finds its limit in the capacity of anyone to copy whatever is in the blog, for saving or dissemination.

Comment Moderation

The blogger's sovereignty also relates to gatekeeping in a different way: Although the blogger is not subject to anyone else's gatekeeping, the blogger becomes a gatekeeper in deciding whether to allow comments by others on the blog and, if so, how to moderate them.

The pros and cons of gatekeeping or moderating comments on your blog are straightforward. Moderating comments, rather than allowing them to be posted automatically, allows the blogger to keep disruptive comments out of the blog. But such moderation also slows the pace of the blog. Unless the blogger is online every minute of the day, an excellent comment, which could spark further excellent comments, could be left waiting for approval.

Is the protection of the blog from undesirable comments worth such a potential slowing and even stifling of worthwhile conversation? It depends upon what the blogger, and the larger world of readers, deem undesirable. Certainly we can see why even strong disagreement with a blogger's political positions, or analysis of a television show, should not be barred from the blog. Indeed, a blogger can usually use such criticisms as a springboard for elaboration of the blogger's initial opinion. "Don't you think 'Lost's' flashforwards were a cheap gimmick?" a comment could ask. "No, I do not," the blogger could respond and go on to explain why the flashforwards in "Lost" were a brilliant gambit.

But this is all a matter of the blogger's opinion. A comment deemed disruptive by one blogger might be deemed conducive to valuable, multiple discussions by another blogger. Or a given blogger might want no comments at all, preferring the blog to be a one-way rather than an interactive mode of communication.

Bloggers can also install a CAPTCHA system (Completely Automated Public Turing test to tell Computers and Humans Apart), which requires commenters to answer a computer-generated question (for example, reproduce a blurry sequence of numbers and letters) designed to distinguish human commenters from automated spam. A CAPTCHA, of course, will not get in the way of a human being bent on entering a nasty or disruptive comment in a blog.

In general, bloggers who want to encourage comments might keep in mind the following principle: Only block or remove comments if you believe they will discourage other comments from you and your readers. A blog without comments is like a flightless bird: The blog may make important contributions or bring satisfaction to its writer, but it will be lacking one of the signature social characteristics of new new media, interaction with the audience. (But see the discussion of Kathy Sierra in the "Online Gossiping and Cyberbullying" section of Chapter 11, "The Dark Side of New New Media," for what can happen when comments become abusive.)

Commenting on the Blogs of Others

As easy as blogging is, writing a comment in someone else's blog, or any online forum, is even easier. All the commenter needs to do is enter the comment in a blog that already exists.

Indeed, entering a comment on someone else's blog can be a very effective way of promoting your own blog. If your comment is about an issue that you are blogging about and your comment is signed by you—not anonymous (see discussion below)—then readers of your comment can easily find your blog. You can encourage this discovery of your blog by including a link to it in your comment, but some bloggers may see this as use of their blog for promotion of other blogs and object (either by entering a comment that says "please don't use my blog to promote yours" or by removing your comment—see "Further Tensions Between New New Media and Older Forms" later in this chapter for details).

As a blogger, I welcome comments with links—as long as the comments and links are relevant to the discussion at hand and not spam for gold sold at low prices or whatever. Because, whatever the motivation of the commenter, comments that are not spam serve to further what Comenius centuries ago called "The Great Didactic" (1649/1896).

Given that blog entries on new media systems such as Entertainment Weekly or USA Today regularly draw hundreds of comments—and on new new media amateur blogs (such as mine) anywhere from none to a few to occasionally hundreds of comments per entry—the comment is clearly the most frequent form of sustained written discourse in the new new media world. At their best, comments serve not only as a voice of the people but as conveyors of truth and correction to a blog post, epitomizing the democratic alternative to expert-driven information that is one of the hallmarks of new new media (and has been developed to a fine art on Wikipedia, which we will examine in Chapter 4). At their worst, comments can be vehicles for trolls to grab attention and can mar or derail an online conversation (see Chapter 11 for more). In between, comments are the ubiquitous Greek chorus not only of blogs but of YouTube videos, Digg's listing of articles from all over the Web, and most new new media.

"Is it a fact—or have I dreamed it—that, by means of electricity, the world of matter has become a great nerve, vibrating thousands of miles in a breathless point in time?" Nathaniel Hawthorne's character Clifford asks about the telegraph in "The House of the Seven Gables" (1851/1962, p. 239). It was indeed a fact back then. But not as much as when Marshall McLuhan talked about the "global village" in "The Gutenberg Galaxy" in 1962. And by no means as much as now, when Hawthorne's and McLuhan's visions have achieved their fullest realization in blogs that buzz with hundreds of millions of comments on more than 130 million blogs worldwide (as per Technorati) at any instant.

Comments as Correctors

Most of my posts on Infinite Regress are either about politics or are reviews of television shows. In the case of the television blogs, I try to get my reviews up within a few minutes of the conclusion of the show's episode on television; making reviews available as close as possible to a show's conclusion maximizes the number of people who will read my review.

But such a tight schedule does not always make for a review that is perfectly factual. I make it a point of mentioning the names of actors and actresses, if they play important roles in a show I am reviewing, but sometimes these may not be available online, either on the show's Web site or on IMDB (Internet Movie Database).

On October 12, 2007, I reviewed the 12th episode of the first season of AMC's "Mad Men" on my blog. It was an excellent episode, and I mentioned in my review that "my favorite sex/romantic scene in this show was Harry (Isaac Asimov!) (played by Rich Sommer) and that secretary (played by xxxx)." The "Harry" was Harry Crane, who, in my opinion at least, looks a lot like science fiction author Isaac Asimov did in the 1950s and 1960s. (You can see their two photographs side by side at my "Interview with Rich Sommer," 2007.)

But to return to comments as correctors, the reason I wrote "played by xxxx" above is that, in my original blog post, I had listed the wrong actress. I had looked at IMDB and every site of relevance I could find on the Web. I could find no actress credited with playing beside Rich Sommer on the couch. So I had pored over whatever photos I could find of actresses who played secretaries on "Mad Men" and came up with the wrong actress as having played "that secretary."

The first I learned of my mistake was via a comment in my blog, written about 30 minutes after I had posted my review. It read, "Hey, Paul. I read your reviews every week. Thanks for the kind words, and for helping to get the word out. We really appreciate it! An important correction: Hildy is played by Julie McNiven. She deserves full credit for her amazing work!"

And it had been entered by none other than Rich Sommer!

We exchanged emails after that, and I interviewed Rich on my Light On Light Through podcast—the "Interview with Rich Sommer"—by the end of the month.

But, aside from the coolness of blogging about an actor and then being contacted by him on the blog—something which has happened to me more than once and which is a good example of the equalization of new new media, in which famous and not-so-famous people can more easily be in touch—the comment by Rich Sommer, with a correction of my misidentification of the actress in his scene, spotlights the important role that comments can serve as correctors in blogging.

The whole world, in principle, is not only reading what you write when you blog but is waiting there as a potential safety net and source of correction for any mistakes you might make. Of course, not all comments are helpful, and some might be hostile. But the correction of your review by the very subject of your review, within half an hour of its posting, is something new under the sun of media, unless your review was on a live television broadcast, and the subject of the review happened to have your phone number.

As for Rich Sommer's helpful correction (his comment is still on the page), I changed the wrong name to Julie McNiven as soon as I finished reading—and taking in the larger significance of—Rich Sommer's comment.

MySpace Message from Stringer Bell of "The Wire"

Everyone is a fan of someone, usually more than one actor, actress, singer, musician or author. As exciting as it was to hear from Rich Sommer after blogging about him, his was not the most extraordinary and unexpected comment I received from an actor, or from a member of an actor's family, after blogging about the actor. In addition to Rich Sommer, I heard from Len Cariou's wife (via a comment still on

the page) after I had blogged in 2007 about how much I had enjoyed his performance in two seasons of "Brotherhood" on Showtime (the character died at the end
of the second season) and from the father of Aaron Hart (via email), one of two
actors who played Don Draper's little boy in the second season of "Mad Men" in
the summer of 2008. But as fortunate as I was with "Mad Men"—hearing from two
actors or relatives of actors on the series—and as much as I enjoy both "Mad Men"
and "Brotherhood", neither achieved the extraordinary quality of "The Wire", which
ran for five seasons on HBO, from 2002 to 2008.

Paramount among "The Wire"'s characters, dominating every scene he was in
for the first three seasons (his tenure on "The Wire") was Stringer Bell, second in
command of the drug operation under investigation by the police. An attendee of
night classes in economics, a copy of Adam Smith's 1776 "The Wealth of Nations"
on his shelf and as ready to kill if necessary as worry about inflation, Stringer Bell
was no ordinary drug chief in the ghetto.

In August 2006, when the only blog I was writing was the very occasional
Twice Upon a Rhyme on MySpace (named after my 1972 album of the same name),
I wrote a piece about "The Wire". The little knowledge I had then of blog promo-
tion led me to post a link and brief summary of the blog post on HBO's
"Community" forum about "The Wire".

A few months later, in the wee hours of a late October morning, I was quickly
reading through a batch of "Friend" requests on MySpace. It was late. I was tired.
I was not thinking at all about "The Wire", and although the name Idris Elba
seemed familiar enough for me to accept his Friend request without looking at
his page, I went on quickly to the other Friend requests and promptly forgot
about Idris's.

Until I received a message from Idris Elba about a week later, which read as
follows: "Hi Paul, I read your comments on my acting in "The Wire" some time
ago. Cheers for the support! I see you have been involved in the music biz for some
time now and just wondered what you thought of my music? I'll be buying your
latest book, because it looks like just my sort of read. Idris."

I liked his music, especially his hip-hop version of "Johnny Was," so much so that
I played it on a special episode of my Light On Light Through podcast, "The Wire
Without Stringer," on November 4, 2006. I received another message on MySpace
from Idris Elba a few days later: "Paul, I just had to take the time out to drop you a
line to say, that it is an absolute honour to have such a scholar like yourself dedicate
an entire podcast to me, my music and my role as Stringer Bell. Incredible dissection
of what made followers of The Wire gravitate towards my character. My music
is about giving that same heart, but with my very own script…. Cheers, Idris."
(This message is currently posted on the right-hand column of my Light On Light
Through podcast page.)

In the realm of new new media that we all inhabit, it is that easy for someone,
anyone, watching television, computer at hand, to strike up a relationship with the
star of that television show.

Changing the Words in Your Blog
After Publication

The blogger's absolute authority over the blog pertains not only to the comments but to the blog post itself, not only before it is posted on the blog but for as long as it remains on the blog, which could be forever after.

Writing used to be the archetypically immutable medium. Writing with ink or whatever chemical or dye on papyrus, parchment or paper gave those words life as long as the papyrus, parchment or paper survived. The words could be crossed out or obliterated, of course, but the obliteration was still observable. Even erasing the marks of a pencil on paper leaves signs of the erasure.

The printing press heightened this immutability. Under pressure from the Roman Catholic Church, Galileo recanted his views that the Earth revolved around the sun. But the thousands of copies of books expressing his original opinion were not changed with the recantation. The Church won a Pyrrhic victory, and the Scientific Revolution continued (see Levinson, 1997, for more).

That happened in the first decades of the 1600s. This immutability of published writing was still very much in effect at the end of the 19th century, at the end of the Victorian age of printed literacy, when Oscar Wilde famously is said to have observed about the process of authoring that "books are never finished, they are merely abandoned" (the quote more likely originates a little later with French poet Paul Valéry in 1933 and is about creating art or writing poetry). Whether of book, poem or painting, the abandonment was as real as a loved one moving out of the home. Once published, a book or a newspaper article was beyond being changed by the author, except via the unlikely means of a new edition or an editor willing to publish an amending note by the reporter in the newspaper. But that was to radically change with the advent of "word processing" and then online publishing by the end of the next century (see Levinson, 1997). And in the 21st century age of new new media, bloggers may be seen to have the reverse problem: The easy revision of a blog means it is never really finished and all but impossible to abandon if the blog is on a site under the blogger's control.

Here is how that came to be: In the last two decades of the 1900s, word processing for the first time in history gave writers the capacity to change their written words with no tell-tale evidence of the original. Spelling errors could be corrected in email prior to sending and ideas could be sharpened in manuscripts with no one other than the writer the wiser.

But email and manuscripts submitted to editors were by and large one-on-one communications. Once a manuscript was printed and published, it was as immutable in the 1980s as were the words wedded to the paper of Galileo's books in the 1600s.

Blogging has made the publication as easy to alter as the initial writing. The most innocuous result is that spelling errors are easily correctable, as are missing words. There is no downside to such correction, nothing nefarious. But what about the capacity of any blogger to easily change the material wording and meaning of a blog post after it has been published?

If no one or few people have seen the original, such alterations pose no problem. But what if many people have read the original and commented upon it, in whatever media available?

On the one hand, changing a text already extensively commented upon can certainly generate confusion. What is Reader "C" to make of a blog post and comment in which Blogger "A" changed the wording of the blog to reflect and remedy a critique made by Commenter "B"? One way Blogger "A" can eliminate any ensuing confusion is to put a postscript in the blog post, appropriately dated, which explains that a change was made in response to a comment made by Commenter "B." But what if the blogger neglects or decides not to do that?

On the other hand, the greater the number of people who have read and commented upon a text, the more difficult for the author to surreptitiously alter the text and pretend the altered text was in the blog post all along. The audience for the initial text thus serves as protection against the changing of the text for purposes of deception, just as the same audience can be a safety net for the blogger by pointing out errors in the blog that can be corrected.

The social group as a guarantor of truth—or, at the very least, accuracy—is a factor we will encounter in other new new media, particularly Wikipedia and Twitter.

Long-Range Blogging and Linking

The duration of blog posts for months, in some cases years, after their posting allows for another kind of self-promotion, in which the blogger keeps abreast of comments about his or her post in other blogs on the Web and adjusts the links in the original post to take advantage of these new comments.

Here is an example: In August 2007, I wrote a short item in one of my blogs with four pieces of advice to would-be writers. The item drew many readers (see "Gauging the Readership of Your Blog," later in this chapter, for how bloggers can keep track on a daily or even more immediate basis of the number of readers). A few months earlier, I had begun a podcast—Ask Lev—with brief, three- to five-minute bits of advice to writers. At some point a few months after my August 2007 posting, I got an email from a reader saying he was trying to locate my "My Four Rules: The Best You Can Do to Make It as a Writer" blog post but could not find it and instead had discovered my Ask Lev podcast, which had answered his questions.

The first improvement of my August 2007 "Four Rules" then occurred to me: put a link in that post to the Ask Lev podcast, since readers of the post would be likely to find the podcast of interest. Of course, that could and should have occurred to me when I first wrote the post. But the infinite perfectibility of any blog allowed me to recover and to put in this link months later.

The story continues: In December 2007, I interviewed Dr. Stanley Schmidt, editor of Analog Magazine of Science Fiction and Fact (the leading science fiction magazine), for my Light On Light Through podcast. That interview drew many listeners, including those on Analog's online site, AnalogSF.com, where it became a topic of conversation. I, of course, kept a happy eye on these online discussions and noticed in October 2008 that someone said one of the best parts of the interview was the advice it gave to writers who wanted to get published in Analog.

This immediately set off another insert-a-link bell, and I proceeded to put a link to the August 2007 "Four Rules" blog post in the text accompanying my podcast interview with Stan Schmidt. (By the way, you can find the URL to "My Four Rules," 2007, in the Bibliography at the end of this book in case you, too, are desirous of advice on how to become a published writer.)

You can see where this is going: Once you begin to look at not just your blog but the whole Web as your oyster for blog promotion, you have entered a realm in which your words do not deteriorate but can improve with time, as you draw ever more readers from different places to your blog. The key is that, although blogging is usually a solitary process, its promotion is inherently social and thrives on the easy linking of the Web.

Of course, if you are not interested in large numbers of readers, or any readers at all, you can always make your blog private and admit only those readers who meet your criteria. This would deprive your blog of many of the social advantages of new new media, but the preeminent principle is nonetheless that the blogger has complete control over his or her online work.

Usually, the blog will be the continuing creation of an individual. But sometimes the very blogwriting itself can be a group activity.

Group Blogging

Entries or articles on Wikipedia are edited by everyone, which is also an option for any blogger who might want to open one or more blog posts to other authors. Such group blogging would be a good example of readers literally becoming writers of the very text they are reading.

Writing has traditionally been and usually is an individual effort, in contrast to talking, which usually entails two or more people (it could be argued that talking to yourself is not really talking since no interpersonal communication takes place unless someone overhears you, in which case you are no longer talking only to yourself). The advent of group blogging thus can be seen as a further erosion of the difference between writing and talking, which began when word processing made correction of the written word almost as easy as the spoken and in some ways more effective, since the digitally corrected written word can leave no trace of the original, in contrast to the listener's memory of a spoken error.

But group writing has at least one disadvantage: Unlike a spoken conversation, in which each voice is identifiable as belonging to a separate person (even if we do not know who that person is), there is nothing in the written word that intrinsically connects it to any author. Wikipedia addresses this problem by providing detailed "histories" of every article, in which every edit is clearly identified. Group blogs are usually less sophisticated and often do nothing more than list everyone who has written or edited a given post.

The main benefit of group writing of blogs is that it can increase the sum total of expertise brought to the blogwriting. For example, in December 2008, I started a blog titled Educated Tastes about food, drink, restaurants, recipes and groceries. Because my expertise in food pertains mostly to consumption, I had a choice of either leaving recipes out of the mix or bringing another writer on board who knew how to cook and write about it. Because my wife excels in both, I invited her to join the blog as a writer.

Whether blogwriting or songwriting or scriptwriting, the same calculus of collaboration applies. If it adds more to the project than any frustration you might feel from sharing your creative control, then it is worth trying.

Monetizing Your Blog

The commercial essence of the Web has always been that it's free—"only suckers pay for content," as David Carr observed about what succeeds most on the Web in The New York Times, back in 2005. That still holds true, and more so than ever, as newspapers such as The New York Times have made much more of their content available for free on the Web, in order to encourage links back to their articles in other blogs (a link in a blog post to a site that requires payment would displease most blog readers) and to be competitive with totally online and free blog newspapers such as Daily Kos and The Huffington Post. (See "Blogging for Others," later in this chapter, for details on these and other blog newspapers.) But none of this means that you cannot earn money from your blogging or other new new media activities.

Here are five general ways of making money from your own blog:

1. Google AdSense is the grandparent of revenue-making by individuals (you and me) on the Web. You sign up, get "code" to put on your blog and you're in business. Text, image and/or video ads, the size and subject and placement of your choosing, appear on your blog. The work required to set this up is easy and less demanding than the writing of most blog posts.

That is the good news. The not-so-good news is that you won't make much money—not only not enough to retire on or earn a living from but not enough in a month to buy a decent dinner in New York. An average of 500 to 1000 visitors a day is likely to earn you no more than about $10 per month from Google AdSense, which pays on clicks and impressions, meaning you get paid for the number of people who click on the ads (clicks) or view them (impressions). As is the case with many online ad services, Google AdSense only pays you when your ads have earned a minimum amount of revenue—in the case of AdSense, $100.

You will likely find that ads about certain topics—usually those that relate in some way to the subjects of your blog posts—attract more clicks on your blog than ads that have nothing to do with the subject of your blog. AdSense automatically runs ads, when available, that relate to the subjects of your posts. Unfortunately, this selection process is keyed only to the subject and can miss the tone or opinion of your blog post. A post on my blog that criticized John McCain in the 2008 presidential campaign attracted Google ads in support of McCain. If such ads are not acceptable to the anti-Republican blogger, Google AdSense provides a means of filtering out any ads on specified unwanted subjects. Unless this is done when the ad code is first created, however, an unwelcome ad can nonetheless appear on the blog. But the code can be revised at any time.

You may find that video and image ads attract more clicks than text ads. Placement of the ads can also increase your revenue. A text ad at the top of a blog can generate far more hits than attractive image and video ads in the sidebar. But ads placed at the top of the blog give the blog a more commercial look than ads placed in the sidebar. The blogger thus has a choice: Which is more important, appearance of the blog or income earned? Of course, if you want your blog to look as commercial as possible, then your course of action is clear.

The key point in all cases is that you have complete control over the kinds of ads (text, image, video) and where on your blog they are placed, as well as some control over the subject of the ads. You can learn via experiment which combinations look best and which produce the most revenue.

2. Amazon Associates has a different approach. You place ads for Amazon's books and other products on your blog page and get paid a percentage every time someone clicks on the ads and buys something from Amazon. The percentage, as of January 2009, starts at 4 percent for the first 6 sales, increases to 6 percent when sales number 7 or more, increases to 6.5 percent when there are 33 or more sales, and so forth. As an author, I find it valuable to have numerous Amazon ads on my blogs for my own books. But the more general guiding principle for this kind of monetization is not that you need to be an author of books sold on Amazon but a blogger willing to do the little research required to see which books on Amazon relate to subjects of your blog posts.

For example, in a review of an episode of "Lost" in its fourth season, in which time travel played a major role, I not only placed Amazon ads for my own time travel novel, "The Plot to Save Socrates", but for such time travel classics as Isaac Asimov's "The End of Eternity" and Robert Heinlein's "The Door into Summer".

Because Amazon sells far more than books, you can use its Associate services to sell a wide range of products on your site. For example, if have a blog about food, you could put Amazon ads for foodstuffs, beverages, cutlery, etc. on your blog.

CafePress operates in a somewhat similar way. You design a logo, which can be placed on coffee mugs, T-shirts, etc. You place an ad for the item on your blog.

CafePress produces an item every time one is ordered—publishing on demand— at no cost to you. CafePress sets its price, and you can add whatever you like, above that price, for your commission. If your logo is some sort of advertising for your blog, you earn not only a commission but also good publicity for every sale.

Unlike Amazon, however, you either need sufficient talent to design an attractive logo for CafePress or will have to hire or persuade someone to design it for you. In contrast, Amazon supplies images of the book covers and all of its products in the ads for your blog.

3. In the case of Google AdSense and Amazon Associates, nothing is changed in the writing of your blogs—the ads are placed at the bottom, the sides, the top or in the middle (if you prefer) of your text. PayPerPost, one of several different such operations, offers another kind of approach to making money from your blog: You are paid to write posts on given subjects.

PayPerPost pays anywhere from $5 to $500 or more for blog posts requested by its clients. Your payment depends mainly upon the popularity of your blog— how many readers the advertiser can expect will see your post about the advertiser's subject.

The great advantage of this kind of blog monetization is the money you see in hand from your blog posts. The leading earner on PayPerPost in 2007 earned more than $12,000 for her written-to-order blog posts.

The disadvantage is you may be tempted to write about subjects you otherwise might not want to write about in your blog. This can undermine one of the crucial benefits of new new media and blogging: writing whatever you want, with no gatekeepers to approve or disapprove of your output. The fine line to be walked is writing reviews of products you already know about and like. But this could be difficult: Would you pass up $500 to write a positive post about a product you thought was just OK, not great?

The principle of being honest with your readers can also come into conflict under this kind of monetized blogging. PayPerPost insists as standard operating procedure that all of its assigned posts have a clearly displayed notice that the blog post was purchased. As a further safeguard, PayPerPost also requires all participating bloggers to publish at least one nonassigned post for every purchased post, which further makes clear to the reader which posts were hired. But several other "blog for money" organizations want otherwise—reasoning, probably correctly, that readers would take the post more seriously if they thought the post came from the blogger's mind and heart and not the advertiser's paycheck. Indeed, even PayPerPost offers a few of these "nondisclosure" opportunities, with the proviso that it did not endorse the approach but would be willing to serve as broker if that is what the advertiser and the blogger both wanted.

Another, related problem can arise from the general topic of the blog post. Favorably reviewing a movie you already saw and liked, or even expected that you would like, is one thing. But what about accepting PayPerPost blogging assignments for political or social issues, in which the assignment requires you to write on behalf of the issue or candidate? Even if you support the issue, and even with the PayPerPost disclosure advisory on assigned posts and no advisory on everything else, taking on such political assignments can cast doubt among your readers that you mean what you say in your nonassigned posts. If you want your readers to be 100 percent sure that the political analyses they read on your blog are 100 percent yours, the safest course of action may be to avoid doing any PayPerPost or assigned blog posts on political and social subjects. (See also "Bloggers and Lobbyists," later in this chapter.)

4. You can put a PayPal donation widget—a digital money tip jar—either on your overall blog or on any specific blog post. PayPal is in effect an online banking service, which receives payments from other PayPal accounts, as well as traditional credit cards, and makes payments to other PayPal accounts. PayPal account holders can transfer funds from PayPal to their traditional bank accounts.

How much money can a PayPal donation button generate on a blog? Shaun Farrell's 2007 podiobook of my 1999 novel "The Silk Code" provides an instructive example. A podiobook is an audiobook available free, online, in weekly installments, from Podiobook.com (see Chapter 10, "Podcasting," for details). "The Silk Code" podiobook placed in the top 20 of podiobooks downloaded in 2007 (its exact placement in the top 20 was not revealed). More than a thousand people downloaded all or part of the novel. Farrell received about $100 in the PayPal donation box on his blog page.

But a podiobook is not a typical blog. Because a podiobook appeals to an audience that might otherwise purchase an audiobook, donations to the author (and, in Farrell's case, the narrator) make some sense. In contrast, authors of written blogs tell me they are lucky to receive even a few dollars a year from their tip jars.

5. A fifth way of making money from one's blog draws upon the oldest form of advertising and predates new new media by centuries: You can accept and place ads on your blog, paid for directly by the advertiser. You can make far more money than via Google AdSense—you can charge whatever the market for blog ads will bear, based on the number of people who read your blog—but the price you pay for not going through the Google AdSense middleman is you have to find the advertisers, or they have to find you.

This kind of advertising goes back to the advent of newspapers in the 1500s, 1600s and 1700s—they were called "pamphlets" back then—and developed as follows: Originally, printers were funded and supported by the monarchs of Europe, and especially fortunate printers were designated "royal presses." But monarchs expected printers to publish stories favorable to the monarchs, and eventually some printers began to chafe under this arrangement.

Merchants with ships laden with goods from the New World provided a way out and indeed a solution that provided the economic basis of democracy. Merchants paid printers to run announcements of their products, what we today call "ads." Other than printing these announcements, the presses could print whatever else they pleased. Printers thereby gained the economic freedom to break free of royal purse strings and political reins. This worked best first in England and then America, which enacted the First Amendment to ensure that the government, even in a democracy, could never control the press. (As I detail in my "The Flouting of the First Amendment," 2005, the First Amendment has not always been adhered to in America; see the "First Amendment" section later in this chapter. See also "The Soft Edge", Levinson, 1997, for more on the advent of advertising and its political consequences.)

The advertising symbiosis, however—merchants get publicity, printers get money, both are beneficiaries—became a bedrock of American media and continued in the age of radio and television, which went a big step further than newspapers by providing content free of charge to their listeners and viewers. Consumers paid for the receiving equipment—radio or television set—but received the content free. Radio and television stations and networks made money by attracting consumers of the free programming and then selling airtime, or exposure to the audience numbers, to sponsors. The free blog, though it is written like a newspaper article, is therefore more like the traditional broadcast media in terms of being free. And, although one of the hallmarks of new new media content is that it costs the consumer nothing, this characteristic began not with new new media but with older broadcast media. Ironically, although free radio and television continue to flourish, the number of network television viewers has been declining for almost two decades, with paid cable and free new new media drawing away audiences (Associated Press, 2008; but see also Cheng, 2008, for a report that 64 percent of viewers between ages 9 and 17 go online when watching television, which suggests a mutually beneficial relationship between the two media for young viewers).

In all such classic cases of paid advertising, the ad is paid for on a cost-per-thousand basis—how many thousands of people will see or hear the ad. Television lives or dies depending on the number of its viewers, as reported by the Nielsen ratings. These ratings are based on statistically valid samples of the total television viewing public. The new new medium of blogging on the Web offers direct counts, not samples, of blog visitors (see "Gauging the Readership of Your Blog," later in this chapter).

The blog also offers opportunities to refine the circumstances for payment for an ad, not available in print or broadcast media, where the reader or viewer can not only see the ad but click on it and purchase the product. The blogger is then paid a percentage of the sale. The additional possibility of seeing an ad and clicking on it, but not buying the product, is used as one of the payment criteria by Google AdSense, as we saw in the first example of monetization described above.

Television, radio and newspapers charge flat rates for their ads, based on how many people can be expected to see or hear the ad (the cost-per-thousand formula). In contrast, although blog ads that come directly from advertisers can also work on such a flat-rate basis, the blogger also can be paid based on the number of impressions, clicks, or actual purchases resulting from an ad. When payments are made based on flat rates or numbers of impressions—or on factors other than number of purchases or clicks, which can be recorded by the advertiser—then methods of gauging the readership of one's blog are crucial.

These five ways of earning money from your blog—Google AdSense, Amazon ads, PayPerPost, PayPal donations and direct ad purchases—all pertain to blogs completely under the blogger's control. In the "Blogging for Others" section later in this chapter, we will consider the opportunities for remuneration when you blog for someone else. But, first, let's consider in a little more detail the degree to which any way of monetizing your blog may be incompatible with the communicative and democratizing ideals of blogging.

Is Monetization Incompatible with the Ideals of Blogging?

Not everyone in the blogosphere is happy about the monetization possibilities of blogging. Jeff Jarvis, creator of Entertainment Weekly and the well-known BuzzMachine blog, put the "problem" he saw with the PayPerPost model as follows: "The advertisers are trying to buy a blogger's voice, and once they've bought it they own it" (Friedman, 2007).

David Sirota, senior fellow at the Campaign for America's Future, sees a different kind of harm arising from advertising in blogging. Criticizing a report that Jonathan Martin gave on Politico.com about President-elect Obama's December 7, 2008, appearance on "Meet the Press"—that Obama was "backing off" (Martin's phrase) his campaign pledges on taxes and Iraq—Sirota concluded with the following: "I'm not linking to [Martin's] story because the entire reason the Politico made up this outrageous lie is to get people to link to the story and build up traffic which it then uses to attract ad revenue" (Sirota, 2008).

Jarvis, then, sees money as putting literal words in bloggers' mouths—or via their fingers in their blogs—while Sirota sees the desire to increase the number of readers, to increase advertising revenue, as leading to the writing of blogs of "outrageous lies."

Both concerns may be warranted. But let's try to put the pursuit of money by the press in historical context. Why and how did advertising as a source of income for the press arise in the first place? And what damage, if any, has resulted to a free press from this?

As we saw in the previous section, advertising was adopted by the press in the first place as a means of freeing the press from economic and thus political reliance on the monarchies of Europe. And as far as we know, there have been but three sources of income for the press, and for media in general, in history.

One is government support, which has always translated into government control of the media. Whether Pravda in the Soviet Union or the BBC in Britain or the royal press hundreds of years earlier in that country under Henry VIII, government financing of the press has always made the press an organ of government. In a totalitarian society this hardly matters, because the government controls everything anyway. In a democracy, government control of the press can undermine the democracy, because it can obstruct the press from being a critic of the government and reporting to the people what the government might be doing wrong. During the Falklands War, to cite just one example, the British government controlled and censored the BBC's reporting on that war (see Levinson, 1997, for details). Indeed, one of the reasons that democracy was able to arise and flourish in England is that printers were able to break free of royal control. Thomas Jefferson, James Madison and James Monroe understood the crucial role of a free press in a democratic society, which is why they insisted on the First Amendment to our Constitution and its guarantee of a press unfettered by governmental fiat.

A second source of income for media is the purchase or rental of the media by the public. Sale of newspapers, magazines, books, DVDs, CDs and movie theater tickets (a form of rental) has worked well for many media. But they have not worked very well for newspapers, especially in recent years. The New York Times thus loses money on every paper it sells, and The Village Voice dispensed with its price per copy altogether and has been distributed at no charge for the past decade. Newspapers do this because they want to keep their number of readers as high as possible, to attract advertising revenue.

Furthermore, or maybe first of all, to charge for reading of a blog would cut far more deeply against the ideal of blogging, and new new media in general, as available to the public for free, than would advertising, if needed to keep the blog free. (But in May 2009, Amazon—a new, not a new new medium—began offering monthly subscriptions to blogs for a dollar or two for Kindle users, in addition to electronic books. [See Brown, 2009.] This might make sense, given that Kindle devices can receive content from the Web without the usual wireless connection, and therefore can make blogs available when would-be readers are away from their laptops or cellphones with Internet access.)

Which brings us to the third source of income for media for the past hundreds of years: advertising. In a Platonically ideal world, perhaps we would not need it—not for blogging or older media such as newspapers and magazines. Independently wealthy bloggers with the best of motives would write just the truth as they saw it and would not contaminate it in either reality or appearance by taking any money for their work. But we do not live in such an ideal realm—in our world, bloggers and people in all media need to eat. I love teaching, but I would never dream of doing it for no payment, because I do have to pay my mortgage and my electricity bill, and, although our children are now adults, we like to help them out with a little money too, from time to time.

And what, specifically, is the evidence of damage done to blogging, either by the PayPerPost approach or the pursuit of advertising? Sirota's post is titled "Politico's Jayson Blair"—after the infamous New York Times reporter who made up stories and plagiarized (Levinson, "Interview about Jayson Blair," 2003)—and unintentionally brings home a telling point: The "newspaper of record," The New

York Times, was plagued by "outrageous lies" on its pages by Jayson Blair. Was that because it, too, was pursuing advertising revenue?

The more likely explanation is that there is no cause-and-effect between advertising and faulty reporting, which arises from the frailties of all human beings, including reporters (though see Nissenson, 2007, for Dorothy Schiff, New York Post publisher, killing a story in 1976 because her advertisers objected to it). Nor is there any evidence that PayPerPost blogging has deluded the public with lies. If a post is clearly identified as written to someone else's specification, right before and after posts that are clearly written only to the blogger's specifications, the reader is no more likely to perceive the paid-for post as the blogger's "voice" than the reader of a newspaper is to confuse an ad with the paper's editorial opinion.

Dressing Up Your Blog with Images, Videos and Widgets

Ads on blogs come in text, images and video. Amazon.com ads have images of the books for sale, and Google AdSense offers options for text, image or video ads, as discussed previously. But images and videos also can be placed on blogs just to make the blogs more interesting, colorful and spiffy—to illustrate blog posts or just attract viewers—with no ad revenue earned from them.

Many blog platforms (such as Blogspot, see "Different Blogging Platforms" later in this chapter) allow the writer to upload images and videos directly to the blog. In the case of videos, they also can easily be embedded by code available from YouTube.

Photobucket is an example of a free site that hosts images. HTML code is generated for every hosted image and can be edited to change the size and placement of the image on your blog. You can align images to the left or right, and the text will wrap around them. Links can also be easily placed in the image code, so that when readers click on the images, they will be taken to the page on the Web in the link. This is the way Amazon and Google image ads work.

Flickr not only hosts images but works, in effect, as a photographic blog, or a photographic equivalent of YouTube, which attracts viewers to its site, as well as provides content embeddable on blogs.

Widgets are a way that blog posts, videos and links of any kind can easily be integrated into a blog or Web page. As distinct from a "button," which usually links to just one other site, a widget is designed to offer numerous connections. MySpace and Facebook, for example, supply "buttons" or "badges," which allow readers to connect to a specified profile. Amazon and Twitter supply widgets, which allow readers to connect to numerous pages on those systems.

Widgets are supplied not only by companies such as Amazon.com to help readers of your blog or Web site see Amazon's products (for which purchases you will be paid a percentage, if you are an Amazon Associate—see "Monetizing Your Blog" earlier in this chapter) but also by networks and organizations that are not selling anything. Twitter's widgets allow your readers to see the twitters, or one-line status announcements, of specified people or everyone on Twitter. In all cases, the widgets are supplied for free. They, in effect, act as little building blocks of the Web, appearing on your page with a bundle of connections to other Web sites.

One of the distinguishing characteristics of widgets in contrast to static links is that the links in widgets change, or are "dynamic," based on the purpose of the widget. Amazon has widgets for its products that provide updating links to those products based on the content of blog posts on the same page. For example, if I post a review about "Dexter", the Showtime television series, my Amazon widget will display the "Dexter" novels and DVDs of earlier seasons. Google AdSense ads work in the same way. Twitter's widgets are constantly updated to show the most recent tweets. I also have a "Politics" widget from an organization called "Widget Box," which takes yet a third approach, displaying headlines with links for the most popular—meaning, most read—political posts on blogs in the "Politics" division of the Widget Box network (divisions exist for television, science and other categories). Widget Box also provides a widget that lists the posts in your blog with updates; this can be very useful if you have more than one blog and want to attract readers back and forth and, of course, if you can get friends to put your widget on their blogs and Web pages. Blogging platforms such as Blogspot also provide numerous widgets, including one—much like the Twitter widget—that lists and links to the most recent posts of other blogs, which you have entered into your "blogroll."

Adaptive Blue offers one of the most sophisticated widgets available. I have one for my novels and another for my nonfiction books. The covers of the books are displayed in the widget. Clicking on a cover will provide links to where the book can be purchased online (Amazon, Barnes & Noble, Powell's), reviews of the book, Wikipedia and Google pages for the book (if they exist), and Facebook and Twitter and other social media where the book can be discussed.

The multiplicity of links in Adaptive Blue widgets brings home another point about monetization of the Web. Although the Adaptive Blue widget is not itself commercial, as is an Amazon or Google AdSense widget, it nonetheless links to sites such as Amazon and to new new media such as Facebook, where ads are displayed. Similarly, political blogs in the Widget Box political widget may display Google AdSense or any kind of ads, even if your blog does not. If for some reason you are not only allergic to making money but to aiding any kind of income generation on the Web, you need to take special care in choosing your widgets.

Gauging the Readership of Your Blog

Unless you blog purely for the pleasure of seeing your writing on a Web page— which is certainly a motivating factor for most writers—you will be interested in how many people are reading your words, and in other statistics that measure the popularity of your blog.

Services such as Statcounter and SiteMeter provide details on the number of people who visit your blog, including raw number of visitors, what pages they read, where the visitors come from (what countries, what Web sites, etc.), how long they stay on your blog and where they go when they leave your blog (what links they click). The basic services are free, with paying options that provide analyses of larger groups of visitors.

Technorati measures a blog's popularity in a different way: how many other blogs have linked to it. Further, Technorati keeps track of the linkage of all blogs that link to yours. Being linked to 10 blogs with 500 links each is more impressive than being linked to 100 blogs with 5 links each. In the first case, many more readers are likely to see your blog than in the second.

Alexa takes another, complementary approach, ranking blogs according to a formula based on number of readers, links and rates of growth. Google PageRank does something similar but over longer periods of time. Both systems are secretive about the precise "algorithms" they use to determine the rankings, to discourage unscrupulous bloggers and Web site developers from manipulating or "gaming" the data to achieve higher rankings.

Such "gaming" is something we will encounter in other systems that measure popularity or base their listings on popularity. Digg, which we will look at in Chapter 5, puts articles, images and videos on its front pages based on the number of "Diggs" and "Buries" submissions may receive from readers. Attempts to inflate this number, and Digg's attempts to prevent that, provide one of the main dramas of its operation and indeed of new new media such as Facebook and MySpace, where status is based on numbers of "Friends."

Different Blogging Platforms

My InfiniteRegress.tv blog uses Google's "Blogspot," or "Blogger," platform. In addition to the virtue of being free, it offers a big assortment of blog templates (which determine what the blog looks like—colors, positioning of blog posts and sidebars, etc.) or allows you to import and therein design your own template. The Blogspot platform also offers extensive control over comments, including notification of new comments and various moderator tools such as CAPTCHAs. Blogspot also allows multiple blogs by the same or multiple authors, all at no charge.

A key feature of Blogspot—perhaps the most important—is that bloggers have access to the HTML code that determines the look and feel of the blog and allows easy insertion of stat counters, automatic Digg counters, etc.

MySpace, Amazon, Vox and other Web sites also offer free blog space to their users but with no access to the HTML code and far less control over the blog in general. Wordpress is most like Blogspot, in that it offers a wide variety of features and is free.

At the other end of the spectrum, some platforms offer features equivalent to Blogspot but are not free. Typepad charges anywhere from $4.95 (basic service) to

$89.95 (business service) per month. Its main advantage over Blogspot is a more distinctive look (assuming you like that), and it comes packaged with stat counters and other features. Movable Type is free for noncommercial use (no ads on your site, and you do not use it to make money) or otherwise costs from $49.95 to $99.95 per year. LiveJournal's basic blogging account is free but offers an "upgrade" with increased image storage capacity for less than $2 per month. (Typepad, Movable Type, and LiveJournal are all owned by Six Apart.)

In the end, if money is no object, your choice of blog platform will likely be most determined by what you find most attractive or consonant with your image of your blog's purpose. For a cheapskate like me, the free cost of Blogspot is irresistible. And I do like its general appearance and the powers I have to sculpt and control the blog.

Are Bloggers Entitled to the Same First Amendment Protection as Old-Media Journalists?

Blogging can be serious business, not only in the money that can be made and the ethical issues involved, which we have examined previously, but in its political and social impact and its relationship to older media ranging from newspapers to television. We turn in this section and the remainder of this chapter to a consideration of some of these issues, starting with the question of whether bloggers are protected from government interference under the First Amendment.

The Supreme Court has generally sided with newspapers and print media on First Amendment and freedom of the press issues in the 20th century. In *The New York Times v. Sullivan* (1964), the Court severely limited the degree to which the press could be sued for defamation and libel; in *The New York Times v. the United States* (1971), the Court stopped the Nixon administration's attempt to shut down publication of the Pentagon Papers (see Tedford, 1985, for a detailed discussion of these and the other First Amendment cases mentioned in this chapter; see also Levinson, "The Flouting of the First Amendment," 2005).

Broadcast journalism, the other old-media part of the press, has not fared as well. *Red Lion Broadcasting v. Federal Communications Commission* (1969) held that, since broadcast stations are necessarily scarce in comparison to print media—only a limited number of stations can fit on the broadcast spectrum, in contrast to no natural or technological limit on the number of newspaper publishers—radio and television stations had to give "equal time" to opposing political opinions (also known as the "Fairness Doctrine"). And although more an issue of social satire than hard reporting, the Supreme Court ruled in *Federal Communications Commission v. Pacifica Foundation* (1979) that the FCC had a right to tell radio stations not to broadcast comedian George Carlin's "Seven Dirty Words" routine (the reason in this case was that listeners could tune in and accidentally hear such objectionable broadcasts, unlike a deliberate decision to buy a copy of Playboy or Penthouse).

New media—or the appearance of old media such as newspapers on the Web—received a major endorsement by the Supreme Court in *Reno v. American Civil Liberties Union* (1997), in which the Communications Decency Act and Attorney General Janet Reno's attempt to use it to punish Joe Shea for publication of "indecent" language (critical of Congress for passing this law) in an online magazine were struck down as a violation of the First Amendment's protection of the press (see Levinson, 1997, for more). The decision in effect held that an online magazine was more like a newspaper than a radio or television broadcast.

And what of new new media—such as blogging?

Here a battle has been waging over government coercion of the press in an area that may be a bit beyond First Amendment territory: shield laws, which protect journalists from being forced to reveal their sources to prosecutors and courts and do not address the right to publish, per se. The Supreme Court held in *Branzburg v. Hayes* (1972) that the First Amendment did not give journalists the right to refuse to testify or reveal sources, but Congress and the courts could enact legislation that gave journalists that privilege. Shield law advocates argue that, without such protection, journalists would be unable to do their jobs, since their sources could not rely on any pledge made by a journalist not to reveal his or her sources in a story. I agree and was quoted in USA Today about New York Times reporter Judith Miller's 2005 imprisonment for failing to reveal her sources in the Valerie Plame CIA leak investigation, "It is wrong to jail a reporter for protecting sources, including flawed reporters" (Levinson, quoted in Johnson, 2005). Miller quoted my comment in the opening statement of her testimony to the U.S. Senate Judiciary Committee, Hearing on Reporters' Shield Legislation, on October 19, 2005.

At present, there is no federal shield law, which is why federal prosecutor Patrick Fitzgerald was able to get a judge to put Miller behind bars. Thirty-six states and the District of Columbia have shield laws, but do they—should they—protect bloggers or journalists who blog?

Judith Miller reported on the "Fox News Watch" (December 6, 2008) that, for the first time, more online journalists than print journalists had been arrested around the world in 2008.

The imprisonment of video blogger Josh Wolf in San Francisco in 2006–2007 shows that, for some people, the very phrase "journalists who blog" is a contradiction. Wolf was videotaping a protest in San Francisco in July 2005 about the G-8 Summit taking place then in Scotland. He sold some of his video to local television stations and posted other clips on his blog. A police offer, ironically named Peter Shields, was assaulted at another part of the demonstration, not videotaped by Wolf, and suffered a fractured skull. Wolf was asked by authorities to turn over his videotapes. He refused and was thrown in jail. Commented U.S. Attorney Kevin Ryan in a court filing, "[Wolf] was simply a person with a video camera who happened to record some public events"; U.S. District Judge William Alsup, apparently agreeing, described Wolf as an "alleged journalist." Wolf's attorney, First Amendment advocate Martin Garbus, thought otherwise and indicated, "I would define a journalist as someone who brings news to the public" (see Kurtz, 2007).

Wolf was released in April 2007, after eight months in prison, when prosecutors withdrew their insistence that Wolf had to testify. I concur completely with Garbus and was pleased to produce several blog posts and one podcast (Levinson, "Free Josh Wolf," 2007) as well as a letter to the federal prosecutors on Wolf's behalf.

One way of looking at this case, and the more general issue of whether bloggers are bona fide journalists, is how to best apply Marshall McLuhan's famous aphorism that "the medium is the message" (1964). Applied superficially, we might well conclude, as Prosecutor Ryan did, that the medium of blogging is different from the media of print and broadcasting, as it indeed is, and different enough to negate or not allow journalists in its online ranks. A more accurate analysis, however, would note that there are media within media—that journalism, a form of communication, is a medium that can be presented via other media, such as newspapers, radio, TV broadcasts and written and video blogs (see Levinson, 1999, for more on media within media). As Garbus observed, the medium or practice of journalism is the bringing of "news to the public." Wolf was clearly working in that medium, within the larger packaging of video blogging.

Wolf's case was likely complicated by the fact he was not only a blogger but also not a traditional blogger, in that he was using video rather than text as his medium (media within media: journalism via video via blog). Text blogging, which is what we have been looking at in this chapter, has significant differences from video blogging, most importantly that the text can be written and uploaded and therein disseminated at least a little more quickly, with less technical requirement or savvy, than videos. But Garbus's definition of what makes a journalist indicates that the capacity for journalism is not among such differences. We will look further at the special qualities of video in new new media in the next chapter, about YouTube. But whatever these qualities, they offer but another opportunity for journalism and all communication, unfettered by editors and experts and bosses—and, one hopes, government—as do all new new media.

Bloggers and Lobbyists

A related issue surfaced in Washington state in December 2008 ("Fox Report with Shepard Smith"), where the Public Disclosure Commission began looking at whether bloggers who are paid to write posts endorsing specific positions are, in effect, lobbyists and therefore subject to the regulations that govern them (these amount to always disclosing that you are a paid lobbyist).

Horsesass.com blogger David Goldstein argued on the Fox segment that bloggers are entitled to First Amendment protection from any disclosures to the government, including whether they are paid for their blogs and who is paying them. But advertising and lobbying are already under substantial governmental regulation, which insists on full disclosure for lobbyists and truth in advertising for commercials on television, radio, the press and indeed anywhere. Are the lobbying laws themselves in violation of the First Amendment? And what about the restrictions on advertising?

The question regarding advertising and governmental insistence on truth is the easiest to answer, because advertising is clearly a form or part of business, which is itself regulated in numerous ways by the government. False advertising is surely a kind of fraud in business and therefore not really in the same arena as reporting and commenting on public policy or any other subject—the job of the press, whether new new media blogs or old media newspapers.

Regulation of lobbying is a different issue, part of the goal of making politics in our democracy "transparent," as in obliging candidates for office to reveal their financial contributors. I am not sure, even aside from blogging, that government monitoring of election contributions is in the best interests of our democracy. An argument could be made that the best policy is for the government to keep its hands and scrutiny totally off election financing, as such supervision could lead to a party in power taking actions that support its continuing dominance. But if, for the sake of argument, we agreed that lobbyist financing should always be made public, there is still the question of whether a blogger being paid to write in favor of a candidate, official, or political position is in effect a lobbyist.

A lobbyist usually works on an interpersonal basis, via meetings with the targets of the lobbying (lawmakers, etc.) to convince, cajole, and pressure the targets to vote or act in favor of or against a certain piece of legislation, or to take a certain position on a package or wide range of bills revolving around a central issue, such as global warming. Although production of press releases may well be part of such efforts, the text is just a component of the campaign.

In contrast, a blog post, whether paid for or created on the blogger's initiative, exists in its own right on a blog page. A lobbyist may well link to it, reprint it or include it in the campaign materials, but if we are talking about a blog post, and not a press release, the text also has a life of its own. Although it obviously has characteristics in common with advertising and should be identified as a purchased post (as discussed previously in "Monetizing Your Blog"), I would argue that government insistence that the blogger reveal all circumstances of the purchase goes too far and does violate the blogger's First Amendment rights. The publisher paid an advance and will pay royalties to me for this book. Newspapers pay reporters salaries. The name of the publisher is on the title page of this book, and the name of any newspaper is clear to any reader. But other than the IRS getting notified of this income for tax purposes, no one would dream of saying the government has a right to know the specific financial arrangements between my publisher and me, or between a newspaper and its reporters. A blogger being paid to write on behalf of a political cause or candidate should be entitled to the same protections.

Anonymity in Blogging

Although bloggers should not be compelled by government to reveal the circumstances of a blog post's creation, good form certainly requires that a blogger should let readers know when a post is hired. This question of what should and should not be revealed about how and why a blog post is written relates to a larger question of anonymity, or whether a blogger (or commenter) should write under his or her name.

Anonymity is antithetical to journalism; most reporters and documentarians, including Josh Wolf, are all too happy to have their names associated with their work, and, indeed, in old media such as newspapers, a byline is rightly considered crucial in building a career.

But The New York Times (Glater, 2008) reported a case in which a district attorney in the Bronx subpoenaed a text blog about New York politics, titled "Room 8," to reveal or help prosecutors discover the identities of several anonymous bloggers. As was the outcome with the Josh Wolf case, the DA's office withdrew the request—this time under threat of a lawsuit by the blog over violation of its First Amendment rights.

The great advantage of anonymous blogging, of course, is that it maximizes the freedom of bloggers to speak or post their minds without fear of reprisal from supervisors, bosses, voters, friends and family. Anonymous blogging goes even further in this direction than blogging under a pseudonym or a nickname unrelated to the blogger's real name—all anonymous blog posts literally have the same "anonymous" attribution, which defeats any attempt to identify a series of blog posts as the work of a single person, obviously apparent when a post is signed by a pseudonym, even though the real name of the blogger is nonetheless not known.

Posting without revealing one's identity has a long history on the Web and online communication. When my wife, Tina Vozick, and I founded Connected Education in the mid-1980s—a nonprofit organization that offered courses for academic credit, completely online, in cooperation with the New School and other land-based institutions of higher education (see Levinson, 1985, 1997)—one of the first things I discussed with a colleague, Peter Haratonik at the New School for Social Research, was whether we should allow anonymous comments in the Connect Ed Café, an online forum for casual discussion. Anonymous comments by students in their online classes were ruled out from the beginning, but we thought that perhaps discussion in the Café would benefit from the opportunity of anonymity by those who wanted it. In the end, we decided against it; people don't like talking to people with "bags over their heads," as Haratonik put it.

But anonymity, and/or pretending to be someone you are not, has evolved into many other uses in blogging and new new media, including not only the capacity to make controversial posts without worry of reprisal but also disruptive, cyberbullying and cyberstalking comments without revealing one's identity (see Chapter 11). Used for such purposes, anonymity serves as a coward's mask for reprehensible behavior.

In an entirely different kind of disruptive application, anonymous and pseudonymous accounts can be employed to inflate the popularity of a blog post or anything with a URL on the Web. All the inflator needs to do is create multiple accounts. This is a significant concern on Digg. It also rears its head on Wikipedia, where "sock-puppets," or accounts created by users to buttress their arguments, can short circuit or bias attempts to build a consensus among online editors. We will look at these abuses in more detail in Chapters 4 and 5.

There may also be a personal disadvantage to both anonymous and pseudonymous blogging for the blogger, in addition to the professional problem of not building your reputation as a writer. I often joke that I would never write under a pseudonym, because I want the girl who sat next to me in seventh grade, and didn't pay much attention to me, to see the error of her ways when she walks into a bookstore. The general principle here is that anonymous writing will not feed your taste for fame, if that is what you seek.

Anonymity is obviously easier in text media than audio-visual media, where disguising of voices and images takes a little work, and any muffling of sound or image is obvious. Indeed, anonymous comments are an option on most blogs, although the moderator can block anonymous comments. If a blogger wants to encourage discussion, blocking or removal of a comment merely because it is anonymous seems counterproductive. As a rough, anecdotal statistic of the popularity of anonymous comments on blogs, more than one of four comments on my Infinite Regress blog are anonymous.

Blogging for Others

Although blogging on your own blog is the newest new media use of blogging—that is, the specific kind of blogging that most captures the qualities of new new media and its differences from older media—numerous blogs on the Web permit, invite and consist of blogs written by people who are not the blog's owner. The crucial difference between writing for these kinds of blogs and your own blog, of course, is that you have far less control over how what you write is published on the blogs of others. In its most extreme form, this kind of gatekeeping can decide whether your post will be published. The applicant blogger is in such cases no different than a freelance writer or reporter submitting a story to an online newspaper. But even when the publication of anything you submit is assured, writing for the blogs of others may leave decisions in the hands of others about where on the blog page your post is placed, in what category and so forth. The blogger may also be deprived of the ability to edit the post after it has been published, remove or moderate comments, keep track of the number of readers, and earn advertising revenue from the blog post. These and other specific limitations of blogging for others differ from blog to blog.

The great advantage of blogging for sites other than yours is that these sites may well have enormously greater numbers of readers than does your blog. The Daily Kos, for example, had some 5 million readers on Election Day 2008, and the number of its readers in the days before and after was no lower than about 2.5 million. Compare those numbers with the readership of USA Today, the highest circulation newspaper in the United States, which is just over 2 million per day, and you can get an idea of the power of the most successful blogs to attract large numbers of readers.

The Daily Kos started in 2002, which makes it one of the oldest of the new new media. It publishes "diaries" submitted by registered users (registration is free and open to everyone). Such blog posts cannot be submitted more than once a day. They are listed briefly on the front page—unless they are "Recommended" by Daily Kos editors, in which case they are listed on the front page longer—or, even better, "Front Paged" by the editors, in which case the blog post is actually published on the front page (this happened to me just once, out of about 50 submissions, "Take It from a College Prof: Obama's 'Missing' Paper Is Another Conservative Red Herring," 2008). The writer can edit the diary after publication, but there is a public indication that the diary has been edited. Other registered users can make comments—diaries on the front page often get hundreds of comments—but the writer has no power to eliminate, reject or otherwise moderate the comments. The writer, however, is free to join in such discussions and respond to comments. Diaries can be recommended by readers. Comments can be rated (not recommended), and writers can also post a special comment titled "Tip Jar," which readers can rate and therein show additional approval and appreciation of the diary.

These features of blogging on the Daily Kos provide an excellent example of a mixture of new new media and new media (or top-down, expert-driven, editorially controlled approaches of older print media applied on the Web).

Op-Ed News has more old media—editor-controlled—characteristics. Submissions to Op-Ed News can be published as either "op-eds" or "diaries." The decision is made by the editors and is significant at least insofar as "op-eds" attract greater numbers of readers. Also unlike the Daily Kos, which publishes its content as soon as submitted, Op-Ed News publishing takes time—a few hours or longer—since each submission has to be approved for publication and characterized as either an "op-ed" or a "diary" by the editors.

At the outer fringe of old media, top-down editing on the Web, Jezebel.com (part of the Gawker Media Network) not only moderates comments but insists that first-time writers of comments "audition to be a commentator." The gist of the guidance Jezebel provides for the basis upon which commenters may be approved? "We only approve the comments we love."

The Daily Kos and Op-Ed News both permit cross-posting, or publishing pieces that have already been published on other blogs, including your own. Not so on Blogcritics, which insists on first publication of all submissions. (It adopted this policy in 2007, as a way of maintaining its readership. Google usually puts the earliest publication of a blog at the top of its search results.)

Neither the Daily Kos nor Op-Ed News pays the writers who submit blogs for publication. But some blogs do. This, obviously, can add a powerful incentive for writing for the blogs of others.

Payment can generally come in one of two ways: payment for publication of the story (either on a per-word or per-story basis) or payment from ad revenues earned from your stories' publication. Internet Evolution and iPhone Matters are examples of the first kind of payment. Tucker Max's Rudius Media employs the second method. Guess which kind of payment is most likely to provide the most income?

The answer should be apparent in the "Monetizing Your Blog" section. Advertising on blogs generates negligible payment unless your daily readership is in the many thousands. And, when you're splitting this income with the publisher of the blog, hundreds of thousands of readers a day may be needed to generate hundreds of dollars a month. In contrast, you could earn that amount with a single post on blogs that pay for your articles or via daily, short posts on blogs that pay even a few dollars for each of your postings.

Open Salon initiated a different, third approach in 2008. The classic Salon site, with roots going back to 1995, is a mix of old and new media strategies. It provides free blogging content, updated daily, but also offers a variety of paid subscription options to readers. Open Salon takes a clearly new new media approach, encouraging readers to register for free and post their own blogs. As on the Daily Kos, blogs can have "Tip Jars," but in the case of Open Salon, these can receive not only kudos but also cash, in the form of donations of $1 or more made by readers. The Tip Jars are thus not metaphoric but real insofar as the tips consist of real money. At this point, the success of Open Salon as a way of generating income from blogging has yet to be fully determined. Presumably the income will be far less than that received for publication of a story on a per-word or per-story basis. (The same applies to the Google AdSense option that Open Salon began providing for its bloggers in June 2009.)

In summary, it is worth noting the obvious: All blogs under the control of someone other than you can not only refuse to publish a given piece by you, but can fire you if you are a regular blogger, or ban you from the blog. The Daily Kos banned Lee Stranahan in August 2008 (Stranahan, 2008) for cross-posting a piece he had written for The Huffington Post, urging John Edwards to tell the truth about his affair first reported in the National Enquirer. Stranahan's banning took place before Edwards admitted to the affair on August 8, but the truth or falsity of Stranahan's or anyone's post is not the issue that concerns us here. The lesson of Stranahan's banning is that any blog other than your own, regardless of how progressive and writer-driven, can still exercise old-style media control any old time it pleases.

The Daily Kos, in terms of the ultimate control it exercises over its pages, is thus no different than The New York Times. Given that the Daily Kos publishes "diaries" written by readers—or, at least in principle, anyone—we can reasonably designate it an example of new new media, in contrast to The New York Times, which is an archetypal old medium in journalism (not really "all the news that's fit to print" but "all the news that we deem fit to print"), with articles written by assigned, professional reporters, even when published on the new medium of the Web. But the Daily Kos is nonetheless very much on the old side of the new new medium continuum, if only because of its power to ban any blogger. In a truer or full-fledged new

new medium, which arises any time anyone writes a blog under his or her control, the blogger may retire or refrain from blogging but cannot be fired or banned.

Of course, a blogging platform—Google's Blogspot or Six Apart's Typepad or Moveable Type—could refuse for whatever reason to provide or sell a platform to a given blogger. But such refusals seem closer to a telephone company refusing to provide service to a given customer—because of the customer's poor credit, for example—than an editor of a blog banning one of its writers.

Changing the World with Your Blog

As in everything we do in life, we may have different motives for publishing our blogs—and often more than one motive. These could include the joy of writing and having other people read what you write, making money, and changing the world—influencing something real in the world, in politics or science or whatever area—by the words on your blog. Words, after all, can be very powerful. And the power of a blog is unique in comparison to older forms of writing, in that the writing, as we have seen, can be instantly published, which means that anyone, including powerful, important and famous people, can read it. A significant limitation, however, is that readers, whether famous, important, powerful or not, are not likely to know about a blogger's writing, are not likely to look for it, and are not likely to pay much attention to it if they stumble upon it, unless the blogger already possesses some of these qualities—that is, the blogger is powerful, important, famous. Nonetheless, when all factors are taken into the equation, the unknown blogger still has a much better chance of being read by the powerful and famous than the unknown writer in older media, mainly because those older, unknown writers had little chance of being published.

How do you know if someone important is reading your blog? Stat counters can tell you the IPs—Internet locations—and geographic locations of your readers. These may include the company or school in which their computer is located but not likely their names. Ultimately, the only completely reliable way of knowing who, specifically, has read your blog is when readers comment, link or refer to your blog in their own blog, or speak or write about your blog in other media.

Rich Sommer's comment on my blog about "Mad Men," discussed previously, would be a case of someone more famous than I not only reading but also communicating to me and the world on my blog. But the world did not change as a result of this. And, indeed, television reviews are not all that likely to have a big impact on the world.

Political blogs of course are different in their potential impact. I have no idea if Barack Obama or any of his close advisers or anyone significant in politics ever read any of my blog posts, let alone was influenced by them.

But on the early afternoon of September 24, 2008, I published a piece on Infinite Regress and cross-posted to Open Salon and several other sites, titled "Obama Should

Reject McCain's Call to Postpone Friday Debate." This was my response to John McCain's announcement that he was putting his campaign on hold, so he could go to Washington to deal with the financial crisis, and his request to Barack Obama to join him in postponing their first scheduled debate of the 2008 presidential election.

I "advised" Obama that postponing the debate would be a big mistake, that the financial crisis called for an affirmation of the democratic process, including a continuation of the campaigns and the scheduled debates, not suspending or delaying them.

I was soon pleased to post the following on my blogs:

> BREAKING NEWS: 4:47 p.m.: Obama just said that he thinks the debates should go on—that this is precisely a time when the American people need to see what he and McCain would do as president. Good!

And, at 6:00 p.m., Joan Walsh, editor of Salon and blogger on Open Salon, posted the following comment on my blog:

> Paul Levinson speaks, Obama listens! I just blogged on this, too!

Did Obama or any of his advisers read my blog? Were they influenced by it? Probably not. Obama's team was far more likely to have read and been influenced by the blog of Joan Walsh, who is not only editor of Salon but a frequent guest on Chris Matthews' "Hardball" and other news shows on MSNBC.

But I've included this true story of my blogging in this book because it highlights the potential of any post, anywhere on the Web, to be read by a presidential candidate or a president him- or herself (especially the case now for Barack Obama, given that we know he is an active BlackBerry user). And this, too, is one of the hallmarks of new new media: You sit at your computer and type your words, and those words can tip the world in a better direction, or at least the direction you think best. You can be a major editor, a college professor, or a sophomore in college or high school.

A Town Supervisor and His Blog

Paul Feiner, who since 1991 has been town supervisor of Greenburgh, New York (an elected two-year term, in Westchester, a little north of New York City), is explicit about his reliance on blogging. When I was a guest on his weekly "Greenburgh Report" radio show on WVOX on January 9, 2009, Feiner explained that he finds comments made on his own, public blog to be helpful, even crucial, in keeping informed of what his constituents are thinking.

Feiner even recognizes the benefits—and drawbacks—of anonymous commenting. "I let people write anonymously on the blog," Feiner told me, even though such commenters can be "very nasty" and "make up stuff that's not true." Feiner appreciates the dividends of this: "I'm able to get a sense from my blog [of] what some of the issues and controversies are going to be well before they hit a Town Board meeting…because sometimes people can say what's really on their mind in a blog....If I hadn't had a blog or used the Internet or just relied on news-papers, I would never know what people are saying, not in my presence."

In other words, for officials and political leaders such as Paul Feiner who perceive the advantages of new new media in governing, we might say that "foreblogged" is forewarned or "fore-informed."

"Bloggers in Pajamas"

The political impact of blogging, however, has not been applauded by everyone. Back in September 2004, Jonathan Klein, a former CBS News executive, defended Dan Rather's "60 Minutes" segment about George W. Bush's lack of National Guard service during the Vietnam War, by observing on Fox News that "You couldn't have a starker contrast between the multiple layers of checks and balances [at "60 Minutes"] and a guy sitting in his living room in his pajamas writing" (quoted by Fund, 2004). Klein, who would soon be appointed CNN/USA president, was attacking the conservative bloggers who were attacking Rather and CBS, and although I thought then and now that CBS and Rather were right to run that story (see Levinson, "Interview by Joe Scarborough about Dan Rather," 2005, and Levinson, "Good For Dan Rather," 2007), I certainly did not agree with Klein's myopic "analysis" of blogging, nor with his confidence in the "multiple layers of checks and balances" in mass media journalism. Jayson Blair's several years of fictitious and plagiarized reporting for The New York Times had already been exposed. And given the power and reach of the Internet even then, and the way all kinds of information could become available in all sorts of unexpected ways, it struck me that pajamas and living rooms were no impediments to the pursuit and publication of truth.

That is obviously much more the case today. But the "bloggers in pajamas" meme lives on, not only as a justifiably sarcastic comment on Klein's 2004 statement and any like-minded old media worshipers still among us—and in the names of successful online news venues (for example, Pajamas Media) and well-read independent blogs such as The Pajama Pundit—but also in the thinking of conservatives such as Sarah Palin, unsuccessful Republican VP candidate in 2008. Palin, shortly after losing the election, told Greta Van Susteren on Fox News that a lot of the media's negative stories about her were due to their reporting on the basis of "some blogger, probably sitting there in their parents' basement, wearing pajamas, blogging some kind of gossip, or a lie" (Palin, 2008). Palin not only demoted the blogger in pajamas from guy to kid, from living room to basement, but later switched the focus of her concern from pajamas and parents' basements to blogging anonymity, telling John Ziegler in the segment of his "Media Malpractice" documentary put on YouTube in January 2009, "When did we start accepting as hard news sources bloggers—anonymous bloggers especially. It's a sad state of affairs in the world of the media today—mainstream media especially, if they're going to be relying on anonymous bloggers for their hard news information. Very scary." (See also Kurtz, 2009.)

In Klein's slight defense, in 2004 new new media were much newer than they are now. The Huffington Post, YouTube and Twitter did not yet even exist, and Facebook was just a few months old. Palin's attack was thus more unwarranted than Klein's.

But her contempt for new new media is nonetheless shared by many in the older media themselves. Or as "John Connor," lead character in Fox's "Terminator: The Sarah Connor Chronicles," sarcastically observed in the 13th episode of its second season (2008), "We all know how reliable bloggers are." That bloggers were mentioned at all on a television series about fictional characters is an indication of how important blogging has become in our lives and culture. But the fact they were cited with disdain shows the degree to which so many people in our real world still distrust them.

Not coincidentally, Facebook took a lashing in the 10th episode of the same season of "The Sarah Connor Chronicles" (2008), a few weeks earlier, when "Riley," John's girlfriend, lambasted her adoptive family and their obliviousness to the real dangers that await them with a remark that all they care about is looking at their "Facebook pages." Meanwhile, over on the premiere of the fifth season of "Weeds" on Showtime in 2009, "Celia Hodes" observed that a Facebook account "would be a waste of time." And "Margene Heffman" on the sixth episode of HBO's third season of "Big Love" in 2009 bad-mouthed yet another new new medium, apologizing that some of the information she had obtained about a Mormon pioneer "may not be right—I got it off Wikipedia."

In incurring this disfavor among some politicians and people who write fiction for older media, new new media continue a tradition that in one way or another afflicted the advent of many nascent media in their time, including the telegraph, motion pictures and television. The London Times delayed printing the news it received about Abraham Lincoln's assassination, because the news was received via telegraph. Motion pictures were considered a "primary school for criminals" early in the 20th century. And first television and, more recently, video games have been blamed for violence in the real world, on the basis of no reliable evidence, or at best a misunderstanding of correlation and causation. Just for good measure, television has been blamed for a reduction in literacy, even though a survey taken in 1978, in the same town in Indiana as in 1944, showed no decline at all, and book sales have risen through the past 50 years of television. (See Levinson, 1997, for details on the initially distrustful reception of telegraph and motion pictures, the continuing attacks on television, and the status of book sales in the 20th century; Maeroff, 1979, for the Indiana literacy study; and Levinson, 2006, for the confusion of correlation with causation in the "evidence" attempting to link violent videogames to violence in the real world.)

The telegraph was replaced in the 20th century by the telephone and, ultimately, by fax and email. But motion pictures and television did just fine, even though the screens on which movies and television shows are viewed are increasingly part of a computer or an iPhone, the same screens on which blogs are read.

And there are those in old media who see blogging as neither bogeyman nor panacea but subject to the same events that threaten to undermine old and new media, and all of society. Or, as Neil Young put it in his 2009 "Fork in the Road" song, in part about the economic crisis: "Keep on blogging, till the power goes out, your battery's dead, twist and shout."

Blogging cannot in itself cure what ails our society. (No communication can.) Blogging certainly cannot solve economic crises or make peace in the world. But it beats the alternative of saying nothing, and it goes a lot further than saying a word to the person next to you or relying entirely on professional reporters and commentators to say it for you.

The Blogosphere Is Not Monolithic and Not All-Powerful

As the initial liberal attack in 2004 on conservative "bloggers in pajamas" and Sarah Palin's 2008 attack on liberal "bloggers in pajamas" indicates, the blogosphere is not monolithic politically or in any other way. And neither are any new new media, which are intrinsically in the business of maximizing individual expression.

But old media continue to encourage monolithic, either/or categorizations and apply these categories to bloggers. On November 20, 2008, for example, Norah O'Donnell had a segment on her afternoon show on MSNBC about how the "liberal bloggers" were "outraged" about the Democrats' decision to allow Joe Lieberman to continue to caucus with the Democrats and keep his position as chair of the Homeland Security Committee. (Lieberman, an Independent/Democratic senator from Connecticut, had vigorously supported Republican John McCain in the 2008 election and had said about Barack Obama, among other things, that whether he was a "socialist" was "a good question.") Markos Moulitsas, founder of the liberal Daily Kos in 2002—after the "kos" in his name—affirmed that, yes, he and liberal bloggers were upset that whereas Barack Obama had promised "change," keeping Lieberman in the caucus, in effect rewarding his attacks on Obama's program of change, could hardly be considered "change."

Similarly, Jim Angle reported on Fox News on December 22, 2008, that the appointment of John Brennan as CIA Chief, intended by Obama, had been "torpedoed by bloggers on the left." Salon's Glenn Greenwald was identified as foremost among this cabal, and Greenwald himself, appearing in that Fox News segment (on Brit Hume's "Special Report"), confirmed that "the Obama team would be foolish if they just ignored what happened on blogs," and he knew "for a fact" that there were "people high up in the Obama campaign and the transition team who read blogs regularly" (confirmation of sorts for what I discussed previously in "Changing the World with Your Blog"). A few days later, on December 26, 2008, CNN's Brian Todd said "people" are referring to Brennan's nixing by bloggers as "blogicide." (The term, however, is more commonly used to describe a blogger's deletion of all of his or her posts, as in Georganna Hancock's "PageRank Promotes Blogicide!" 2007, or a desire to end one's blog in response to a low "PageRank" or measure of popularity by Google.)

If we accept Greenwald's observations as true, and the consequent perspective of this book that presidential advisers who read blogs are doing well for the president and the country by keeping informed of diverse opinion, does that mean that Moulitsas and Greenwald were speaking for all liberal bloggers? Not that they were presenting themselves that way, but MSNBC and Fox presented them as representative of the liberal blogosphere. Would a more accurate depiction have been that the two bloggers were speaking for themselves and offered views shared by many but by no means everyone on the left?

For example, regarding Joe Lieberman, I had written a blog on November 6, 2008, titled "The Shame of Joe Lieberman," which concluded, "I would rather see the Democrats have one vote less in the Senate than ever see you counted as part of our party." So, clearly, I was very angry at Lieberman's behavior in the election, and "outrage" would be an apt description of what I felt.

But by the time Lieberman's continuation in the Democratic caucus was announced two weeks later, I had moved from outrage to something closer to mild annoyance—I didn't like it, but I could see the wisdom in keeping Lieberman in the Democratic fold.

Or consider the Let Joe Stay blog (2008), with the following description on its masthead: "I'm a Democrat counting down the days to President-elect Obama's inauguration. However, in the promised new climate of hope and change, I find it upsetting to see Senator Harry Reid and many of his Democratic colleagues turn against one of their own simply because he chose his longtime friend over his party."

Now, the Let Joe Stay blog is anonymous and, for all we know, was created by a member of Joe Lieberman's family or staff, or by Joe Lieberman himself. And someone could well quibble and say that I, a self-described "progressive libertarian" (2008), am not really a "liberal," even though I favored massive government intervention to help with the 2008–2009 economic crisis, etc. But that's precisely the point—or the mistake of characterizing segments of the blogosphere in monolithic political terms. In reality, the left side of the blogosphere, the part of the blogosphere that enthusiastically supported Barack Obama's election, includes Moulitsas (founder of a blog with millions of readers daily), the Let Joe Stay blogger (whose profile had a total of just 108 views as of January, 2009), and millions of other bloggers (most with very few readers, a few with very many) who write a wide and subtle diversity of political and all manner of opinion.

In contrast, a newspaper has an editorial opinion on its editorial page, along with the opinions of a handful of commentators. These opinions may be similar or contradictory, but they can be accurately summarized at any time. We could count the number of newspapers, survey whether they are primarily liberal (such as The New York Times) or conservative (such as The Wall Street Journal), and obtain a reliable indication of the political valence of newspapers in the United States (or the world), and the points of view espoused in its liberal, conservative, or other segments.

But the blogosphere is less like the realm of newspapers and more like a brain, in which a myriad of thoughts race and can change at any time. Indeed, the blogosphere is even less predictable than a brain, because, although any individual may or may not change his or her mind, the sheer number of inputs into the blogosphere provides a guarantee that at least some part of its "mind" will be changed, somewhere, from minute to minute.

A better way, then, of discussing the impact of any given blogger or bloggers is to give their names and their political identifiers, if known—liberal, conservative, whatever—but resist painting them as part of a "liberal blogosphere" or "conservative blogosphere," which implies a unity of purpose and opinion that does not really exist, except in the perception of some in the old media.

Further Tensions Between New New Media and Older Forms

As we will see throughout this book, media rarely live in harmony. In fact, media throughout history have competed for our attention and our patronage in a struggle for survival that Charles Darwin would have recognized. The only difference is that, in the Darwinian evolution of media, we humans make the natural selections, or decide which media survive (Levinson, 1979).

The competition between new new and older media is therefore no surprise, and it plays out, as we have seen, in the disdain and misunderstanding of new new media by people working in and through older kinds of media. Because blogging is the most prevalent form of new new media, especially in its characteristic of consumers becoming producers, it has received most of the hostility.

Another clear example can be found in the attitudes of official television blogs—message boards set up by television networks for discussion, i.e., promotion, of their shows—to the posting of comments with links to other blogs. Over the past few years, as a low-key experiment, I posted comments on Fox's official blog for "The Sarah Connor Chronicles", NBC's official blog for "Heroes", and ABC's official blog for "Lost". Many of these comments contained links to my reviews of these same television shows on my own Infinite Regress blog.

Moderators from all three blogs occasionally moved or removed my comments, and "The Sarah Connor Chronicles" blog removed my account—i.e., blocked me from its blog completely. Here is the listed policy on links, posted on Fox's official forum about "24": "The only links that are allowed are ones to articles about the show, cast, etc., in the mainstream media, or the official sites of the cast. Links to fan sites, personal sites, competing sites, commercial sites, links to download sites, jpgs, MP3s, etc., are not allowed."

In terms of the tensions between new new and older media we have been tracing, we might put the above policy as follows: "The only links allowed on our new media site, about the old medium of television we are promoting, are links to other new media or official sites such as those in the old, mainstream media or official, professional sites about the show, cast, etc. Links to new new media fan sites, personal sites, competing sites, etc. are not allowed."

A moment's reflection shows how destructive those restrictions are to the purpose of the Fox blogs, which is to promote the television programs. Although links to "unofficial" blogs in comments posted on official blogs may indeed draw readers from the official blogs to the unofficial blogs, the readers of the unofficial blogs are still reading discussions of the television program that is the subject of the official blog.

The phrase "competing sites" in the original statement of the rules shows, in particular, just how illogical and counterproductive this policy is. What is a "competing site"? Is not any site that posts blogs and reviews of the same television series a site not in competition but in support of the same goal as the official site? A blog site not allied with any television series—such as BuddyTV, TV.com, or Television Without Pity—might at least have a logical point in forbidding links to other sites, since what these sites want is not necessarily an increase of viewers of any television show but an increase in readers of their site. I would still disagree with such a strategy—because I think the profusion of links raises all boats in the blogosphere, or all blogs—but I could at least understand it. (Of the three blogs mentioned, only Television Without Pity—perhaps apropos to its name—zealously removes links and bans writers for posting them.)

Conceivably, the official blog moderators do not actually read any blog posts with links to other sites, do not click on the external links posted in the official blogs, and as a result assume the external links are nothing more than spam, with no connection to the television show. But, in that case, the old media top-down approach of deciding what gets published, rather than letting all readers become writers and publishers, is still to blame.

For well-established television shows such as "Lost" and "Heroes", such self-destructive actions—or inoculations against the very advantages of viral marketing and promotion—likely will not have much ill effect on the success of the shows. But as we move into a world that increasingly expects unfettered participation of viewers—one of the hallmarks of new new media—the difference between a show that gains a reliable audience and a show that does not may well reside in how fully the online discussion boards divest themselves of old media habits. (It may be worth noting, in this context, that "The Sarah Connor Chronicles" was not renewed by Fox for a third season.)

The misunderstanding of new new media by older forms manifests itself in other ways. As "Mad Men", the AMC television series about early 1960s advertising executives, gained popularity and notice in the first part of 2008, people with names of characters from the show—"Don Draper," "Peggy Olson"—began showing up "tweeting" on Twitter. MySpace has for years seen accounts from users ranging from Socrates to Jack Bauer (hero of Fox television's "24"). These, like the Twitter names, are a form of role-playing that people enjoy, and which therefore help promote the show. AMC at first did not see it that way and filed a copyright violation notice that forced Twitter to take down the accounts. Fortunately for all concerned, AMC's ad agency had more new new media savvy than AMC and talked it into backing off (Terdiman, 2008). Don, Peggy and the gang are happily tweeting, at least as of June 2009.

The Associated Press and bloggers have been embroiled in a different kind of copyright conflict. AP regularly files "take down" notices to bloggers who extensively quote AP articles without permission and payment. (AP is a news agency, or wire service, which sells news reports and stories to newspapers and broadcast media. It has roots going back to 1846 and the advent of the telegraph and is the only surviving international news service headquartered in the United States.) Bloggers retaliated by threatening to boycott AP (Liza, 2008). So far, neither side has annihilated the other, but copyright continues to be a major bone of contention between old and newer media, and we will look at that issue in more detail in Chapter 3, about YouTube.

But it would also be a mistake to conclude that old media and their practitioners have nothing of value to teach or impart to new new media. We turn now to hard-line, investigative reporting, at the opposite end of the journalistic spectrum from the commentary that thus far has been the lifeblood of blogging.

The Need for Old-Media Reporting in an Age of New New Media Journalism

Marshall McLuhan astutely observed back in 1977 that "the Xerox makes everyone a publisher"—but, like his recognition in 1962 that electronic media were turning the world into a "global village," his observation about the Xerox machine was more prediction, based on a powerful trend he noticed, than a depiction of how the media and the world of that day actually were.

It would take the rise of new new media in general, and the internationally interactive participants they created, for the global village to be fully realized (see my "Digital McLuhan", 1999, for more). For the global village of the 1960s was neither global (television was a national medium) nor interactive like the residents of a village (television viewers across a nation could not talk to each other, except in very small groups).

As for photocopying creating publishers, almost all of the output of such machines, even today, is also for very small numbers of readers. That limited kind of publishing would finally be surpassed—and in a way that rivaled older publication of newspapers and magazines—with the advent of blogging, as we have seen in this chapter.

And what of the older vehicles of journalism—The New York Times, the Washington Post, and other paper press? Their numbers have been declining, in circulation, number of different newspapers, and the size of the newspaper operations that have survived (Perez-Pena, 2008). The New York Times reported a 5 percent drop in circulation from 2007 to 2008, though it is still more than a million. These older media have to some extent migrated to the Web. (See "themediaisdying", 2009, on Twitter for hourly or more frequent reports about cutbacks, layoffs and closings in old media. The title gives cause to think that grammar may be dying, too—"media" is plural for "medium".)

But there remains, as of this writing in 2009, a crucial resource in older media that newer media such as the Daily Kos, Huffington Post and Politico have yet to fully and in many cases even partially re-create for themselves, and thus continue to seek from old media. As Jeff Jarvis noted in an NPR interview (2008) about "How Will Investigative Stories Fare in an Era of Layoffs and Slashed Newsroom Budgets?": "Bloggers rely on the resource that mainstream media put into this.... The whole business is still in trouble and investigative journalism is in peril..."

Ironically, the Daily Kos and new new media blogging first achieved prominence as important media of journalism in the aftermath of the failure of old media journalists to report the absence of weapons of mass destruction in Iraq and in general to supply sufficient criticism in the buildup to that war. (Daily Kos began on May 26, 2002, and The Huffington Post on May 9, 2005.) One could say, cynically, that new new media would do well to field their own investigative reporters, who could not do much worse than the old media professionals on the crucial issue of going to war (see Reilly, 2009, for a similar point). That might be all well and good, but given that new new media do not have their own investigative teams in place, where would investigative journalism come from, if the older media ceased to exist?

The good news from the history and evolution of media is that new media rarely replace, utterly, their ancestors. For every hieroglyphic or silent movie that did not make it into the future—because it could not survive the competition of alphabetic writing in the case of hieroglyphics or talkies in the case of silent movies—there have been hundreds of media, large and small, that have taken the path of radio (which amply survived the advent of television) and still photography (which easily survived the rise of motion pictures).

The key, as I alluded to above when I said that humans decide the survival of media—and I explain in "Human Replay: A Theory of the Evolution of Media" (1979) and "The Soft Edge: A Natural History and Future of the Information Revolution" (1997)—is that media survive if they uniquely satisfy a human communication need. Radio survives in an age of television because it caters to our need to sometimes hear one thing when seeing something else. Imagine driving down the highway and watching television; if you were the driver, you would not get very far. Similarly, just look at a wall or a landscape in the distance or even a person's face at rest, and a still photograph can usually capture all you might like to see of that. In contrast, the world grows dark every night but never really silent, and our eyes close but not our ears, which spelled the end of silent movies and their presentation of images without synchronized speech. (See Chapter 13, "Hardware," for more on this "anthropotropic" evolution of media, as I call it, toward more human communication.)

Words on paper still have their advantages. They are inexpensive, easily portable and require only the power of the sun or any ambient light to be read. As long as that advantage continues in contrast to words on a screen, old media newspapers and magazines will survive in some form, which, one hopes, includes a cadre of investigative journalists. And if and when that advantage fades, presumably at least some blogs by then will be generating enough steady income to field their own investigative reporters.

Old Media and New New Media Symbiosis: Easter Eggs for "Lost" and "Fringe"

Not everything in the natural, Darwinian world is competition. Organisms also live in mutually beneficial relations, as do bacteria in our digestive system, which help us digest our food, as we give them a nice warm place to live. Bees eat pollen, which helps plants reproduce, as the bees carry some pollen from one plant to another. And we humans also benefit, doubly, since we like both honey and flowers.

The old medium of television clearly benefits from publicity given to its shows by the new new medium of blogging; the new new medium of blogging benefits from television or any medium that gives bloggers something to write about. News blogs benefit from the work of old print media investigative journalists, while old print and broadcast news media draw upon analyses and opinions expressed by bloggers. And old media such as television shows and newspapers advertise extensively on blogs, just as blogs such as Television Without Pity advertise on Bravo Television.

The symbiotic or mutually catalytic relationship of old and new new media is thus undeniable and vibrant. And although conflicts can get in the way of such cooperation—as when an official television blog prevents links to reviews on other blogs—there are also cases in which television deliberately works new new media into its programming and promotion.

The virtual "game" of Second Life—in which users appear as avatars—figured in a "CSI" television episode in 2007, in which characters from the television show pursued an investigation in Second Life and entered there as characters (Riley, 2007; see Chapter 9 later in this book for more on Second Life). "Lost" tried something even more ambitious, setting up a real Web site for "Oceanic Airlines"—the fictitious airline which flew the lost flight that started the show—on which users could look for "additional" flights. "Lost," as well as J. J. Abrams' more recent show, "Fringe," offer "Easter eggs," or clues on the Web, which fans can then find to gain special insight into the ongoing stories on television.

As "Fringe" Executive Producer Jeff Pinkner told TV Guide's Mickey O'Connor in an online interview (2008), "There are many Easter eggs, several of which have yet to be discovered by anybody—either on the show or out there on the Internet. There's a clue in every episode that tells you what the next episode will be about."

So "Lost" and "Fringe" deliberately seeded the Internet with clues to enhance the viewers' enjoyment of the show, not just by giving them valuable information but by making the viewers more than viewers, turning them into researchers, and in effect much more active participants in the unfolding fiction of the show. And, to complete the cycle, some of these viewers who were transformed into researchers were so inspired that they blogged about the show. (And the cycle continues in the university classroom. Sarah Clarke Stuart's Spring 2009 "The Infinite Narrative: Intertextuality, New Media and the Digital Communities of 'Lost'" course at the University of North Florida, for example, uses blogs about "Lost," including one of my reviews in Infinite Regress, as part of the course's required reading; see Stuart, 2009; Aasen, 2009.)

But the new new media of the Web are doing more than making anyone who so desires to be a publisher. New new media of sound and image are also making some of us producers.

YouTube

IF TEXT IS CLOSEST TO THE OLDEST PERMANENT FORM OF HUMAN communication—the oldest form, period, if we include the cave paintings in Altamira and Lascaux as a kind of picture writing—then audio-visual recordings are surely the newest.

Even though the ancient Alexandrians knew about persistence of vision—the characteristic of human perception that keeps images in our vision a split second after they are in front of our eyes, and makes motion pictures possible—motion pictures themselves did not become a mass medium until the 1890s. The first movies back then were voiceless. Talkies arrived in the late 1920s, around the same time as television was invented. Commercial television started making a big impact in the late 1940s and was being watched in nearly 90 percent of American homes by the end of the 1950s. VCRs were introduced in the mid-1970s, and cable as an independent source of programming in the early 1980s. The history of audio-visual media prior to YouTube, in other words, only goes back less than a hundred years.

YouTube was created in February 2005—the work of Chad Hurley, Steve Chen and Jawed Karim, who had been colleagues at PayPal—and publicly debuted in November 2005. It has certainly thrived on clips from network and cable television, a striking partnership of old and new media. But its most unexpected and long-lasting impact has come from videos made by nonprofessionals, or, rather, by people who are not cable or network television producers. Its trademark, along with the YouTube logo, is "Broadcast Yourself."

Consider, for example, the story of Obama Girl, now a YouTube and new new media classic.

"Obama Girl"

The story of Obama Girl begins in December 2006 on an old medium. "Saturday Night Live," on NBC television, aired a hilarious skit originally titled "My Dick in a

Box." Thanks to the FCC, however, NBC was afraid to broadcast the comical routine with its original wording. "My Dick" was replaced by "Special Treat."

But the singing and dancing with the original wording somehow made its way onto YouTube, where it attracted millions of viewers, likely more in the long run than had seen the bowdlerized skit on television. (Although Congress has tried to impose language restrictions on the Internet, and Bill Clinton actually signed the Communications Decency Act of 1996 into law, it was struck down by the Supreme Court.)

Enter Ben Relles, who, with singer/songwriter Leah Kauffman, had an idea for an answer or a response video to "My Dick in a Box": "My Box in a Box." Answer videos or video responses are a YouTube equivalent of text comments on blogs, and they give new producers a good way of attracting attention by literally appending the response video to a video that already enjoys a big audience, or large number of views. YouTube also has a thriving text comment section. Popular videos generate thousands of comments, in contrast to a handful of response videos.

"My Box in a Box" did not do nearly as well as the original "My Dick in a Box," which received more than 24 million views in the first six months it was on YouTube (see Catch Up Lady, 2007). "Box in a Box" has been taken down and put back up numerous times since then, so its statistics as of January 2009 of more than 4 million views since its posting in December 2006 are not strictly comparable to "Dick"'s. But those numbers were more than enough to get Ben Relles and his team, BarelyPolitical.com, interested in YouTube as a medium to showcase their productions.

Fox's "24" started a new season ("Day Six") in January 2007. Relles and company had an idea for a video, "I've Got a Crush on Jack Bauer." That's the way Kauffman wrote the song. Obama announced he was running for the presidency in February 2007, and that gave Relles the idea that Obama would be an even more exciting object of a video crush than Bauer. Amber Lee Ettinger was brought in to act the part. "I've Got a Crush on Obama" was put up on YouTube in June 2007. It received more than 2.3 million views in the first month (Sklar, 2007) and, as of January 2009, more than 13 million views. Obama Girl became a popular icon. Further video with Obama Girl followed, as well as a bevy of similar or answer videos for other candidates, including Hillary Clinton and John McCain. When Ben Relles and Amber Lee Ettinger visited my "Intro to Communication and Media Studies" class at Fordham University in September 2007, there wasn't a man or woman in my 120-student class who had not already seen or heard about Obama Girl (Levinson, 2007).

Did Obama Girl have an impact on the 2008 election? Who would admit to voting for a candidate because of a saucy, funny video? But this much is clear: Obama did very well with the under-30-years-of-age voter—in the primaries and the general election—and this was precisely the group that did not go to the polls in numbers needed by Democratic presidential candidate John Kerry in 2004, and the group that most watched Obama Girl on their computer screens in 2007. And the Obama Girl video went viral at a very early and therefore crucial time in the campaign, when many people were still first learning whatever they could about

Obama. The video, at the very least, showed Obama as someone cool, interesting, and attractive.

Linda Wertheimer reported on National Public Radio (June 24, 2008) that the number of voters under age 30 in primaries and caucuses across America was two to three times greater than four years earlier. Fifty-eight percent of these voters identified themselves as Democratic, and they voted for Obama over Clinton by 3 to 1 margins in states such as Georgia, which Obama won, and 2 to 1 margins for Obama in states such as Pennsylvania, which Obama lost in the primaries.

The trend held through the November general election, in which at least 50 percent of 18- to 29-year-olds voted in America for the first time since 1972, and 66 percent of them voted for Obama, "up 12 percent from those who voted for John Kerry in 2004 and 18 percent from those who supported Al Gore in 2000" (Grimes, 2008; see also Dahl, 2008). As we will see throughout this book, and especially in Chapter 12, "the Obama campaign was able to leverage many types of new and social media" (Baird, 2008).

YouTube Presidential Primary Debates

The 2008 presidential campaigns also saw the debut of YouTube primary debates in 2007, in which questions for the candidates were submitted via YouTube video clips. CNN, under whose auspices the candidates assembled to answer the questions, selected the video clips, making these debates a little less than a breath of totally direct democracy, or an example of completely new new media in politics. But the origin of questions directly from American citizens was a significant improvement over questions asked by news commentators, presumably asking questions on our behalf. No doubt some of the questions were coached and perhaps even prepared by surrogates for the candidates. But even with such inevitable abuses, the YouTube debates marked an important step forward in the democratization of the debate process.

What follows are my blog posts, entered immediately after the Democratic CNN-YouTube primary debate on July 23, 2007, and the Republican CNN-YouTube primary debate on November 28, 2007:

> The first YouTube/CNN Presidential Debate—this one with the Democrats—just concluded. I said I would wait until I saw it, to say how much of a revolution it was. Having seen it, I think it was revolutionary indeed—and, in fact, as much a leap forward in the debates and democracy as the first presidential debates on television in 1960.
>
> I don't ever recall seeing a debate in either party with such a refreshing, humorous, frank and incisive series of questions. The people asking the questions in the YouTube videos were far more on the money than any panel of experts.
>
> And the candidates rose to the occasion with honest and important answers.

Barack Obama, when asked about whether he is a legitimate African-American candidate—given his access to power—quipped, "Ask the New York cabbies!" (African-Americans unfortunately have a tougher time getting a cab to stop for them and pick them up than Caucasian New Yorkers—I'm Caucasian, I've lived in New York all of my life, and maybe this problem has lessened a little, but it still exists.)

Hillary Clinton, responding to a question about the election of Bush in 2000, responded that, actually, Bush was not elected president.

John Edwards, on health care, gave an impassioned plea for the need for all Americans to have it—he did this even though he had exceeded his time, and Anderson Cooper was trying to cut him off.

Joe Biden answered a YouTube question about gun control, asked by someone who was armed with an automatic weapon, which he called his "baby." Answered Biden: if that's your baby, you need help....

And that's just a sampler.

Even Anderson Cooper, who did seem to unfairly cut off the minor candidates—such as Mike Gravel—more than the major candidates, was in fine form tonight. The final questioner asked each candidate to cite something liked and disliked about the candidate to the left. Kucinich quipped that there was no one standing to his left on the stage (true). Cooper replied—we tried to find someone to your left but there was no one...

There's nothing like the fresh air of democracy to energize a debate and give people clearer choices. There was concern, before the debate, about CNN exercising too much control in choosing the YouTube questions to be shown—I agree that CNN should not have selected the questions, but I don't see how the choices could have been any better.

I'm looking forward to the Republican rendition of this fine experiment—which will become the norm—in September.

But added July 27 [link to new blog post]: *Republicans Now Thumb Noses at YouTube as Well as Evolution.*

The last line was added because, as of July 27, 2007, only John McCain and Ron Paul had committed to a Republican primary CNN-YouTube debate in September 2007, so CNN was obliged to cancel it. The Republicans eventually did see the YouTube light, and their YouTube debate took place on CNN on November 28, 2007. I posted the following on my blog immediately after the debate:

I didn't find tonight's Republican YouTube/CNN debate as refreshing and provocative as the first YouTube debate among the Democratic contenders for president a few months ago. Possibly the YouTube bloom is off the rose. More likely the questions weren't as humorous or provocative tonight as those received via YouTube for the Democrats.

Otherwise, it was a good, punchy debate, which showed most of the candidates off to their best advantage. McCain, in particular, was more eloquent and forceful than usual in his support of the war and his denunciation of torture. Romney was on the receiving end of McCain's torture lecture—Romney falling back on his all-too-typical letting the experts decide—but Ron Paul had a fine moment in his cogent explanation, back to McCain, on the difference between being an isolationist and a noninterventionist (Ron Paul is the latter). And Ron Paul also spoke truth about why violence has decreased in southern Iraq—that it happened because the British left.

But Romney was excellent in knocking down Giuliani's attack on Romney's alleged employment of illegal aliens—Romney reasonably replied that he contracted with a company to work on his home, he did not directly hire illegal aliens.

I should note here, however, that although I admired Romney's rhetoric in this exchange—a rarity—I think most of the Republicans and many of the Democrats are making too big a deal about illegal aliens (not that terminology matters all that much, but I can't help thinking of people from outer space whenever I hear that phrase). One of America's greatest strengths has always been its openness to people from other countries and cultures.

Huckabee was probably the best on stage about this issue, refusing to back down from his funding of education for children of illegal immigrants.

Giuliani, other than the exchange with Romney on the employment of illegal immigrants, was pretty much on top of his game, and Fred Thompson was a little more animated than usual tonight, too.

So where do we stand: Huckabee is personable and gaining in the polls and could conceivably pull an upset in Iowa. Even if he comes close, he could be a good running mate for Giuliani. I'd say it's too late for McCain and Thompson, whatever they do or say from now on. Romney is still Giuliani's major competition.

And Ron Paul still has by far the best positions. He alone among the Republican candidates continues to speak the truth to authority about war. We'll soon find out how many votes this translates into in the primaries.

Huckabee went on to win in Iowa, McCain was not too late to win the Republican nomination, Ron Paul in fact did very poorly in actual primary voting—even though articles in favor of his candidacy were "Dugg up" to the front page of Digg every day in the primary campaigns, and phone-ins after presidential debates frequently declared him the winner. We will explore in Chapter 5 on Digg why this was so—why Ron Paul, who did so well in new new media, did so poorly in the primaries, in contrast to Barack Obama, who did very well in new new media, and won. Part of the reason is that Obama also looked very good on the older medium of television.

Telegenic + YouTube = Cybergenic

Barack Obama was first described as "cybergenic" by Paul Saffo in June 2008, an observation picked up by Mark Leibovich in The New York Times in August 2008. The logic of the appellation is that just as FDR was a master of radio (see "Radio

Heads" in Levinson, 1997, for more on FDR's—as well as Churchill's, Hitler's and Stalin's—political wielding of radio), and JFK was a natural for television (in contrast to Nixon), so was Obama a perfect Internet candidate, especially in comparison to John McCain. (We might now say he is an ideal Internet president.)

The historical analogies, however, are not completely apt. FDR and his advisers understood and harnessed the power of radio, whereas JFK merely looked better than Nixon on television. On the other hand, Kennedy and his advisers knew after the debates that he performed well on TV—a majority of people who heard the debates on radio thought Nixon did better, in contrast to the majority of television viewers who liked Kennedy (see McLuhan, 1964, p. 261)—and televised press conferences became a hallmark of his administration. Indeed, JFK's press conferences are still the high watermark for élan and style of a president talking to the media, though Obama may well equal or surpass that.

But, more importantly, the designation of Obama as cybergenic, in contrast to telegenic, misses the crucial role that looking and sounding good on television plays in making a candidate cybergenic.

In fact, there is a synergistic, mutually catalytic relationship between old and new new media, which can be easily missed when focusing on the revolutionary impact of new new media. We saw it in the previous chapter on blogging, in which investigative reporting from old print fuels much of the reporting and commentary on new and new new media such as The Huffington Post and Daily Kos, and successful television series such as "Lost" enlist the viral Internet for promotion. In the case of the "cybergenic" candidate, most of the political video clips that appear on the Web, embedded from YouTube or directly from news sites such as MSNBC.com, originated on traditional cable television.

This means that a candidate must look good on television to look good on the Web. No matter how judicious a YouTube clip of me is from an appearance on "The O'Reilly Factor", I am not going to look like George Clooney. Similarly, Obama's YouTube superiority over McCain flowed from Obama's looking and sounding better on television. For all the magic and power of YouTube, it cannot make a new new media silk purse out of a TV sow's ear.

Indeed, so crucial is the old medium of television in new new media politics that, even if a candidate is successful on the Internet, he or she still has to look and sound good on the traditional tube. Consider Howard Dean's story in 2004, in which he raised a lot of money and seemed to be catching fire as a presidential candidate on the Internet, only to lose it all in one bad television moment after losing the primary in Iowa.

The relationship of new and old media, of new new media to the preexisting real world, will be one of the main areas of focus in this book. The gist is that success in new new media is not in itself enough—or is not really success unless it is aided and abetted by older media, and reflected in the world offline.

YouTube Undeniability and Democracy

At the opposite end of the professional production spectrum, we have YouTube clips not taken from a television talk show or news show and not even created by non-network producers such as Ben Relles. We have clips taken via cellphone or other lightweight, hand-held video cameras that could be in the hands of…well, anyone.

And though the producers of such clips taken on the fly can be anonymous or completely unknown, the subjects of the videos could be the same politicians and celebrities we see on traditional television.

Sen. George Allen, for whatever reason, called upon a questioner at a public event on August 15, 2006, and referred to him as "Macaca." The term is a racial epithet in some parts of the world. Allen denied that he uttered the term; he said he had no recollection of saying it. YouTube knew better. A clip of George Allen saying "Macaca" was up for all the world to see. Allen lost his bid for reelection to the Senate that year and, along with it, his position as a likely contender for the Republican presidential nomination in 2008. Rolling Stone aptly titled an article, shortly after the incident, "The First YouTube Election: George Allen and 'Macaca'". The subtitle was "George Allen: Digital Foot in Twenty-First Century Mouth" (Dickinson, 2006).

Michael Richards, the comedian who played Kramer on "Seinfeld", also discovered that cellphone videos and their dissemination on the Web were no laughing matter. Richards' response to a heckler at the Laugh Factory in West Hollywood on November 16, 2006, was to refer to the heckler as a "nigger"—six times (TMZ staff, 2006). Richards later apologized but will always be something much more—and worse—than a funnyman in the public eye.

Jonathan Alter of Newsweek, talking on Keith Olbermann's "Countdown" on MSNBC on June 9, 2008, captured this facet of the YouTube revolution, what it means for politicians, and, by extension, anyone in the public arena. In 2000, Alter said, a videotape of a politician talking would be in some vault in some network backroom somewhere, after its airing on television. (This was the case in 2004, as well.) But nowadays—in 2008 and thereafter—anything a politician says can be up in the bright, unblinking lights of YouTube minutes later, out of the custody and control of both the network and the politician.

Alter was talking about John McCain's claim that he never commented on the media's impact on politics and elections—a claim already refuted by a McCain statement just a few days earlier that the media had been unfair to Hillary Clinton in her race for the Democratic nomination, "The media often overlooked how compassionately she spoke to the concerns and dreams of millions of Americans" (McCain, 2008), in a speech widely available on YouTube.

And a politician's words cannot only be posted on YouTube a few minutes after they have been spoken, but they can stay on YouTube for years—in effect, forever. Words in a YouTube video clip are not only undeniable, they are indelible. The lights are not only bright and unblinking but permanent.

The public is well aware of this YouTube resource for democracy. On November 13, 2008, I published a blog post on Infinite Regress, Open Salon, and my MySpace page, titled "Katie Couric, Hero of the Revolution." I identified what I saw as the single most decisive moment in the 2008 campaign—the instant, if there was one, when the McCain-Palin ticket irrevocably lost the election.

There were several contenders in my mind, including John McCain's announcement shortly before the first presidential debate in September 2008 that he was putting his campaign on hold and going to Washington to help with the financial crisis. McCain also called on Obama to postpone the first debate, a request that Obama refused. All of this proved to be very damaging to McCain, but none of it contained an indelible moment that the public could instantly call upon. Indeed, as the weeks progressed, McCain's first response to the financial crisis became diluted by other events.

Not so a response that Republican VP candidate Sarah Palin gave to "CBS Evening News" anchor Katie Couric in an interview. Asked what newspapers she read, Palin could not name a single one. That exchange, in my view, implanted an image of Palin's unsuitability for the office of vice president in the minds of many Americans, and it never left them. They could furthermore see that image any time they wanted, on YouTube.

The exchange was first broadcast on the "CBS Evening News" on September 30, 2008. But as an Open Salon reader pointed out about 10 minutes after I called Katie Couric a "Hero of the Revolution" in my blog several months later, it was not on CBS Television that he had repeatedly seen Palin give that nonanswer to Couric. It was on YouTube, where the video clip as of late November 2008 had received nearly 2 million views.

Anything recorded via any audiovisual device is a candidate for universal dissemination on YouTube—and that includes not only what politicians and other celebrities are saying now but what anyone said or sang or otherwise communicated since the invention of motion pictures in the 1880s and the phonograph in 1876, if a motion picture or a recording was made of that communication.

YouTube Usurps Television as a Herald of Public Events

By all accounts including mine (e.g., Sullivan, 2008; see Suellentrop, 2008, for a summary of blog reviews; Levinson, "Superb Speeches by Bill Clinton and John Kerry," 2008), 2004 Democratic nominee for president John Kerry gave one of the best speeches of the 2008 Democratic Convention in Denver, and probably the best speech of his life, on August 27, 2008. Unaccountably, the speech was carried in its entirety on none of the three major all-news cable television networks. Instead, MSNBC, CNN, and Fox News went for their own talking heads. As Andrew Sullivan aptly noted, "Cable believed their pundits were more interesting than this speech. They made the wrong call."

Or perhaps we can indeed account for why the television networks cut out Kerry. Driven by the need to attract a maximum of viewers, required in turn to attract a maximum amount of revenue from advertisers, the program directors at the networks probably figured that John Kerry, not known as an electrifying speaker, might well lead viewers to other channels with more scintillating programming. Or, the networks at least thought that Chris Matthews, Wolf Blitzer and Brit Hume—on MSNBC, CNN and Fox News, respectively—would bore fewer viewers than Kerry.

C-SPAN and PBS, not beholden to advertisers, did broadcast John Kerry's speech. My wife and I had C-SPAN as an inset on our television screen—we were watching MSNBC—and we switched to get an idea of what Kerry was saying. We kept our television on C-SPAN for the rest of Kerry's speech.

Noncommercial television thus saved TV as an instant herald for John Kerry. Beyond that, the speech was posted on YouTube within an hour. It attracted thousands of viewers in a few hours. Television increasingly counts only in the immediate run—in the short, medium and long runs, YouTube has become the medium of record.

The relationship of YouTube to television in the coverage of public events complements the relationship of blogging to newspapers and helps pinpoint the position of new new media in our culture. Blogging provides commentary far faster than the op-eds of any printed newspaper. YouTube provides audio-visual records of events on television that would otherwise be gone the instant they conclude—or, in the case of John Kerry's 2008 speech, incompletely broadcast or not at all. Television, of course, can replay parts or all of any programming, but such replays are not accessible 24 hours a day, from most places in the world, as is any video on YouTube. Anything on television can be captured on TiVo or DVR, but those records are private, not publicly accessible. The new new media herald of events is thus faster in the case of blogging and more reliable in the case of YouTube than their old media counterparts. For the time being and near future, newspapers will continue because they do not require batteries to read, and television because it is still often an effortlessly accessible first word. But the better heralds of new new media are likely to continue to supplant and replace them.

YouTube Is Not Only Omni-Accessible and Free to Viewers—It's Free to Producers

Barack Obama paid $5 million for a 30-minute address (Sinderbrand & Wells, 2008), carried by most of the major television networks, a week before the presidential election of 2008. Some 33 million people saw his address (Gold, 2008), so the money was well worth it.

But YouTube charges nothing for placement of videos on its site. As Joe Trippi remarked, Obama "can do a half-hour YouTube address every Saturday, addressing millions. The networks would never give the president that much television time each week, but the press is still going to have to cover what he says on YouTube" (Fouhy, 2008). A presidential candidate would certainly not get 30 minutes free of charge every Saturday to talk to the nation via network television, but Trippi astutely observes that likely neither would a president. Broadcast media have become more protective of income earning from their rented time today than back in the 1930s and '40s, when FDR delivered 30 "fireside chats" to the American public in prime time via radio from 1933 to 1944 (Dunlop, 1951).

Trippi, author of "The Revolution Will Not Be Televised: Democracy, the Internet, and the Overthrow of Everything" (2004), first came to America's attention as the manager of Howard Dean's unsuccessful campaign for the Democratic nomination for president in 2004. Trippi chronicles and assesses the Dean campaign in his book. Dean became known as the "Internet candidate," and Trippi was the Internet mastermind, but new new media back in 2004 were not what they are now. Blogging was thriving, but Facebook had just been created, and You Tube and Twitter were still a year or two away.

Obama as the New FDR in New New Media as Well as the New New Deal

The famous November 24, 2008, cover of Time magazine that depicted Barack Obama as the new FDR—the then president-elect in specs, gray suit and hat, sitting in a car, cigarette jutting optimistically upward—was captioned "The New New Deal."

The comparison, of course, was to FDR and Obama both first taking office in the throes of financial crises and catastrophe, and to Obama's plans for public works projects—"infrastructure" in 21st century parlance—to help Americans get back to work and lay the foundations for more efficient commerce, just as FDR did in the Great Depression of the 1930s.

But the announcement—a day after the Time cover became public on November 13, 2008—that Obama's radio address on November 15, 2008, would also be made available on YouTube, showed that Obama would be the new FDR not only in New Deal economic terms but in the employment of new media to communicate to the American people.

Roosevelt's "fireside chats" had used the new medium of his day, radio, to communicate directly to the American people, as no president had ever done before. Roosevelt and his advisers understood the advantages of new radio, which allowed anyone talking through it, including the president, to sound and seem as if he were talking directly to Americans, in their living rooms, bedrooms or in whatever room their radio happened to be situated. The effect was powerful, unprecedented, profound. My parents, who grew up in the Great Depression, often told me how they regarded Roosevelt as almost a kind of father—which makes sense, for whose deep voice would otherwise be talking to you in the inner sanctums of your home, if the economy and then the war were making you feel almost as helpless as a child? When World War II came, my parents, in their late teens and early 20s, felt especially comforted by Roosevelt's voice. They felt that, as long as FDR was talking to them and all Americans, the country would be OK. (See my 1997 "The Soft Edge" for more on radio and FDR.)

Americans stopped listening to radio that way in the 1950s, when television became the predominant political broadcast medium, and radio became a vehicle of rock 'n' roll. By 1960, people who saw the Kennedy-Nixon debates on television thought Kennedy won, in contrast to those who heard the debates on radio, as we considered previously ("Telegenic + YouTube = Cybergenic"). Unfortunately for Nixon, 87 percent of American households had televisions in their homes by 1960 (Roark et al., 2007). And by the election and its aftermath in 2008, YouTube was replacing television as the predominant political audio-visual medium—though, as discussed in the "Cybergenic" section, this by no means indicates that television is becoming unimportant in politics. To the contrary, a lot of what is on YouTube comes from television.

But Obama's YouTube addresses, in particular, take advantage of all the characteristics of this new new medium, just as FDR's fireside chats did with radio in the 1930s and '40s. In place of the voice in the home, the fatherly reassurance that radio conveyed for FDR, Obama on YouTube suits today's world, in which people want to be in touch with their president, or at least hear and see him, at times of their rather than the president's choosing. Like a president on radio, a president on YouTube is still conveying reassurance, but it is a reassurance for people on the move, accustomed to being in the driver's seat about when and how they receive their information, getting their news on screens on the go, including presidential addresses, whenever and wherever they want it. In the fast-changing 21st century, the biggest reassurance about information is knowing that it's there.

Amateur YouTube Stars and Producers

Because YouTube is fed by anyone with a video camera or camera phone, the people in the video—the subject of the clip—can just as easily be unknown as famous. The amateur or unknown YouTube producer can point the camera at him- or herself, friends, the general public or celebrities with almost equal facility.

As of February 2009, the YouTube videos with the most views were "Evolution of Dance" with Judson Laipply and "Girlfriend" with Avril Lavigne. Both had more than 110 million views, but Laipply was a little-known comedian before his YouTube success and Lavigne a Grammy-winning star vocalist. (Her YouTube numbers have been questioned as being at least in part the result of automatic replays on some Web sites and "gaming" the system, or repeated brief views by her supporters; see Chapter 5, "Digg," in this book for more on gaming, and MacManus, 2008, for more on the most-viewed YouTube videos). These videos vividly demonstrate that success on YouTube is not dependent upon celebrity status (Lavigne was a celebrity, Laipply was not). The exceeding of 100 million views compares well with the more than 95 million viewers of the February 2009 Superbowl, the third most watched show on the old medium of television (Superbowl 2008 was second with 97.5 million, and the finale of "M*A*S*H" the most watched television show, with 106 million viewers in 1983—see Armstrong, 2009). Of course, the Superbowl broadcast was live, over several hours, while the YouTube views accrued over several years. So the comparison of YouTube and television viewers is not completely equivalent, although it nonetheless shows that YouTube and television are both in the same huge audience ball park, and you need not be a superstar to play in it. The extraordinary success of Susan Boyle in April 2009, first appearing on television's "Britain's Got Talent," but with video clips receiving more than 100 million views on YouTube within a month after, provides another example both of the power of YouTube in contrast to television and the symbiotic relationship of these two media. Boyle would be an example of someone such as Laipply who was not yet a celebrity, but was brought to public prominence by both television and YouTube.

Meanwhile, Chris Crocker, a total unknown, had achieved more than 11 million views for his hilarious "Leave Britney Alone" clip, and the original "I've Got a Crush on Obama" video had received more than 13 million views by February 2009. These videos are in effect amateur/celebrity hybrids, with the producer or creator an amateur prior to the making of the video (Chris Crocker for "Leave Britney Alone," Ben Relles for "Obama Girl"), but the subject already a big star (Britney Spears, Barack Obama). Amber Lee Ettinger, who played Obama Girl, was also unknown prior to the video.

"Food Fight" provides a more purebred example of how lack of previous fame is no impediment to success on YouTube. "An abridged history of American-centric warfare, from WWII to present day, told through the foods of the countries in conflict," the YouTube description tells us about this sage and funny video. It was produced, written and animated by Stefan Nadelman, a complete unknown, as the expression goes. And, indeed, nothing about the animated video was well known beforehand—no stars, no voices, just animated. It was uploaded to YouTube on February 27, 2008, and as of February 2009 had attained more than 3.6 million views.

How could such a video, however superb, but with such utter lack of celebrity status, attract millions of viewers? (Even Judson Laipply was a professional comedian.) I first saw "Food Fight" when a friend and colleague at Fordham University—Professor Lance Strate, who was also a "Friend" on MySpace—placed it in a comment he entered on my MySpace profile. Such accidental, nonprofessional promotion can be every bit as effective as a multimillion-dollar publicity campaign. Indeed, most public relations and publicity firms these days spend a lot of money in attempts to simulate such word-of-mouth, in-the-street promotion.

This is known as viral marketing, and it is the unpredictable, wildly successful promotional engine of the new new media age. Nadelman's "Food Fight," while not the most successful video on YouTube—100+ million for pure celebrity or at least professional, 10+ million for celebrity/amateur hybrids, 3.6 million for amateur Nadelman—is an archetypal example of the unadulterated viral video on YouTube.

Viral Videos

Viral marketing, viral videos—viral any product or activity relating to popular culture—operates via one person who loves a song or video or whatever on the web or elsewhere letting another person know of this enjoyment. When millions of people let millions of other people know about this video, it can become enormously popular—as much as or more so than a video promoted by old-media advertising and publicity.

This used to be called "word of mouth." But "viral" is something more, because digital word of mouth can reach anyone, anywhere in the world, and millions of people, instantly, in contrast to old-fashioned spoken word of mouth, which can only reach the person right next to you or, in the days of just landline telephone, the other end of your phone connection (nowadays, cellular phones, especially when texting, are part of viral communication).

But why "viral"? In the biological world in which we and our physical bodies reside, a virus spreads by hitching a ride on or infecting a host cell, which every time it reproduces takes along with it a piece of the virus. The viral video does much the same, by infecting or hitching a ride in the mind of every viewer who may see it. When these minds have access to new new media, where they can talk about, link, even edit the video, the viral dissemination can become epidemic. Whether in the world of biology or popular culture, in other words, the virus or viral video sells itself.

Richard Dawkins was the first to apply this viral metaphor to human mentality in his discussion of "memes" in his 1991 essay "Viruses of the Mind." Human beings become hosts—happy, unhappy, conscious or otherwise—of ideas. And the words all humans speak, and the books and articles that authors, reporters and now bloggers write, then proceed to disseminate these ideas, these "memes," to other people, just as viruses disseminate their genetic materials from cell to cell, and just as DNA perpetuates itself through the reproduction of living organisms. Dawkins is here picking up on Samuel Butler's famous observation (1878) that a chicken is just an egg's way of producing more eggs—in Dawkins' schema, living organisms are machinery used by DNA to make more DNA. Dawkins first presented this perspective on DNA in his 1976 breakthrough book, "The Selfish Gene," some 15 years prior to his equation of memes or infectious ideas with biological viruses.

Prior to Dawkins' "Viruses of the Mind," and well before the advent of the Web as a major fact of life, the virus analogy became prominent in the computer age in the popular designation of certain kinds of destructive computer programs as "computer viruses." (Dawkins prominently acknowledged and built upon the computer virus metaphor in his 1991 paper.) Attached to a computer program or code that did, or was purported to do, something useful—something the computer owner desired—the virus, once set loose on the computer, would erase files and do all manner of things that interfered with the user's work, to the point of shutting down the computer. This virus analogy obviously has a lot in common with the biological virus (more than does the virus metaphor in viral marketing), since both biological and computer viruses can result in the breakdown of their hosts—illness and possible death in humans and animals, uselessness and incapacity of computers.

The migration of the analogy to popular culture, however, resulted in "virus" not necessarily signifying anything bad. A viral video, after all, may be instructive and humorous—as is "Food Fight," as an example—with no damage done to any of the hosts, unless they happened to be warmongers in this case, and, even then, they could learn something from this video. (As an aside, we could say that the very growth and expansion of the use of the adjective "viral" has been viral, and not at all in a bad way, because the term indeed helps us understand how YouTube, new new media, and popular culture in general increasingly work in the 21st century.)

We might say, then, that, unlike computer viruses, which are always taken to be destructive, a viral video, or any kind of viral popular culture, can range from being destructive to beneficial. The viral aspect does not in itself make the video good or bad. Because viruses in biological reality are not always or necessarily destructive to their hosts, the viral video may actually be closer to the general virus in nature than is the always-malicious computer virus, after all.

Nonetheless, there is a growing abuse on YouTube in which videos of beatings and other mistreatment of people and animals are uploaded for the perverse satisfaction of their creators and the perverse enjoyment of some viewers.

Viral Videos Gone Bad

The inevitable drawback of all open systems, the tradeoff for the democratic benefits of all new new media, is that open systems can admit bad eggs. In the case of Wikipedia, which we will look at in the next chapter, the damage done by disruptive writer/editors is to the words in Wikipedia—its online articles. Such despoiling is easily discovered, removed or otherwise remedied.

A video portraying a beating or "beat down" can be easily removed from YouTube, as well. But because real people are being beaten, the damage is to far more than information, and removal of the offending video cannot reverse or undo the beating or other depredation.

The upside of the ubiquitous video in such cases is that there is a permanent record of the crime, which makes it easier for the offenders to be brought to justice. But YouTube—and like video repositories—is nonetheless open to the question: Did the culture it created, in which anyone can be a star given the right (i.e., massively attractive) viral video, provide too easy an invitation to mentally unbalanced or ethically vacant people?

This is a question that arises whenever people as a whole are empowered by a new technology. The new device rarely creates the appetite for or the practice of depredations; I recall kids in my schoolyard, alas, being beaten up by what the teachers called "toughs" back in the 1950s (when I was a student, not yet a teacher). Would people who toss babies across rooms (see O'Brien, 2008) and puppies over cliffs (see Wortham, 2008), just so they can be videotaped and see themselves on YouTube, not be likely to do similar things in the absence of YouTube?

We will examine the beat downs and other abuses conducted via or on behalf of YouTube and other new new media in more detail in Chapter 11, "The Dark Side of New New Media." For now, we might well consider Salon's Farhad Manjoo's (2008) thought that "the idea that the Web has desensitized kids to beatings and that MySpace has given rise to teen brutality is extremely dubious.... despite high-profile news stories, we've got no evidence that that's the case—that bullying, fighting, or generalized teen angst has worsened during the MySpace era. Also, doesn't it seem just as plausible that headline-making incidents like this could deter, rather than provoke, violence in kids?"

Manjoo's last point suggests that kids with any brains will see that a beating that features them as the beaters, on YouTube, will provide both legal evidence against them and continuing shame in the future. Whether this would restrain all potential abusers eager for publicity, we don't know, but we can nonetheless assume that they would probably sooner or later do something deplorable, with or without YouTube, and YouTube contributes a lot more to the public good than to its undermining. We will continue to consider some of those beneficial effects below, but we should not lose sight of the abuses, and always stay on the lookout for ways to reduce or remove them, while maintaining and increasing the benefits.

The YouTube Revolution in Popular Culture

It was Harold Innis (1951), one of Marshall McLuhan's inspirations, who first wrote about how all media either space-bind or time-bind—make communication easier across space or distance (as in the case of written documents carried across Roman roads), across time (as in the case of hieroglyphics carved on walls), or both (books produced by the printing press). As McLuhan (1962, 1964) noticed, new technologies in the 19th and 20th centuries continued to facilitate these kinds of "extensions," usually either across space or time, primarily, not both. The telegraph and telephone were space-binding extensions, while the photograph was time-binding.

Here in our 21st century, all new new media are both space-binding and time-binding, due to the speed (across space) and retrievability (across time) of any information conveyed on the Web. But YouTube, especially, does both, par excellence.

Last year, I was watching a DVD of Martin Scorsese's 2005 masterpiece about Bob Dylan, "No Direction Home". The documentary has a clip of Dylan and Joan Baez singing Dylan's "With God on Our Side" at the Newport Folk Festival in July 1963. Baez takes Dylan by the hand out onto the stage, and they start singing.

After the movie, I searched on Baez and "With God on Our Side" on YouTube and found her complete rendition of the song in Stockholm, Sweden in 1966. I embedded the YouTube video on my Web site, InfiniteRegress.tv, and commended it to people running for president. In particular, "If God is on our side, He'll stop the next war."

There are as many examples of this as there are videos with music performances on YouTube, which has turned every computer and an increasing number of cellphone screens into on-demand television at your 24-hour disposal or an easily accessible window across space and time.

Roy Orbison's Guitar

The Traveling Wilburys were—in my opinion and that of many critics and fans (e.g., Gill, 2007)—the best rock supergroup ever to have existed. Bob Dylan, George Harrison, Jeff Lynne, Tom Petty, and Roy Orbison recorded under that name from 1988 to 1990. Their best-known songs were "Handle with Care" and "End of the Line."

Roy Orbison died at the age of 52 in December 1988. When the time came to record a video of "End of the Line," the Wilburys put Orbison's rocking guitar in a rocking chair in the part of the song starting at 1 minute 44 seconds, where Orbison carried the lead. You can also see the rocking guitar at the very end of "End of the Line."

You can read all about that in the Wikipedia entry on the Traveling Wilburys.

You can see the video and this moving tribute to Orbison any time you like on YouTube—in your home, office or, if you have a mobile device such an iPhone that connects to YouTube, from any place you happen to be.

YouTube, in other words, has robbed death of some of its meaning—at least insofar as it pertains to popular culture. The end of the line for audio-visual popular culture has become immortality on YouTube.

"My Guitar Gently Weeps" Through the Ages

Roy Orbison's is not the only immortal guitar on YouTube. George Harrison, another member of the Traveling Wilburys who is no longer with us, also has a guitar that plays across YouTube, in a way that brings home another one of YouTube's signature characteristics: presentation of numerous, slightly different takes of the same real-life event or numerous versions of the same song or creative work.

Slightly different takes of the same event can come from numerous people in a live audience with camera phones and other hand-held vid-cams. Numerous renditions of the same song can also come from professional recordings of different performances throughout the past decades.

YouTube has at least a dozen versions of George Harrison's "While My Guitar Gently Weeps," beginning with Harrison's performance at his 1971 Concert for Bangladesh, which also features Eric Clapton on guitar, and proceeding through the years to Eric Clapton and Paul McCartney's rendition of the song at the 2002 Memorial Concert for George, and the 2004 performance (my favorite) by Tom Petty and Jeff Lynne, with incandescent guitar work by Prince, when Harrison was posthumously inducted into the Rock 'n' Roll Hall of Fame for his solo work.

We see Harrison progressing through 20 years in these videos, Clapton through 30 years, with the song poignantly surviving its author. We see blurry videos with unclear sound taken by "bootleggers" at concerts, and we see top-of-the-line clips made for television broadcast. We see a library, hear a record album through history, which we can add to or subtract from at any time, including—if we happen to have recorded it—even adding a video clip of our own making.

We see, in short, the essence of YouTube and new new media.

We can also see on YouTube about 10 renditions of George Harrison's "All Things Must Pass," including one sung by Paul McCartney after Harrison's death. (My favorite, however—McCartney's performance at the Memorial Concert for George held at the Royal Albert Hall in London on November 29, 2002, one year after George's death—was gone from YouTube when I looked in November 2008. The reason was copyright violation, which we will examine in the "YouTube's Achilles' Heel" section later in this chapter.)

A standout line in the song is "daylight is good at arriving at the right time." Not only good things, but bad things, don't last forever.

All things must pass. But it is tempting to now add to Harrison's perceptive lyric: except for performances captured on video and added to what may well be the eternity of YouTube. For although YouTube itself, as it is currently configured, may well come to pass or be transformed or subsumed into something different, there is no reason to suppose that videos currently on YouTube, especially those of groups such as the Beatles and the Traveling Wilburys, or of Michael Jackson or any great contemporary artist, will not be included in such post-YouTube media.

YouTube Retrieves MTV

"Video Killed the Radio Star," the UK New Wave group The Buggles sang to everyone in 1979, heralding the success of music videos on MTV in the 1980s and being the very first video played on MTV when it began in 1981.

Here is what really happened:

To begin with, the enormous and rapid dissemination of television sets in the 1950s was thought by many observers to spell the end of radio. (A famous New Yorker cover in 1955, Perry Barlow's "Another Radio to the Attic," shows a radio languishing next to a crank-up Victrola in a dusty corner, as if it was an artifact from some long-ago era. Carl Rose's 1951 New Yorker cartoon similarly depicts a little girl and her mother in the attic, with the little girl pointing to a radio and asking, "What's that, Mama?") Television had co-opted radio's original and highly successful network programming of soap operas, serials and news.

But radio not only did not fade away, it thrived and became the most profitable medium, dollar spent for dollar earned. Radio did this by playing rock 'n' roll records, supplied free of charge by record companies and sometimes even with payments (which the U.S. government soon cracked down upon, calling this "payola"). And radio capitalized on the capacity of all acoustic media to be listened to when doing other things—in the case of radio, when driving, getting up in the morning, etc. This rock 'n' roll and multitasking propelled Top 40 radio in the 1950s and '60s, and FM radio in the 1960s and '70s (see Levinson, 1997, for details).

The debut of MTV in the early 1980s indeed diverted some of the limelight from radio to the television screen. But MTV hardly "killed" radio or the radio star, and by the mid-1990s, CDs and even more importantly MP3s were tipping the scale of attention and prominence in the popular culture back to acoustic media.

This was the situation when YouTube opened its virtual doors in 2005. But the music videos easily available on YouTube, from decades past to the present, have given the video a new, expanded lease on life in the popular culture.

In sum: video didn't kill the radio star in the first place. But YouTube has made the music video even more of a major player than it was on MTV in the 1980s—an example of a new new medium (YouTube) supplanting a new-ish old medium (MTV or cable television.)

Will YouTube Put iTunes Out of Business?

As we have seen, new new media (blogging, YouTube) compete not only with old media (newspapers and television) but with new media on the Web, or media on the Web that charge for their information, operate via strict editorial control and employ other procedures of old, mass media.

How long can iTunes, which as of January 2009 charges 69 cents, 99 cents or $1.29 per song (Mintz, 2009), survive YouTube's free competition? iTunes, Amazon.com and online newspapers that charge for subscriptions are classic examples of "new" in contrast to "new new" media. Old media exist offline. New media exist online but retain old media ways of doing business. Some new media retain more old ways than others. iTunes charges (but not for podcasts) and has strict editorial control over what appears on its pages. The Huffington Post, which can be considered about halfway between new and new new media, is free but still wields strict old media gatekeeping or editorial control. New new media co-exist with new media online but have shattered all old media confinements of payment and editorial control.

iTunes is still not without its advantages in comparison to YouTube—mainly in the great number of songs it offers and their easy organization. The quality of the music for sale on iTunes is likely better than the sound of most, but not all, YouTube videos, but as high-quality videos become more prevalent on YouTube, this difference is likely to vanish. Further, the accessibility of YouTube and videos on iPhones makes them competitive with MP3s played on iPods—ironic, since Apple is the maker of both iPhones and iPods. Indeed, sites such as ListentoYouTube.com "rip" music or any sound from YouTube videos and render MP3s, which can be listened to on computers, iPods and iPhones.

Perhaps such concerns are what led iTunes to say in October 2008 that it might shut itself down if artists and record producers received higher royalties for sale of their songs on iTunes (Ahmed, 2008). The Copyright Royalty Board in Washington, D.C., was convinced by iTunes and supported its refusal to raise royalties from 9 to 16 cents per download (Frith, 2008).

But, in the end, Apple will win either way. If iTunes goes out of business, Apple will still be doing well with its iPhones and iPods (which increasingly provide easy access to YouTube).

YouTube Refutes Lewis Mumford and Turns the Videoclip into a Transcript

Lewis Mumford (1895–1990) typified the attitude of many critics of television when he compared watching it with being in a state of "mass psychosis," in his 1970 "The Pentagon of Power" (p. 294). Mumford's objection to television was that it provided no sense of past or future, allowing viewers no way to look back or skip ahead when they were watching a television series or news show, as readers easily could when reading a book or newspaper.

VCR technology began to give viewers some control over the past in television as early as 1976. DVR and TiVo technology has expanded that control from the past to the future, by allowing users to program the recording of episodes weeks in advance.

But YouTube ratchets up this viewer control a significant step by allowing people to watch what is on YouTube not only at any time but from any place, if the viewer happens to have an iPhone or other portable, Internet-accessing device at hand. Via the combination of YouTube and mobile media, the audio-visual image is at last as controllable by the viewer as pages in a book are to a reader. (See my "Cellphone: The Story of the World's Most Mobile Medium," 2004, for a history and current impact of mobility in media, and Chapter 13 of the current book for more on the role the iPhone and similar media play in the impact of new new media on the Web.) Mumford's hyperbole was incorrect in the first place. But YouTube has decisively consigned it to the attic of bygone intellectual history.

In effect, YouTube has made the online video as accessible and "readable" to the viewer as a written transcript online or in hand. Just as the reader of a written transcript can stop, go back, browse forward and read a section again, so can the viewer of a YouTube video do the same with the moving images on the screen. From the point of view of the new new media user, there is indeed no significant difference between an online transcript and video, other than that one must be literate to read the transcript. We can make the following analogy: a transcript or book or newspaper in hand is to VCRs and DVDs as a transcript or book online is to YouTube and other videos online. The goal or target of all new new media—or, in Aristotle's terms, their "final cause"—is to make their worldwide contents as accessible as a book in hand.

Tim Russert, 1950–2008

YouTube has also made the immediate past unforgettable and universally retrievable. Tim Russert, "Meet the Press" moderator and NBC Washington News Chief, died unexpectedly on June 13, 2008. The story was covered all that day and most of the weekend on three all-news cable networks in the United States—MSNBC, CNN and Fox News. YouTube played a different role, with more than 500 clips of Tim Russert added in the first 24 hours after his death.

The YouTube contribution underscores another significant difference between new media (cable television) and new new media (YouTube). Although CNN International is available in many parts of the world, it appropriately moved on to other stories in the days following Russert's death (MSNBC and Fox have much less international reach). In contrast, the YouTube clips of Russert were instantly available everywhere in the world and will continue to be instantly available for years to come—or, as indicated previously regarding the music videos of Roy Orbison and George Harrison, in principle forever. (But see also Chapter 4, "Wikipedia," for controversy involving new new media in the initial reporting of Russert's death.)

YouTube's Achilles' Heel: Copyright

The following has happened to many a blogger: You write a nice post about a favorite song or a musical performance—as, in fact, I did, in June 2008, about Paul McCartney's rendition of George Harrison's "All Things Must Pass" at the 2002 Royal Albert Hall Memorial Concert—and flesh it out with a video of the performance, via an embed from YouTube. It looks and sounds great. You put links to your post on Digg, Fark, Reddit and all the appropriate places. You receive complimentary comments. But a few months later, you also receive an email from a disappointed reader, who got a message that the video is "no longer available." You check on your blog site, and then on YouTube, and, sure enough, you find that the video has been taken down from YouTube, because it violated its "terms of service"— or, in plainer English, some person or corporation told YouTube that the video violated its copyright. The hand of old media copyright enforcement, withered but not without power, has just pulled the rug and the fun out from under your new new media blog creation. Or, to try another appendage metaphor, you have just been kicked by YouTube's Achilles' heel, copyright enforcement.

YouTube's one flaw is that there is no guarantee that a video clip available today will be there tomorrow, or even five minutes from now. This means there is no guarantee that any links to it elsewhere on the Web, and embeds of the video, will continue to work. The Internet, on the one hand, has gone a long way to achieving even more stability and permanency than lots of paper—"reliable locatability" (see Levinson, "The Book on the Book," 1998; Levinson, "Cellphone," 2004 and Levinson, "The Secret Riches," 2007)—via "permalinks." But even permalinked text and videos can be taken down, and YouTube's vulnerability to copyright enforcement, in addition to the person who put up a video in the first place deciding to remove it, is a significant, retrograde old media step backward. The great asset of YouTube and new new media, which is that anyone can become a producer and everyone can see the results, forever, has found a limitation. If carried to the extreme, this would be a dagger in the heart of YouTube and its liberation of videos.

There is software readily available that allows users to download videos—not just link to or embed them—with the result that these users can then put the videos up on their own Web pages, without recourse to YouTube or other video storage and dissemination sites such as Blip.tv, Metacafe and the Daily Motion.

But this might well be a copyright violation, also. And though the violation might never be discovered, its possibility keeps us on one of the prime battle lines of old and new media, on the one hand, and new new media on the other: copyright.

Copyright—literally, the right to copy—started as a royal prerogative in Europe, after the introduction of the printing press in the middle of the 15th century. Monarchs gave printers the right to make copies and thereby controlled the output of written information in their realms. But in 1710, Parliament in England enacted the Statute of Anne, which made copyright a right to be claimed by authors and protected on behalf of authors by the government (see Kaplan, 1966; Levinson, 1997).

This is where copyright resides today. It protects the author's interests in three ways. The owner of the copyright determines who, if anyone, can (1) make copies of the work, (2) make money from copies of the work, or (3) use portions of the work in new creations, not of the original creator's making.

Details in the application of copyright are complex and have evolved. At the beginning of the 20th century, authors had to claim copyright. By the end of the 20th century, copyright was accepted as a right belonging to authors, inherent in the authorship of the work (registration of copyright with the government makes enforcement of copyright easier but is not required for an author's assertion of copyright). A hundred years ago, the term of a copyright in the United States was 28 years, with one renewal possible. It is currently for the lifetime of the author plus 75 years. (The Berne Convention, of which the U.S. and 163 other nations are signatories, provides copyright protection for the life of the author plus 50 years.

Signatories are free to provide longer protection.) "Fair Use" is a custom supported in courts of law, which allows inclusion of small portions of work for educational and similar uses, without obtaining the approval of the copyright holder. But all rights deriving from the copyright can be assigned, or bought and sold.

Someone who embeds on his or her Web site a YouTube video of someone else's creation likely has none of the above in mind. The burgeoning millions of embeds on the Web—done without any attention to the copyrights that YouTube boilerplate says must be observed and adhered to—in itself speaks loudly of the reality that the traditional old media mold of copyright is irrevocably broken in the new new media age.

But is copyright completely shattered, or are there parts worth preserving and applying, if possible, to YouTube and new new media? The fundamental right to make copies seems lost, and that is likely for the best. But the copyright holder's right to share in any income generated from the work—and, indeed, to determine whether another person or corporation can make money from the work—seems a reasonable right to insist upon. Further, because income is more easily tracked than placement of embeds on a Web page, this commercial aspect of copyright is not impossible or even very difficult to enforce.

Plagiarism is also worthy of prevention and punishment. In its worst forms, the plagiarist takes work created by someone else and not only passes it off as his or her own but seeks to make income from it. Here the Web is not the plagiarist's best friend. The universal access that makes everything available to everyone on the Web means that, sooner or later, someone familiar with the original work will come across the plagiarist's version and report the plagiarism to the original author or the current copyright holder.

Bottom line: Dissemination of copies of a work, whether an MP3 of a recording or a YouTube clip of a video, is impossible to prevent in the realm of new new media, and probably should not be prevented, unless money is made from the dissemination or the work is plagiarized (disguising the original author's creation of the work), in which case the dissemination should be stopped if possible.

In practical terms, the Recording Industry Association of America's (RIAA's) attempt to prevent dissemination of MP3s purely for the purpose of sharing and not for making money will not succeed in the long run (see Marder, 2007, and Levinson, 2007, "RIAA's Monstrous Legacy," for discussions of how the RIAA has alienated segments of the music-loving public). Neither will the Associated Press (AP) succeed in its attempt to require payment for posting of quotes from its articles in the free blogosphere (see Liza, 2008). As for the future of copyright, it will have to evolve to something closer to the "Creative Commons," in which the creator specifies what kinds of rights are given to the world at large—for example, right to copy but not commercialize—if copyright is to survive (see creativecommons.org).

"Net neutrality" and "open source" systems are consistent with this post-Gutenberg, post-Marconi—or post–mass, old media—approach to intellectual property. Net neutrality wants the digital architecture or operating systems and widgets of the Web to be entirely useable by any personal computer system, including nonproprietary, noncommercial systems, or those that may access the Web with programs other than Microsoft's, Apple's or others', or not protected by copyright and patent. Open-source systems permit anyone to see the code that makes a Web page work the way it does. The viewer can then capture and use this code to create new pages. Both approaches, which have yet to be universally realized and implemented, give the amateur, nonprofessional Web builder and programmer—that is, everyone—the same producer possibilities that new new media bestow to all readers, listeners and viewers. Or we could say that net neutrality and open sourcing are to the structure or architecture of new new media as blogging, YouTube and everything else we are considering in this book is to the content of new new media, and the production and reception of this content.

Comments as Verifiers on YouTube: The Fleetwoods

As is the case with all new new media, the open invitation to everyone to upload video clips to YouTube means that some of the information that accompanies these videos—the brief descriptions of what is on the little screens, even the titles—could be wrong, intentionally or accidentally. Text and video comments, which can be written or uploaded by anyone (if the original video uploader allows this option), provide a mechanism for correction of such errors, just as text comments do in blogging.

Consider the case of The Fleetwoods. The California trio had two hugely successful No. 1 records in the 1950s, "Come Softly to Me" and "Mr. Blue," which featured mellow vocals and beautiful harmonies. The group was unusual in its membership, consisting of one male and two female singers: Gary Troxel, Gretchen Christopher and Barbara Ellis. YouTube has a fine, vintage video of the group performing "Come Softly to Me" on "American Bandstand" in 1959. (I actually remember seeing that, with Dick Clark's introduction and all, when I was a kid. The Fleetwoods were and still are one of my favorite groups.)

YouTube also has half a dozen other videos of The Fleetwoods, including performances in August 2007 on a PBS special and in November 2007 in Las Vegas. But, on closer inspection, these two performances are not quite by the original Fleetwoods. Gary Troxel is still singing a mellow lead in the PBS performance but with two other women. And Gretchen Christopher is the only original member of the group performing in Las Vegas.

But how would someone watching these video clips know this? Not from the titles or descriptions, which give only the name of the group, song and venues. Fortunately, the comments entered by savvy viewers provide the clarifying details.

Of course, there is no guarantee that all or any comments for any video with misleading information will provide accurate corrections. But their capacity to do so—to draw upon the general wisdom of the millions of YouTube viewers—is an example of the self-corrective quality of new new media, which we will see in even greater prominence in Wikipedia, to be examined in the next chapter.

YouTube also added an "annotation" option in 2008, which allows uploaders of videos, at any time, to insert brief phrases of text (annotations) into the video. These can also help clarify who and what is seen in the video.

The Pope's Channel

January 2009 brought the news that "Pope Benedict XVI has launched his own dedicated channel on the popular video sharing website, YouTube" (BBC, 2009). A subsequent Associated Press article (Winfield, 2009) observed that "The pontiff joins President Barack Obama, who launched an official White House channel on his inauguration day, as well as Queen Elizabeth, who went online with her royal YouTube channel in December 2007."

According to Winfield, the Vatican's embracing of what we are calling new new media is by no means free of proviso and controversy. On the one hand, "In his annual message for the World Day of Communication, Benedict praised as a 'gift to humanity' the benefits of social networking sites such as Facebook and MySpace in forging friendships and understanding." On the other hand, the pontiff "also warned that virtual socializing had its risks, saying 'obsessive' online networking could isolate people from real social interaction and broaden the digital divide by further marginalizing people."

As we saw previously in "Viral Videos Gone Bad" and will see in more detail in Chapter 11, "The Dark Side of New New Media," and in the chapters about MySpace and Facebook in this book, social media certainly have their dangers, ranging from cyberstalking and cyberbullying to even use by terrorists. But the concern about social media taking the place of real-life interactions and isolating people from in-person contact has been raised not only about new and new new media but as far back as motion pictures early in the 20th century (McKeever, 1910) and is the basis of concern about "book worms," or people who spend too much time reading books and not enough in the "real," flesh-and-blood world (see Levinson, 2003, for more on the relationship of virtual and physical interactions; see also Chapter 9, "Second Life," in the current volume). Not only is there no evidence of any such deleterious effect, but Barack Obama's use of the Internet in bringing together millions of people in small and large groups for "meet-ups," or rallies, during the 2008 presidential campaign, on Election Day and on Inauguration Day 2009 soundly refutes the proposition that social media get in the way of real-life meetings and interactions. Obama's Internet success, which we will examine more fully in Chapter 12, "New New Media and the Election of 2008," similarly refutes the notion of a burgeoning "digital divide," in which socioeconomic lower income groups are locked out of the process. Blogging, YouTube, Wikipedia, MySpace, Facebook and all new new media are, after all, free, and available via any kind of computer and increasingly via cellphones.

The Church, indeed, has given a mixed reception to the new media of the day at least as far back as the introduction of print in Europe in the 1450s. Although writing was regarded as the "Apostolate of the Pen," the printed word was held suspect by some Church fathers as a debasement of the written manuscript, in which the hand that wrote was thought to be guided by the soul (see Eisenstein, 1979, for more). The dependence of the Protestant Reformation in 1519 on the printed Bible—Luther urged people to read the Bible for themselves, which would not have been possible without mass-produced printed Bibles—ironically substantiated the Church's concern about printing (see Levinson, 1997), but the Jesuit Counter Reformation was quick to recognize the pedagogic and propagandistic value of print. In the second part of the 20th century, the Church was once again a little slow to recognize the power of television, but the Vatican II Council from 1962–1965 rectified that. Like the Jesuit endorsement of print and the Vatican II's appreciation of one-way electronic mass media, Pope Benedict's YouTube channel demonstrates that, despite the Church's unwarranted misgivings, it is correct that in order to effectively disseminate its teachings in the 21st century, it needs to utilize the new new media of our day—in the case of YouTube, the ability to view a video message any time of day, from any place in the world, whenever one desires.

YouTube as International Information Liberator

Just as YouTube in America is available both to heads of state and to people on the street, as both consumers and producers, so too is YouTube internationally available not only to the Queen of England and the Pope.

Yulia Golobokova is 24 years old. She was born in the Soviet Union and is presently a citizen of Russia. In December 2008—the last meeting of my fall 2008 graduate class "Media Research Methods" at Fordham University—Yulia presented a 10-minute summary of her final project, a proposal for research into some aspect of media or communication. Her topic was YouTube. Among the important points she made, many of which I introduced to the class and have discussed in this chapter, the one that struck me the most was this: YouTube, Yulia said, enabled her to find out what was going on in the world, find out the truth, when she was living in Moscow. Unlike television in her country, YouTube is not controlled by her government.

The beauty of YouTube is that it is not controlled by any government—neither the Russian nor the American. I already knew that, and it is easy to take for granted, but the value of YouTube—and, indeed, of all new new media—to the world at large was brought home to me and became more than a theoretical point with a student from Russia standing up in my class and talking about it.

I first met Yulia in September 2008 when she walked into my office, a few days before our first class, and introduced herself. She said how happy she was to meet me and that I looked and sounded just as she had expected.

"How is that?" I asked, wondering how and why she might have some preconception of what I looked and sounded like.

"I've seen your videos in Moscow, lots of times, on YouTube," Yulia replied. In the realm of new new media, there is no difference between a computer screen in New York and in Moscow—they are equidistant, technically, from YouTube.

Of course, governments can attempt to ban YouTube, as Pakistan did for at least two hours in February 2008 because of "anti-Islamic content" (Malkin, 2008). The ban apparently caused worldwide problems with YouTube service, showing the system is far from invulnerable and indeed is interconnected with and dependent upon all kinds of systems and servers and hence potentially weak or vulnerable links, as is the case with all new new media. Pakistan lifted the ban when informed that its "erroneous Internet protocols" had caused problems outside of Pakistan.

Fortunately, attempts of dictatorial governments to regulate media have had a poor record of success, as Nazi Germany found out with the "White Rose" anti-Nazi photocopiers (Dumbach & Newborn, 1986) and the Soviet Union discovered with its "samizdat videos" in the 1980s (Levinson, 1992). As for Pakistan, the resignation of Pervez Musharraf in August 2008 restored its democracy. (See also Chapter 8 for the use of Twitter by protestors in Iran in June 2009.)

Resistance to authorities, whether in government or media, has never been easier in our age of YouTube and new new media. In the next chapter, we will look at how Wikipedia has overthrown the tyranny of the expert, at least insofar as the information and wisdom we expect to find in an encyclopedia.

4

CHAPTER

Wikipedia

WE COME FROM A TRADITION IN WHICH KNOWLEDGE HAS TO BE vouched for, authorized and approved by experts before it is allowed to reach us. Whether clerics or professors or newspaper editors, the effect is the same: Knowledge must be vouchsafed and deemed acceptable by professionals, before it reaches the eyes and ears of people in the world at large. Of course, all kinds of knowledge, information, facts and falsities can be seen, heard or discovered by anyone and everyone. But our tradition, common to both Western and Eastern and all cultures in between, with roots deep in the ancient world, requires that knowledge have the imprimatur or seal of expert approval to be considered worthy of study and further dissemination.

Before we scoff at this vetting, we should understand its logic. It is as easy to create and disseminate a falsehood as it is a truth. We might be flooded by such falsehoods, were gatekeepers not carefully regulating what can reach us.

On the other hand, is not our very rationality in the business of separating truths from falsehoods, lies and spins, and recognizing truth in the crowded field? Certainly John Milton thought so. In his "Areopagetica", published in 1644, Milton argued that truth and falsity must be allowed to fight it out in the marketplace of ideas. Milton was confident that truth would be recognized, unless censorship kept some ideas from entering this battle and thereby warped the results. Thomas Jefferson wholeheartedly agreed, which is why he and like-minded Founding Fathers from Virginia insisted on the First Amendment to our Constitution: "Congress shall make no law…abridging freedom of speech, or of the press."

Boards of experts that determined what went into encyclopedias prior to Wikipedia were certainly not governmental censors or in any way in violation of the First Amendment. But they nonetheless embodied and practiced a kind of censorship, or gatekeeping, which prevented the people at large from determining the truth or falsity of a factual statement, or the more complex question of its relative importance.

Wikipedia, which was brought online in January 2001 by Jimmy Wales and Larry Sanger—Wales continues to play a predominant role in Wikipedia's administration—and by February 2009 had more than 2,750,000 articles written in English, overthrew that reign by philosopher-king experts. None of those articles was written by an appointed expert—or, if experts wrote the articles, the knowledge embodied in their Wikipedia writing not their official expertise was what decided whether those articles survived.

Pickles and Pericles

Almost anyone can write and edit entries on Wikipedia (the "almost" refers to people who have been banned, which will be discussed in detail in "All Wikipedians Are Equal, but Some Are More Equal Than Others" later in this chapter). Age, education, location, gender—none of this makes a difference, or is supposed to make a difference, on Wikipedia. Even intention to help with the writing of an entry, or the opposite intention—to destroy it—makes no difference, at first. Hence, entries on Wikipedia are teeming with the work of pranksters—deliberately introduced errors. These are quickly corrected by readers/editors (they are the same on Wikipedia). Indeed, there is an ever-waging war on Wikipedia, between those who attempt to make and keep entries truthful and those who seek for whatever reason to disrupt this process.

My favorite example, because it is so trivial yet instructive, comes from a few years ago, when an entry on Pericles made the front page of Wikipedia (different entries are chosen for the front page by groups of readers/editors). In the first line of the entry, an alternate spelling of Pericles—Perikles—was given. When I logged on to that page, I immediately noticed that Perikles had been changed by some anonymous vandal to Pickles. I changed Pickles back to Perikles (in those days, I did not even have an account on Wikipedia—I was also an anonymous user, with just an IP, or numerical Internet address). Another vandal (or at least someone with a different IP address from the first vandal) soon changed Perikles to Pickles, and this pickle fight went on with various combatants for at least a few hours.

There, of course, are far more serious battles of this sort being waged daily, even hourly, on Wikipedia concerning character assassinations of public figures and celebrities, calumnies (to use that great 18th century term) posted about political candidates and other misleading information. Barack Obama being falsely described as a Muslim was among the most common of misreprestations on Wikipedia in 2008. In all cases, trivial and profound, the dynamics are the same: armies of light, or immune systems, or good cops—whatever metaphor appeals to you—fighting armies of darkness, infection to Wikipedia, marauders of the truth.

The medical analogy might work best to underscore the difference between expert-driven, gatekept encyclopedias such as the venerable Britannica and mass-intelligence-driven encyclopedias such as Wikipedia. In an expert-driven system, the only people who can write are those who have been certified as free from mental maliciousness or other incapacity. In the people-driven system, since anyone can write, all readers/editors serve as antibodies to correct infection—false information—introduced by marauding germs.

But the battlefield on Wikipedia is even more complicated.

Inclusionists vs. Exclusionists: Battle Between Wikipedian Heroes

Life would be simpler if battles between heroes and villains were the only kind that afflicted our world. But, in fact, battles—or at least disagreements—often break out in the ranks of defenders of the truth.

On Wikipedia, a battle constantly is waged between two kinds of reader/editors, who are both trying to make the online encyclopedia the best it can be. Both do their utmost to root out vandalism whenever they see it. But their battle is not primarily about vandalism but what kind of truthful information should be allowed on Wikipedia. Their battlefield is thus not about truth but about relevance and worthiness to be included in an encyclopedia.

As their names suggest—names proudly touted by the two factions themselves—the "exclusionists" or deletionists want to limit the entries on Wikipedia, while the "inclusionists" want to keep and expand them. But there is a lot of room between no entries at all (which, of course, the exclusionists do not want) and anything truthful that anyone writes about anything, however unimportant (which, of course, the inclusionists do not really want either). And there are subtleties and variations within the groups. "Deletionists" focus on removing complete articles deemed unworthy for an encyclopedia, while "exclusionists" are more concerned about removing irrelevant or unimportant sections of otherwise acceptable articles. "Mergists" are a school of deletionists who want to merge two or more articles into one, because some of the articles are deemed insufficient in importance to stand on their own or merit their own article. If these groups sound to you almost like religious or political factions, you would be right. Except the subject matter need not be political or religious and can indeed be on any topic. What makes these factions seem religious or political is not the subject of their focus on Wikipedia but the intensity and specificity of their editing philosophy.

Expert-driven encyclopedias such as Britannica were and are exclusionistic, and, given the limitations of print on paper, had and have no choice but to be. After all, would anyone purchase an encyclopedia of 1,000 or 10,000 volumes? The Encyclopedia Britannica thus not only restricts the number of new entries but also removes or reduces older entries that its editors deem less relevant. (I have pointed out in the preface of my novel "The Plot to Save Socrates" the value of a Britannica from the mid-1950s or earlier—entries on ancient history were shortened in the mid-1950s to make room for the enormous growth of scientific knowledge and political developments in that and ensuing eras.)

Inclusionists point out that an online encyclopedia labors under no such draconian paper master.

Among the most frequently debated issues on Wikipedia is the "notability" of possible subjects of articles—is the person, current or historical, important enough to warrant a Wikipedia entry? Among the many guiding principles used by editors/readers in making such decisions is one that holds that "notability is not inherited." For example, you will find no entry on Francine Descartes, daughter of the great philosopher. But a major entry, of course, is found on Wikipedia for John Stuart Mill, son of James Mill, who was also an important philosopher (though James Mill was not as significant in impact as his son). The point here is that John Stuart Mill would have merited an entry even if his father had been an unknown stable hand.

Incidentally, you or any reader can post an entry on Francine Descartes on Wikipedia any time you like. It would likely be put up for immediate deletion, however. (See "All Wikipedians Are Equal, but Some Are More Equal Than Others," later in this chapter, for much more on the process of deletion on Wikipedia.)

The "notability is not inherited" principle is not at all controversial or difficult to apply in the cases of Francine Descartes and John Stuart Mill. But it can be and has been highly contentious in many other cases.

Consider, for example, the article for Lolo Soetoro, Barack Obama's Indonesian stepfather. The brief history of the man, as it relates to Obama, is that Barack Obama's mother, Ann Dunham, married Soetoro after she and Obama's biological father (Barack Obama the elder) were divorced. Barack Obama the future senator and president lived in Indonesia for four years, from ages 6 to 10. He returned without his mother or Soetoro to Hawaii, where he lived with his grandparents and completed his secondary education through high school.

So does Lolo Soetoro warrant a Wikipedia entry? "Notability is not inherited"— whether forward to descendants or backward to ancestors—would suggest not, but the question became contentious in the 2008 American presidential campaign, for reasons having little to do with traditional exclusionist/inclusionist debating points. Obama supporters on Wikipedia thought readers/editors in favor of a Soetoro entry wanted it as a way of drawing attention to Obama's Muslim upbringing in Indonesia and thereby painting him as an un-American candidate. This led some readers/editors who were usually inclusionists to oppose the article—that is, delete it, merge it or redirect it (for example, to an article about Ann Dunham).

The Lolo Soetoro article was at first removed from Wikipedia, with searches for it redirected to a more general "Family of Barack Obama" article, which contains a section on Soetoro. (Technically, then, the article was not deleted but merged in the "Family" article.) But the Soetoro article was reinstated in June 2008 and survived at least one additional attempt to remove and merge it. (See Wellman, 2008, for a detailed account of the Wikipedia battles over the Soetoro article.

My wife, Tina Vozick, who edits on Wikipedia as "Tvoz," was a "mergist" in these discussions, departing from her usual "inclusionist" perspective.)

A nonpolitical example of what exclusionists and inclusionists argue about on Wikipedia is the "category" about "Fictional Jews." A category on Wikipedia is a link that can pull together diverse articles. The links appear at the bottom of articles and all together on compilation pages that display the titles of the articles, or the names of the subjects. Not all categories are controversial. "Fictional detectives," for example, is accepted by exclusionists and appears on pages for Sherlock Holmes, Hercule Poirot, Sam Spade, Mike Hammer, etc. This is not the case for "Fictional Jews," which once appeared on pages ranging from Shakespeare's Shylock, James Joyce's Leopold Bloom and "Law and Order's" John Munch to my barely known character Dr. Phil D'Amato. The category was removed in March 2008, along with other categories of "Fictional characters by religion," of which the "Fictional Jews" was a subcategory. (An article called "List of fictional Jews," however, continues. A "list" is a less dynamic component of Wikipedia than a category—the list items do not appear at the bottom of articles about the people or items in the list.)

The "Fictional characters" deletion provides a textbook case of the ongoing inclusionist/exclusionist debate. On the exclusionist side, there is clearly nothing essential in such a category—nothing not already available on the subject entries themselves, about Shylock, Bloom or others. But on the inclusionist side, the category provided another way of accessing the information, another method of linking and learning. And since the storage and bandwidth capacities of Wikipedia are in effect infinite in comparison to words printed on paper, what harm is done by including such a category?

Neutrality of Editors and Conflicts of Interest

As the author of novels and short stories in which Phil D'Amato appears as a character (for example, "The Silk Code," 1999), I had a professional interest in wanting any category in which he appeared to continue on Wikipedia. I actually found out about the "Fictional Jews" category after it had been deleted and did not take part in any of the online discussions pro or con, but the ideal editor on Wikipedia is nonetheless a reader who has no vested interest in the article or page he or she is writing or editing. This means the editor has nothing to gain or lose financially, personally or professionally from the words on the page. Friedrich Engels, the Wikipedia guidelines on conflict of interest (COI) helpfully inform us, would not be the best person to edit an entry on Karl Marx.

But day to day, more current situations on Wikipedia may not be as clear-cut. Should someone who supports Obama refrain from editing pages about him and his work, or should Obama supporters, if they are known, be called out by other editors or warned by Wikipedia administrators not to edit Obama's pages? If this seems extreme to you, as it does to me, would you feel the same way if what were at issue were pages about Sarah Palin?

And staying in the political realm, but moving up the ladder of possible conflict of interest, what about a Democratic Party precinct captain? What about David Axelrod (a senior White House adviser) or Howard Dean (former Democratic National Committee chairman)? What about Michelle Obama? Should she be editing President Obama's Wikipedia page?

The last three people would seem, ipso facto, to be courting conflict of interest if they edited any Wikipedia pages in which Obama was the subject. But would it be fair for them to be banned from such editing?

In the end, the only objective way of enforcing neutrality in Wikipedia entries might well be to confine the appraisal to the words on the page and not the person who wrote them. As literary critic I. A. Richards warned us way back in 1929, the intentions of the writer are often inscrutable and have no real connection to the impact of the text. All that should count in analysis and criticism of a text, Richards wrote, is the text itself.

Furthermore, this problem of looking at the identity of the editor and assessing his or her neutrality is exacerbated on Wikipedia by the ease of creating pseudonymous accounts.

Identity Problems

Authenticity of users (readers, writers and commenters) is a problem everywhere in the worlds of new and new new media, where setting up a false identity is as easy as creating an email account on Gmail or Yahoo, under any name you choose, and then using it as the verifier on MySpace, Facebook, here, there and everywhere.

But the problem is especially acute on Wikipedia, since it initially operates via consensus achieved in online discussions of readers/editors ("initially" meaning before a problem may be passed on to and looked at by administrators, for discussion of which, see "All Wikipedians Are Equal, but Some Are More Equal Than Others" later in this chapter). Wikipedians even have a name for accounts created by individuals solely or mainly for the purpose of bringing additional support for their positions in consensus discussions: "sock puppets."

Creating accounts on Wikipedia is actually easier than on MySpace and most online systems; verification via email to an already existing Gmail or other account is not required. Indeed, editors can work on Wikipedia with no account, in which case they are identified by their IPs. Wikipedia is in the business of encouraging and maximizing participation. As in all things participatory and democratic, the process works better with more participants.

But this ease of creating accounts also has the result of making sock puppetry easy to pursue. And a clever creator of sock puppets can be difficult to identify. The bogus accounts can be created on different computers, with different IPs, and can lay dormant for months or get involved in Wikipedia discussions that have nothing to do with the sock puppeteer's real motives. When the sock puppet eventually springs into action and begins writing on behalf of articles near and dear to him or her, urging their retention or deletion in any debates that may ensue, there is no reason for anyone to think that this reader/editor has a vested interest in the article. Used in its most intelligent and effective forms, the sock puppet is thus the new new media equivalent of a sleeper cell. A sharp-eyed participant in the discussion may suspect something amiss, especially if the sock puppet writes in a style that is in some way idiosyncratic, but such suspicions can be difficult to prove when based solely on similarities in writing style.

An interesting back formation from the sock puppet, which is actually very different, is the so-called "meat puppet"—or a real account, created by a real person, for the purpose of supporting a friend's or associate's project on Wikipedia. The problem with equating sock puppets and meat puppets, however, is that the motive of any living human can be unclear. If I come to the aid of a friend in a discussion about whether to delete or keep an entry on Wikipedia, who other than I can know for sure whether I really support my friend's position, and would have had the same opinion if my friend did not exist, or whether I don't care at all about this issue and entered the online discussion only at my friend's behest? Or perhaps the truth is that I spoke up in the discussion because of a mix of the two factors: I believe in the issue but wrote what I wrote because my friend encouraged me.

Issues such as sock puppets versus meat puppets, and the difficulty of identifying and protecting against them, show that online life is by no means immune to the complexities and complications of real life. The two are both subject to vandals and troublemakers, who may be more or less difficult to deal with online. The saving grace of anything destructive online, however, is that it can in itself cause no physical damage in the real world—no damage, that is, unless we act upon it or allow its misinformation to guide our actions in the real world. This is the case whether we are dealing with cyberbullies on Facebook and MySpace or vandals of knowledge on Wikipedia.

All Wikipedians Are Equal, but Some Are More Equal Than Others

Wikipedia is the most thorough-going, consistently user-driven system on the Internet. It is the pick of the new new media litter, at least insofar as its primary, revolutionary characteristic of allowing consumers to become producers. But although all readers can indeed be editors of Wikipedia, a preliminary survey reported that 90 percent of Wikipedia edits were made by the top 15 percent of the most active Wikipedia editors (working paper by Mikolaj Jan Piskorski and Andreea Gorbatai cited in Heil & Piskorski, 2009)—an intrinsic shortcoming of all democratic processes, in which capacity to participate (as in voting) only partially equates to actual participation. And although editors usually decide via discussion and consensus whether an article, or part of an article, is worthy of Wikipedia, what happens when editors cannot decide? Or what happens when an editor acts as a vandal or creates sock puppets to support his or her position? Or what happens when an entry is so controversial that it is rent with constant deletions and reinstatements to the extent that it is changing back and forth every few minutes?

Enter the Wikipedia administrators, who are nominated and chosen by a public discussion and consensus of editors (an editor may nominate any other editor including her- or himself). A special super-kind of administrator—a "bureaucrat," also chosen by community consensus—determines if consensus has been reached in favor of promoting the editor to administrator and, if so, bestows the promotion. A few administrators also act as "checkusers"—they are given the authority to see the IPs of named or account-holding reader/editors (see "Transparency on Wikipedia Pages," later in this chapter).

One of the two prime powers of administrators is blocking the accounts of errant editors. Vandalism is one way to be errant but so is violation of the "three-revert" rule, which insists that no editor can revert changes—reinstate after something is deleted, delete after something is reinstated, etc.—more than three times in 24 hours on a given page or entry. Administrators, in fact, have the power to block an editor's account after fewer than three reversions, but three is the stated and usually followed number.

An account can be blocked for an hour, a day, a week, a month or indefinitely. The blocked editor can appeal, and any other administrator can reverse the decision of the blocking administrator or reduce the sentence (the duration of the block). However, since part of the purpose of blocking is to reduce or defuse so-called "edit wars"—two editors undoing each other's work—administrators try not to initiate a similar war of their own by repeatedly blocking and unblocking editors (which constitutes a "wheel war," in Wikipedian parlance).

The second major power of administrators is "protecting" a page or entry—preventing any reader/editor from making any further edits. As with blocking of accounts, the protection can be for any length of time, and any administrator can unprotect a page or open it for renewed editing. So "wheel wars," or administrators reversing one another's actions, are a pitfall to be avoided here, too.

Protection of pages, however, can be a tricky business. Let's say, for example, that on a given day, vandals and other people of ill intent are busy inserting on Barack Obama's page the falsehood that he is a Muslim. Well-meaning editors are doing the best they can to delete the falsehood. (An important exception to the three-revert rule is that it does not apply to correction of obvious falsehoods and the work of vandals, but the falsehoods have to be obvious.) An administrator who becomes aware of this continual dousing of brushfires set by info-arsonists on Barack Obama's page may well act to protect the page or lock it from further edits, but the administrator needs to be sure that no falsehoods exist on any part of the page prior to the protection. Otherwise, a page with a blatant error would not only be up on Wikipedia for the entire world to see, it would be immune to any editor's correction. Clever vandals, indeed, might well put a variety of more and less obvious errors in a targeted page, in the hope that an administrator protected the page, thinking all errors had been corrected, when in fact one of the less obvious errors remained.

Pages can also be semi-protected, or blocked from anonymous and new account edits. Obama's page has been intermittently semi-protected since 2007. (See Vargas, 2007, for discussion of vandalism on Obama's Wikipedia page.)

But Wikipedia has at least one additional, built-in defense against vandals.

Transparency on Wikipedia Pages

A major feature of Wikipedia that puts even the most diligent vandal at a disadvantage is the complete history of edits easily available on every page or entry. This means that any and all changes, additions, deletions, profound and trivial, can be seen on the screen by any reader/editor. A vandal may seek to disguise an important piece of dirty work by bundling it with a lot of obvious vandalism, and a revision, helpful or destructive, may be missed by a casual reader of the History page, but every single revision is nonetheless listed. Wikipedia also shows what every page looked like before and after the edit.

The transparent History pages on Wikipedia make it radically different from most blogs on the Web, which at most indicate when a page has been edited, and, in the case of Google's Blogspot (of which my Infinite Regress blog is an example), it gives no indication that a page has been edited at all. Similarly, profile pages on MySpace and Facebook give no indication of when or how often they have been edited, though users do have the option of making public the last time they logged on. Given that a page on Wikipedia can be edited by a myriad of people, in contrast to only the blogger being able to edit his or her blog (and only the account holder on MySpace and Facebook), this hyper-transparency of editing history on Wikipedia makes sense.

This level of transparency on Wikipedia, however, extends to pages and not to readers/editors. As indicated above, one need not have an account to edit on Wikipedia, in which case, you are identified by your IP. An IP is unique to your computer connection to the Internet. If you take your laptop to a friend's house and log on via Wi-Fi available there, you will be using his or her IP. (Mobile media such as iPhones have their own IPs.) IPs are thus not a foolproof way of identifying a particular reader/editor.

If you register for an account (free) on Wikipedia, you are thereafter identified by your account name, not your IP. But this allows individuals to register for any number of accounts and serves as the basis for sock puppetry (though an individual may want to have more than one account for nondisruptive purposes). Only specially appointed administrators—"checkusers"—have the ability to see the IP of any given account. These can be helpful in rooting out sock puppets, though the recalcitrant puppeteer can resort to different IPs for the puppets—for example, in libraries, Apple stores, and schools.

Wikipedia vs. Britannica

So, with all of these potentials for error and safeguards, with the battles waging on Wikipedia between vandals and editors, between editors and editors, between editors and administrators, and sometimes between administrators and administrators—all for the purpose of making sure that the articles on Wikipedia contain only accurate and relevant information—how does Wikipedia fare? An error is easier to identify than an irrelevance. If Wikipedia's reader-written, constantly in-flux pages were as free from error as, say, the distinguished, expert-written pages of the Encyclopedia Britannica, that would tell us something very important about how the democratic antibodies of a new new media book of knowledge compared with the strict gate-keeping of our older, trusted reference sources.

As of February 2009, Wikipedia seems to be holding its own against the Encyclopedia Britannica—a remarkable accomplishment—but the jury is still not entirely in.

Nature—one of the two leading science magazines in the world (along with Science)—reported the results of a study it conducted in 2005, in which experts examined 42 articles each from Wikipedia and Britannica (Giles, 2005). The experts found an average of four inaccuracies per Wikipedia article and three per Britannica article—in other words, not much of a difference at all. This result was widely publicized (for example, Associated Press, 2005) but drew an outraged objection from Britannica, which charged that Nature's investigators were the ones who got their facts wrong and, in other cases, offered mere opinion not expert judgment (Orlowski, 2006). Britannica called upon Nature to retract its report. Nature (2006) replied with a lengthy explanation of its methods and findings and concluded, "We do not intend to retract our article." Three years later, Nature stood by its 2005 findings (Giles, 2008).

The clearest lesson of these dueling experts may be that expert opinion is not as reliable as it holds itself out to be—either Nature was in error or Britannica in its criticism of Nature, or both—which in itself provides another strong argument in favor of encyclopedia by democracy on Wikipedia, or what Nature's study suggests.

Old vs. New New Media in Reporting the Death of Tim Russert

Wikipedia competes not only with old media encyclopedias but also with old media news reporting in newspapers, radio and television. When "Meet the Press" moderator Tim Russert died unexpectedly, shortly after 2:20 p.m. on June 13, 2008, NBC and other traditional news media understandably waited until relatives were notified before informing the general public. That occurred at 3:30 p.m., when Tom Brokaw broke into the afternoon programming on NBC, CNBC and MSNBC and announced Russert's death. ABC, CBS, CNN and Fox News all waited for Brokaw's announcement to broadcast their own announcements and stories.

Wikipedia did not. According to a New York Times June 23, 2008, account of the events of June 13 (Cohen, 2008), Russert's page on Wikipedia was updated at 3:01 p.m. to reflect Russert's death. (You can see this in the "History" of Russert's page on Wikipedia.) Also according to The New York Times, the person who made the change on Wikipedia was "a junior-level employee" of Internet Broadcasting Services—an organization that supplies services to local NBC-TV stations and other companies— who was subsequently fired. (The New York Times put the story of Russert's death on its own Web site five minutes before Brokaw's announcement.)

The difference between Wikipedia's and television's treatment of the Russert story highlights the radical departure of new new media from the way old and new media operate. In the case of NBC and all of the broadcast and cable media, an executive—a gatekeeping editor of some sort—made the call as to when the story would be aired. This is the procedure for any and every story we see on broadcast and cable TV, hear on the radio or read in the newspaper. In contrast, no one in the employ of Wikipedia made such a decision, because that is not the way Wikipedia works. (The Wikimedia Foundation and lawyers who work for Wikipedia do not make initial publishing decisions.) An employee of a company totally unrelated to Wikipedia updated Russert's page. Anyone could have done that—you or I. Or we might have put up a completely false story about Russert or about anyone.

It is not that Wikipedia has no standards for what is published in its online encyclopedia. It does, but the standards are applied, again, by you, me and anyone who happens to read an article. One of Wikipedia's primary standards is that facts need confirmation in other media before they stand on Wikipedia. Since no confirmation existed at 3:01 p.m. of Russert's death, the update announcing it on Russert's page was deleted 10 minutes later (according to The New York Times, by someone using another Internet Broadcasting Services computer). And, soon after, it of course was reinstated.

But would any new reader/editor know about this or any of the other many guidelines for articles on Wikipedia? There are extensive, detailed descriptions, explications, and summaries of standards posted on Wikipedia, and these are accessible in numerous ways (for example, see "Category: Wikipedia Behavioral Guidelines"). As is the case with any democracy, it can only work if citizens have easy, reliable access to its laws. As is also the case in any democracy, the laws or guidelines are constantly debated and refined.

Wikipedia Wrongly Reports the "Deaths" of Ted Kennedy and Robert Byrd

And, indeed, the egregiously wrong Wikipedia report of Ted Kennedy's and Robert Byrd's "deaths" on Inauguration Day, 2009, led Jimmy Wales to urge a new level of editorial review, in which "trusted editors" would need to approve all biographical entries by new and anonymous editors (see Pershing, 2009; Kells, 2009). In reality,

Ted Kennedy had a seizure and was taken out of the postinauguration luncheon by medics. Byrd, age 91, was apprehensive and decided to leave the luncheon as well. Kennedy recovered, and Byrd was not really ill in the first place, but in the initial confusion, Wikipedia listed both senators as deceased.

Whether by accident or vandalism, such erroneous posts call into question the reliability of Wikipedia. They were removed within five minutes—a testament to the correcting power of numerous readers/editors—but numerous readers nonetheless saw the incorrect reports. Instating a layer of editorial review would certainly help with this problem, but it would also undermine Wikipedia's fundamental policy of anyone can write and edit and publish on its pages. As of February 2009, several proposals addressing this issue were under discussion on Wikipedia. (Wikipedia in Germany already has such a review policy in place—for all articles, whatever the subject. See Wales, 2009, for preliminary details. And see also Perez-Pena, 2009, for how Wales and Wikipedia administrators kept news of David Rohde's kidnapping off of Wikipedia to help enable his eventual escape.)

Encyclopedia or Newspaper?

The immediate announcement of Tim Russert's death on Wikipedia—and the erroneous reports about Kennedy and Byrd—underlines another contentious issue: Is Wikipedia an encyclopedia or a newspaper? Publishing news as quickly as possible is, after all, what a newspaper does. But Wikipedia and newspapers are nonetheless not the same.

News media, in general, are supposed to report events that are true and significant in some sense and as soon as possible. Certainly an encyclopedia subscribes to the first two—everything in it should be true and significant—but instead of speed an encyclopedia presumably wants to publish information that has some kind of enduring relevance. And the very definition of enduring means it cannot cohabit with immediate, unless one wants to take a leap of faith and predict or assume that an event that occurred yesterday will be of interest to general readers 10 years later.

Sometimes such predictions are easy to make with confidence: Regardless of who wins an election for president of the United States, we can rest assured that the results of that election will continue to be of at least some historical importance. But what about the unexpected death of a prominent news moderator such as Tim Russert?

In the days following his death in June 2008, not only was his already existing page on Wikipedia updated hundreds of times, but additional pages were put up, with reactions to Tim Russert's death by famous people and other information. Was Wikipedia working as an encyclopedia or a newspaper with such entries?

Newspapers of course report not only immediate and breaking news but publish follow-up and retrospective stories as well. To the extent that enduring Wikipedia articles are as well researched as stories in newspapers—assuming that the newspapers have researched their stories—then the Wikipedia article becomes less distinguishable from a follow-up newspaper story. Ironically, Wikipedia guidelines require stories to be sourced, and although no firm ranking of sources (of which sources are preferable to others) is insisted upon, old media newspapers are held in higher regard as sources than blog posts, and world-renowned newspapers such as The New York Times are preferable to high school newspapers as sources. This provides yet another example of the interdependence and love/hate relationship of old and new new media that we saw in Chapter 2 about blogging and that we will see elsewhere in this book, for example, in Chapter 7 about Facebook, where we will encounter a group organized on the new new medium of Facebook to help save the old medium of newspapers.

In the end, the dominant principle in determining whether Wikipedia is an encyclopedia or a newspaper or both is that Wikipedia editors and administrators really have little say in how the rest of the world sees and uses Wikipedia. All that really matters is how people at large actually use it. If readers use Wikipedia as they would a newspaper—a more up-to-date version of The New York Times—then how can Wikipedians stop that?

This, once again, is a cardinal principle of new new media: Not only do consumers become producers, but consumers—not necessarily the same consumers but all consumers, in general—always determine how the new new medium is used. This gives a new meaning to the concept of user: not just one who consumes or uses a medium but, in that very use, helps determine what that medium is. John Dewey (1925), the American philosopher who argued that truth is best perceived and reached through real use and experience, not pre-existing thought and analysis, would have approved.

Does Wikipedia Make Libraries Unnecessary?

If Wikipedia is not quite yet, but may be becoming, a kind of newspaper, how does the online encyclopedia, which in principle has an infinite number of articles, compare with book and brick libraries?

Colin Powell, secretary of state in George W. Bush's first administration (2001–2005), was an early appreciator of Wikipedia. He told Fareed Zakaria on Zakaria's CNN "GPS" program on December 14, 2008, that, when he arrived at the State Department in 2001, he advised everyone to "get rid of all the books in your office. You don't need them anymore, as long as you have a couple of search engines and Wikipedia. And then I challenged my people to try to keep up with Wikipedia in terms of changes in countries."

Powell—whatever history may say about his presentation to the United Nations, prior to the Iraq War in 2003, that Saddam Hussein had weapons of mass destruction when it turned out later he apparently did not—was alert to something significant about Wikipedia and its advantages over older media, and alert to this very early. Books on the shelf suffer from an utter inability to be corrected or updated. All print media, in which words are wedded to paper, are similarly unchangeable and no different in this crucial respect than hieroglyphics carved into a pyramid (see Levinson, 1997, for more).

Newspapers do the best they can in this rigid realm by putting out new editions daily—they did this even more often prior to the triumph of electronic media in the mid-20th century—and offering follow-ups and updates on stories, as well as corrections. But unlike last year's books, last month's newspapers are far more likely to fill in packing boxes than provide missing information.

Books in libraries, then—and even online or digitally delivered, in read-only formats—carry the burden for reference media. But like the facts in printed encyclopedias, the information in such books and libraries may well be out of date, as Colin Powell noted back in 2001.

That's the argument in favor of Wikipedia over books in libraries. Yet Powell went a little too far when he said we "don't need" books anymore, whether in the State Department or the world at large, and such a statement would still be going too far in 2009.

Wikipedia has two disadvantages in comparison with libraries in 2009. The first is that it no doubt does not have some information available in books, whether about international politics and geography or any subject. But this is a classic example of what I call a "caterpillar criticism" (Levinson, 1988)—assessing a medium's incapacity at a given time as if it were permanent, rather than a work in progress, just as we might note that one problem with a caterpillar is that it cannot fly. There is no reason to think that, in ensuing years, knowledge will exist in any book on any shelf that will not be on Wikipedia. Indeed, Colin Powell's advice about not needing books, though still not correct today, is more correct now in 2009 than it was in 2001. And we can expect it to become more correct every year, every day, every hour.

But Wikipedia suffers from a second disadvantage in comparison with books, which is far more chronic, with no solution presently in sight. As we considered in Chapter 2 about blogging and Chapter 3 about YouTube, anything online, anything dependent on a link to a URL for retrieval, lacks what I call the "reliable locatability" of books. If you are currently reading these words—or the words on any page of this book, page 33, 63, any page—and the book consists of bound pages, those words will be there, on the same exact pages, tomorrow, next year, even a hundred or more years from now if you put the book in a safe place. The act of just putting the book on a shelf is usually enough to ensure that the words will be there for you the next time you look for them, in the exact same place in the book on the page.

The exceptions to this expectation would be a real bookworm that ate some pages or some other unforeseen cause of damage to the pages of the book. A book even on a shelf (see Petroski, 1999, for the history and impact of bookshelves) may be destroyed, the page may be torn out or obliterated, and this means reliable locatability is not an absolute guarantee that the text will survive in place. But the wedding of printed words to paper is permanent, and this means that their readers can have a much greater assurance than with anything on the Web that the words and images will be where expected, remembered, noted or cited for future reference.

Wikipedia, to be sure, is probably the most reliably locatable source of information on the Web. Its myriad reader/editors take great care to make sure any changes in links to articles are automatically redirected, often from more than one path or alternative spelling of a name or title of an article. And, as indicated previously, Wikipedia maintains complete and accessible histories of every change or edit made on any of its pages. But the system is still not perfect. For example, an article that is completely deleted may be available only to Wikipedia administrators and not the general editing public. And the sheer ease with which anything can be deleted online, if someone with the necessary access wants something gone, makes even the most secure online entry less secure than any old book. In fact, Wikipedia recognizes the inherent evanescence of Web sources in comparison with books and other old media sources by putting in its Web citations at the bottom of articles not just the date of the cited Web page's creation but also the date it was entered into the Wikipedia article. For the same reason, I indicated in the Bibliography to this book that the links supplied were good as of February 2009.

The future of books, libraries and offline digital media such as CDs and DVDs thus seems under no near jeopardy from Wikipedia and other new new media, though we can expect the offline media to play a decreasing reference role in our lives. (In the realm of entertainment, Netflix has been offering an increasing number of movies and television shows on its Web site, rather than DVDs in the mail.) Books, as well as newspapers, also retain an advantage in convenience over all digital media, online and offline, in that anything printed on paper can be read under any nearby light and requires neither batteries nor electric outlets.

And, although books have been banned and burned throughout history, the practical impossibility of rounding up all copies of a book, once printed and distributed, makes them invulnerable to complete banning by government, commercial or religious fiat—as we saw in Chapter 2 with the Church and Galileo (see also Levinson, 1997).

That's not the case for anything online, including Wikipedia, as we will see in our concluding section of this chapter.

The United Kingdom vs. Wikipedia

An encyclopedia is about the last kind of text one would expect to be banned—the very word breathes something stodgy—especially in the United Kingdom, where the Encyclopedia Britannica was first published, in Scotland in the 1770s. On the other hand, encyclopedias have been politically troublesome to some regimes, but this was not the problem that Wikipedia encountered in the United Kingdom in December 2008 (Kirk, 2008).

It was an album cover posted on Wikipedia—"Virgin Killer" by The Scorpions, from 1976—that attracted the concern of the U.K.'s Internet Watch Foundation (IWF), which put the album on its blacklist, due to the image of a nude young girl on its cover (the genital area, however, cannot be clearly seen, due to a cracked glass effect in the image). The IWF is not affiliated with the British government, but its blacklist is taken very seriously by British Internet providers who are expected to maintain standards of decency by the U.K. government. The result: some 95 percent of British Internet users were blocked from Wikipedia for three days, until the ban was lifted by the IWF (Raphael, 2008; Collins, 2008). That's right: British Internet users were blocked from *all* of Wikipedia on account of one album cover. Although the intent was to block the offending page, "The initial move last Friday by the IWF, which acts as a watchdog...for Internet content visible in the U.K. meant that some people could not see any pages on Wikipedia at all, while others were unable to edit pages on the user-generated encyclopedia" (Arthur, 2008).

As with Pakistan's ban of YouTube for several hours in February 2008, the blocking of Wikipedia in the UK over a questionable page highlights a deep vulnerability in new new media. Although new new media may be outside of the scope of FCC supervision—for now—in the United States, it is subject to control and banning in other parts of the world. In the case of Wikipedia, this can be especially destructive, because every reader unable to access Wikipedia is also an editor, unable to write or work to reach consensus in editorial discussions, which are the lifeblood of the online encyclopedia. (Arthur, 2008, reported that the ban "left millions of Britons unable to make edits on the Wikipedia site.") And the interconnectedness of everything in new new media—in the case of Wikipedia, of all of its pages to one another—meant that the banning of a single page took the whole encyclopedia offline and beyond access to everyone attempting to access the Internet in the country where the ban was in effect. This is equivalent to putting a padlock on a bookstore or library, just to keep one book out of the public's hands.

Indeed, in the case of the Pakistani ban, not only was that country affected but so was access to YouTube around the world. Not just the bookstore was boarded up; bookstores around the world were, too.

Presumably, digital surgical techniques sooner or later will be able to take out just the offending page, or remove from public access what the censor considers a tumor, rather than shutting down a vital new new media organ. But the fundamental problem remains: The current architecture of new new media and their conduits makes them all too easy to ban by central authorities. A glaring irony of new new media is that the digital engineering that make them the most democratizing media in human history also gives governments and other authorities more power to ban them than the Church ever had over Galileo's books nearly 400 years ago.

The problem with the global village, from the perspective of combating censorship, is that the entire globe can be censored just by shutting down a few of the vendors of information on Main Street.

Fortunately, as we will see in the next chapter about Digg, the means have never been better to shout about it from every digital tower.

5

CHAPTER

Digg

IF WIKIPEDIA WAS CONCEIVED AS AN ONLINE ENCYCLOPEDIA, also used nonetheless as an online newspaper, Digg was conceived by Kevin Rose, Owen Byrne, Ron Gorodetzky and Jay Adelson in December 2004 as an index for all news published on the Web, and it serves as an instantly updating digest of news, or an online newspaper of newspapers. Along with Reddit, Buzzflash and at least half a dozen other online news-listing services, the articles that appear on Digg are published elsewhere online and selected—in the case of Digg, "Dugg"—by readers to appear on its front pages. Digg is the biggest and best known and was number 32 in the top 100 American online sites as listed by Alexa on June 25, 2008.

Digg's ranking had dropped to 294 in December 2008 and 272 in February 2009—a significant decline from the previous June, likely due to a reduction in interest after the presidential election, but still impressive (my paullevinson.blogspot.com blog, the blog address of Infinite Regress, was 492,000 on Alexa in February 2009 in comparison). As CNET News reported in May 2008, "with the 2008 presidential election on the way, Digg has caught on among another very vocal set of news junkies: the political crowd. It's helped boost the site's numbers for sure: Digg now boasts 230 million page views per month, 26 million unique visitors, and 15,000 stories submitted per day" (McCarthy, 2008).

Registering as a user of Digg is a bit more exacting than on Wikipedia: an email account is required. Once registered, a user can post anything with a URL— any blog post, online newspaper article, photograph, video—on Digg. All users can Digg or Bury as many posts as they like. The names of those actions mean just what they sound like: A Digg is an approval, a Bury a dislike of a posted link.

When a post or submission receives an undisclosed number of Diggs, and no minimum number of Buries (Digg keeps this Digg/Bury algorithm secret), the submission becomes "Popular," or is put on the front page of Digg.

Users can also comment on a submission, and the number of comments also works on behalf of a submission becoming "Popular." Comments can be supportive or critical of a submission and can be made by users who Digg, Bury or do neither for a submission. Abusive comments can be reported. And as is the case with Wikipedia, disruptive commenters on Digg are disciplined not by Digg users (which would be the equivalent of reader/editors on Wikipedia) but by the Digg administration, which can ban a user as an ultimate sanction.

Thus, in contrast to The New York Times' "all the news that's fit to print," Digg publishes—i.e., makes "Popular," or puts on its front page—all the submissions that its users endorse via Diggs, comments, and not many Burys. The Times' motto, of course, was never true in the first place, as pointed out in Chapter 2.

But neither does Digg's method always function in complete accordance with its ideal. As is the case with all people or nonexpert-directed new new media, Digg is subject to abuse or "gaming"—or users teaming up to get stories to the front page, rather than Digging what they genuinely see as worthy.

This is an abuse as old as democracy itself: The more that any process, government or news publication is open to the will of the people, the more vulnerable it is to small groups of people using the democratic levers to make the process work in their favor. In government, we call this process "lobbying." On Digg and in new new media, it is called "gaming." In this chapter, we examine some of Digg's democratizing techniques, how they have been utilized by "gamers," and what impact both the democratizing and the gaming may have had on the world at large.

Shouting, Paying for Diggs (and Buries)

In principle, stories are supposed to be Dugg or Buried on Digg according to the assessments of each individual reader. In practice, Diggs and Buries are often amassed via deliberate campaigns of readers. As is the case with the "meat puppet" problem on Wikipedia (sock puppetry is alway unethical), a question always remains as to the validity of such sought-after Diggs and Buries: Would the Digger (or Burier) on his or her own have been moved to Digg or Bury the story? Is the mere fact that the Digg or Bury occurred after the reader received a solicitation enough to invalidate the Digg or Bury?

Digg, itself—which has an administration more active in the daily operation of its system than Wikipedia's and is therefore more top-down, or old media, than Wikipedia—is not consistent in its response to solicited Diggs and Buries. A powerful feature on Digg from 2007–2009 allowed users to "Shout" to up to as many as 200 "Friends." Such Shouts could encourage Diggs or Buries. (Encouraging Diggs was a little easier, since the default Shout was "sharing." To elicit Buries, the shouter had to attach a brief note urging a Bury.) Digg retired the Shout feature in May 2009, and encouraged Diggers to continue shouting about Digg stories on Twitter and Facebook, via buttons provided on Digg's pages (Milian, 2009).

Of concern to the Digg administration, then, was not Digg's own "Shouting" feature or informal sharing and promotion of Digg stories on Twitter and Facebook, but deliberate campaigns on and off the system to Digg or Bury stories, including operations purported to deliver X number of Diggs for a given story for $1 or more per Digg (Newitz, 2007). A blogger might be tempted to use such a service, not only to obtain more readers, but for the advertising revenue that a monetized blog with a larger number of readers could generate.

And the numbers are considerable. Of the ten stories written by me and posted on my blogs that went "Popular" on Digg in 2007–2008, the least number of additional readers attracted to my blog was 15,000, and the most was 50,000. But in terms of my book sales and advertising income received from that number of visitors, having "Popular" articles on Digg was not only not enough to retire on, but it would not even have been enough to pay for the purchase of Diggs (assuming a minimum number of 150 Diggs at $1 each to get the article to the front page, though most articles take at least 200 to 300 Diggs to be promoted to the front).

But Digg is by no means averse to promotion of Digg stories off the Digg Web site. It provides a variety of "buttons" and widgets that bloggers can put directly on their sites, with the result that readers can Digg a story directly from the blog. Some blogs, such as The Huffington Post and Blogcritics.com, have widgets indicating which of their stories are surging on Digg at any moment.

These are the ethical bottom lines, then, for promoting stories on Digg: Stories promoted on Web sites on which the stories appear and stories promoted (and trashed) to and by "Friends" on Digg are fine. Stories promoted and trashed by groups outside of Digg, especially if an exchange of money is involved, are not. And, of course, sock puppets set up to Digg or Bury stories is a practice that, as on Wikipedia, is also not allowed on Digg but, as is the case on Wikipedia, no doubt can, and do, take place until uncovered (see Saleem, 2006 and Saleem, "Ruining the Digg Experience," 2007, for analysis and cautions about gaming Diggs).

Or, as Digg advises in its posted "Terms of Use" (2009): Digg is not to be used "with the intention of artificially inflating or altering the 'digg count,' blog count, comments, or any other Digg service, including by way of creating separate user accounts for the purpose of artificially altering Digg's services; giving or receiving money or other remuneration in exchange for votes; or participating in any other organized effort that in any way artificially alters the results of Digg's services."

What Digg is aiming for, therefore, in addition to individual preferences for stories, is a sense of genuine or nonartificial community. But what is genuine about an online "friend"?

"Friends" in New New Media

Digg is the first place we have fully encountered "Friends" thus far in this book. But online "Friends" are the core of MySpace and Facebook and play a major role in Second Life. "Friends" are the essence of "social media," a significant subset of new new media.

And the essence of online "Friends"—their first and foremost principle—is that they have little in common with real-life friends, or friends offline, in the real world. To be friends with someone offline, to be even a casual acquaintance, means you know many things about them, including what they look and sound like. Offline impersonations are, of course, possible, but they happen much less frequently than online. Indeed, by far the best of way of authenticating an online Friend's identity is to know that person offline—we might say that online Friends are bona fide to the degree that they are offline friends.

But is the online Friend a totally inapt and deceptive usage, a metaphor with nothing in common with its offline referent? No. Successful, widely used metaphors usually share at least some significant characteristic with their referents, and, in this case, online Friends do have something crucially in common with offline friends: both have a similarity or community of interests.

In the case of Digg "Friends," the common interest is presumably a taste for the same kinds of stories. As a first step toward such "friendship," any user can become a "Fan" of another user on Digg, signifying that the Fan enjoys or for whatever reason wants to follow or easily find or know more about the user's submitted stories, Diggs, comments or any of the user's activities on Digg. If this user reciprocates and becomes a Fan of the Fan, then the two are "Friends" (this allowed the two to send Shouts to one another).

This two-step approach to online "friendship" is also a feature of Twitter, where users can elect to "follow" the posted notes of other users and in turn can be followed. In other systems, including MySpace and Facebook, a request for "friendship" bestows no privileges, until it is accepted, in which case the two parties become "Friends."

In most new new media systems, including Digg, users can put relevant links to their blogs, photos and other information in their profiles, and they can decide whether to make such information available to everyone or just to "Friends." But no one can ever be sure that photographs on a profile, for example, are actually photographs of the name on the profile or if the person described in the profile is even real—unless, again, the person in the profile is already known to the user visiting the profile.

Such issues of authenticity get to one of the fundamental questions about new new media—what impact do they have in the real world? At one end of the spectrum, we can have users under pseudonyms writing and otherwise participating online in ways that no one offline knows or cares about. At the other end, online activity can have profound consequences in the real world. We will consider the personal impact of online relationships, including its dangers, in subsequent chapters about MySpace, Facebook, and "The Dark Side of New New Media."

In the next section, we examine the impact of Digg and its online activities on the real world activity of politics.

Ron Paul vs. Barack Obama on Digg

Stories about Ron Paul, a contender in the Republican presidential primaries in 2007–2008, were enormously popular on Digg. CNET News reported in August 2007 that he "enjoys about 160,000 mentions on Digg.com, more than the next four most popular candidates combined" (McCullagh, 2007) but also advised that "Paul's poll numbers award him less than 2 percent of the vote among Republican candidates." And, in fact, Ron Paul obtained less than 5 percent of the votes in Republican primaries in most states. Stories about Barack Obama were also highly popular on Digg, though, in the primaries, not as successful as Ron Paul's. Why did Obama succeed in real, offline politics, while Ron Paul did not?

The easy explanation that Ron Paul's success on Digg was inflated, manipulated or otherwise gamed, while Obama's was not, is probably not correct, because, although we have no reliable, proven knowledge about what either of the candidates' supporters did to promote their candidate on Digg, there is no reason to think that Ron Paul's supporters did anything more or different from Obama's.

Ron Paul's high profile on Digg did attract much more general attention than Obama's, because Paul was so low in offline polls and primary votes. First heralded and decried by various observers as a "fringe politician" taking "over the Web" (Spiegel, 2007), Ron Paul's success on Digg soon came under more serious analysis by social media practitioners such as Muhammad Saleem, who wrote in July 2007 that "A few months ago, I was surprised by the candidate's [Ron Paul's] popularity on the various socially driven sites and thought to myself that was simply the result of an online democracy in action. A couple of days ago, however, this image was shattered…" The cause of the shattering was an "expose by Ron Sansone" (2007), another social media analyst, whose investigation convinced Saleem that Paul's "apparent popularity was simply a result of mass manipulation" on Digg, or encouragement of Ron Paul supporters on various Web sites to join Digg and vote up Ron Paul stories. Saleem later noted (November 2007) that "Ron Paul submissions can now get over 100 diggs in an hour" and that Shouting had exacerbated this problem.

Ron Paul's supporters responded throughout 2007 that more stories about their candidate should have made the front page of Digg, and did not because they were hit by an anti-Ron Paul "bury brigade" (Jones, 2007). Mainstream online media such as Wired.com had been reporting about possible "bury brigades," or organized efforts to vote down a variety of articles posted on Digg (not just about Ron Paul), for several months (Cohen, 2007), and, ironically insofar as Ron Paul, Saleem had offered screenshot "proof" of bury brigades at work, several months earlier (February 2007), concluding that although Buries are "supposed to be used to remove superfluous or irrelevant content from Digg, the mechanism is often abused to remove useful and insightful content by malicious users for self-serving and vindictive reasons."

Obama was recognized early on and throughout the primaries as the other Internet candidate (Stirland, 2007; VanDenPlas, 2007) and in the general election as the Internet candidate, period (see Chapter 12, "New New Media and the Election of 2008," for details and analysis). One observer at the end of August 2008 noticed multiple stories about Obama on Digg "having over 2 thousand votes on them and hundreds of comments" (Gladkova, 2008), or easily being at the top of the front page. An article in Business Week from the same time reported that "Obama's people may ask you to Digg an article that is favorable to Obama or critical of his opponent" (Hoffman, 2008). But, interestingly, such reports stopped short of claiming that Obama's supporters had outrightly gamed the system. Scott VanDenPlas's report from a year earlier sums up the enduring perception about the successes of Ron Paul and Barack Obama on Digg: "Paul's surge seems to be more manufactured, based on rigging the democratic systems of the web to return results favorable to the supported candidate. Obama's support has more of an organic feel with power in numbers" (VanDenPlas, 2007).

But what is the difference between being asked "to Digg an article that is favorable to Obama" (Hoffman, 2008) and "manipulation" of Digg (Sansone, 2007, about Ron Paul)? As an alternative to the "Ron Paul gamed the system and Obama did not" explanation of why Ron Paul's excellent showing on Digg bore such meager results in the primaries while Obama's excellent showing on Digg correlated with his getting the Democratic nomination and going on to win the election, let me offer a hypothesis that has to do not with the ethics and sincerity of pro-Paul and pro-Obama Diggers, but their ages.

Users must be 13 years of age to register on Digg, and registration is needed to submit articles, Digg or Bury, comment, etc. The registration process, however, does not insist on any proof of age, so it is a safe assumption that children under the age of 13 are submitting stories, Digging and so forth on Digg. But even if the 13-year-old requirement were 100 percent honored, that would leave five years of people—ages 13 to 17—who could Digg stories but not vote in primary or general elections.

That discrepancy is probably the best place to start looking for why a political candidate could do splendidly on Digg—have stories about him or her dominate the Digg front pages—but fail, and by large margins, in actual elections. Socialmediatrader.com reported that, in a snapshot analysis of Diggs on January 11, 2008, Ron Paul had the greatest number of Diggs in popular or front-page stories—close to 3,000, some 50 percent more than the candidate with the second biggest number, Hillary Clinton with close to 2,000. The other candidates were just hundreds of Diggs below Hillary Clinton. Rudy Giuliani was third, Mike Gravel fourth, Dennis Kucinich fifth, Mike Huckabee sixth—all ahead of Barack Obama, who had only the seventh greatest number of Diggs, a little under 1,500, on front-page stories about him, on this day. John McCain was in eighth place, with about a hundred fewer Diggs than Obama. This was eight days after the January 3 Iowa caucuses, in which Obama came in first for the Democrats and Hillary third, while Ron Paul came in fourth or about midway in the field of Republicans. In the January 8 primary in New Hampshire, Clinton came in first for the Democrats, McCain first for the Republicans and Ron Paul fifth. Clearly, the January 11 Digg activity was already way out of synch with what was happening in caucuses and primary voting booths, most especially concerning Ron Paul.

Was this because Ron Paul's supporters were already gaming Digg, while Barack Obama's supporters were not, at least not at that point in the primaries? That may have been a contributing factor, but let's look at the discrepancy between Diggs and the results in the primaries from another angle. Obama's campaign clearly worked the "grassroots" well enough to win in Iowa and come in second in New Hampshire. Ron Paul's campaign did poorly in both states. This means that Obama's campaign galvanized a far greater number of people who caucused or voted, age 18 or above, than did Ron Paul's campaign. Let's assume that a similar percentage of those Obama and Paul voters—anywhere from 0 to 100 percent—found their way to Digg, or were already on Digg at the time of the primaries. An alternate explanation to Paul's supporters gaming or manipulating Digg is that, in addition to the 18 or older supporters, Ron Paul also had a large number of supporters on Digg ages 13 through 17, or even younger, and that theirs were the Diggs that lifted Ron Paul's articles so high up on the front page.

But how was it that Barack Obama, the widely acknowledged "youth" candidate, as we saw in Chapter 3 about YouTube (see Wertheimer, 2008; Baird, 2008), did not attract large numbers of 13- to 17-year-old supporters of his own to Digg? The answer, I would suggest, is that Obama's campaign wisely focused on people aged 18 to 30, who could go out and caucus or vote. Ron Paul's campaign had no equivalent grassroots operation and did the best it could with extensive Internet promotion, which reaches people below the age of 18 as easily as people above that voting age. Obama's Internet campaign, in other words, built on the foundation of a powerful in-person campaign directed at potential voters and partnered with it. Ron Paul's campaign started with the Internet and never got beyond it.

No scientific statistics exist for the age of Digg users. But a poll reported in September 2006 shows 5 percent of Digg users are between the ages of 13 and 16, 22 percent ages 17–20, 28 percent ages 21–24, 20 percent ages 25–28, etc. (Ironic Pentameter, 2006), which certainly indicates a tilt toward younger users and a significant percentage (more than 5, less than 27 percent) of Diggers under 18. A more recent impression, widely shared (at least insofar as mental age), "is that the average age of Digg users is about 15" (MacBeach, 2008).

I thus think there is sufficient reason to think that, as an alternative to the "gaming" effect, or at least a more significant factor, the below voting-age of Ron Paul's supporters on Digg resulted in his success on Digg and failure at the polls. Obama's campaign concentrated from the outset on young voting-age people, who helped propel him to first- and second-place finishes in the primaries and eventually to a position on Digg almost as powerful as Ron Paul's and, ultimately, to a revolutionary victory in the general election. Ron Paul, in contrast, never succeeded off of Digg and the Internet. He was defeated in the primaries not by the failure of gaming on Digg to translate into votes but because Digg demographics had little correlation to the demographics and views of American voters.

Ron Paul and the Older Media

The possible gaming by Ron Paul's supporters, and their likely young age, figured in a similar story off of Digg, in the older medium of television and its coverage of the primary campaigns and debates.

ABC neglected to mention on at least one occasion that Ron Paul came in first in its post-debate poll. It removed comments from Ron Paul supporters on its online board and then proceeded to shut it down. And ABC also showed a lone Ron Paul supporter before the Iowa caucus, in contrast to big crowds for Mitt Romney, when in fact Ron Paul had big crowds of supporters, too (see Levinson, "Rating the News Networks," 2007, for a summary of these and other network shortcomings in their coverage of Ron Paul, with links). CNBC removed a post-debate poll that Ron Paul won (Wastler, 2007; see also Levinson, "Open Letter to CNBC," 2007). Sean Hannity denigrated Ron Paul's first-place finish in another post-debate poll on Fox, as due to repeat dialing by a small number of supporters, in contrast to Alan Colmes, who insisted on reporting Ron Paul's first-place result without spin (Hannity & Colmes, 2007; see also Levinson, "Hannity & Colmes Split," 2007).

Obama was generally spared such dismissive treatment by the old media, but MSNBC's professional pollster Chuck Todd discounted Obama's success in a post-debate poll on that cable network as due to his supporters dialing repeatedly on cellphones in responding to the poll (Levinson, "Now Obama's Poll Results Are Denigrated," 2007).

Hannity may have had cellphones in mind, too, and he and Todd may have been right that cellphones were the medium that propelled Paul and Obama to victories in the phone polls—but not because of repeat dialing or the same small number of supporters casting numerous phone votes. A 15-year-old, after all, who cannot vote in a primary, could respond via cellphone to a post-debate poll as easily as a 25-year-old. And although I would not put it past supporters of any candidate to cast repeated votes in a post-debate poll, apparently that was not possible with the Fox texting poll on October 22, 2007—I tried to vote twice, as a test to see what would happen, and my second vote was not counted. Of course, I could have cast additional votes on different phones or texted my friends to vote for my candidate on their phones. But the explanation for Ron Paul's success in post-debate phone polls may well be much the same as for his success on Digg: some gaming and manipulation, no doubt, but the younger-than-voting-age of the callers also was likely a significant factor. Since Obama did as well in the primaries as in post-debate polls, his success in the phone polls requires no further explanation, though it is likely that under-voting-age people cast phone votes for him as well.

Restricting phone polling to people 18 or over is no more appealing or easy to accomplish than allowing only people 18 or older on Digg or any place else on the Web. The discrepancy between Ron Paul's success in the phone polls and his performance in the primaries thus is probably best chalked up to unavoidable noise in the phone poll system.

The networks, however, would have done better to offer such an analysis, rather than remove polls that showed Ron Paul winning and disparage his supporters without proof.

Reddit, Fark, Buzzflash and Digg Alternatives

Digg is not the only user-generated headline news service on the Web. Some of the niches of new new media are filled with solitary giants, such as Wikipedia in encyclopedic reference and Twitter in microblogging, which dominate to the point of being the only real games in the global town. On the other hand, MySpace and Facebook, which we will examine in the next two chapters, have carved up the world of social media into two, titanic, competing spheres, much like the two superpowers in the Cold War. YouTube is somewhere in between in this continuum, closer to Wikipedia and Twitter in dominating the video field but with competition from such sites as the Daily Motion, Blip.tv and Metacafe, as well as cable networks such as MSNBC and CNN, which increasingly put up videos from their shows on their own sites, and sites such as Hulu and tv.com, which post episodes from television. If we place Wikipedia and Twitter on the extreme left of a continuum, representing no competition, and MySpace and Facebook on the extreme right, representing competition between two giants, then YouTube could be placed on the left, about 10 percent to the right of Wikipedia and Twitter. Digg might be placed somewhere in the middle, about equidistant from Wikipedia and Twitter on the left, and MySpace and Facebook on the right.

Reddit is the most Digg-like of the Digg alternatives. Readers submit stories just as on Digg and vote them up or down. Readers also make comments, which can be voted up or down. Stories that receive the requisite net number of "up" votes make the front page. As of December 2008, Reddit was second to Digg as the most popular new new media news site—though Reddit's Alexa ranking was 5,122, way below Digg's 294.

Fark represents the least new new media of reader-driven online news listings. Although any reader can submit an article with a link, Fark's editors choose which articles make its front pages. Very few are selected. As of February 2009, only three of my hundreds of submissions made the Fark front page: a blog post I wrote about Dennis Kucinich wanting the voting age lowered to 16 (I think it should be lowered to 14), a video clip from my appearance on the History Channel a few years ago in which I talked about the history of science fiction, and a review of an episode of "Life on Mars", which I titled "'Life on Mars' Meets Itself on TV." A large part of what drives Fark's selections is humor, in particular, clever headlines—I'm sure part of the reason my "'Life on Mars' Meets Itself on TV" review was chosen was because it was published on my Infinite Regress blog (two video cameras pointing at each other is one way of producing a visual infinite regress).

Articles that do not make the Fark front page—Fark says "less than 5 percent" (2009), and in my experience that's been less than 1 percent—are made available to the "Total Fark" community, which can extensively comment on these articles. But the only people who can see such articles and comments are members of Total Fark, and this membership is available only via paid subscription. So, in sum, Fark does draw on stories submitted by readers and in that sense is a new new medium, but its editorial selection (rather than reader selection) and its charging for Total Fark membership (rather than being free) is decidedly old media in approach.

Buzzflash differs in several important ways, the most significant of which is that Buzzflash is directed to a "progressive" political audience. Although it can and does publish links to items that may be antiprogressive—or, at the very least, critical of Barack Obama, for example, from both the left and the right—these are usually attacked in the commentary and not "flashed" to the front page. Buzzflash can thus be considered the new new media equivalent of The New Republic, The Nation and other progressive news and commentary magazines.

Buzzflash also differs from Digg in providing two ways to get to the front page. One works much like Digg, with users "flashing" stories they like and commenting upon them. Stories with the requisite number of flashes—usually 25 in 24 hours, in contrast to Digg, which requires at the very least hundreds (Reddit is in the middle)—ascend to the front page. But Buzzflash editors can also select a story for another front page—BuzzFlash.com, in contrast to BuzzFlash.net—and in this way the Buzzflash operation seeks to get the best of both old and new new media worlds.

Given that the very purpose of Digg, Reddit and the other headline-ranking services is to vote news stories up or down, it is not surprising that they often post stories about themselves and each other and proceed to rank them, as well, in a fiercely partisan way.

A story on the front page of Reddit on December 25, 2008—in the top 20, in fact, with 3,378 up votes and 1,170 down votes for a net of 2,258 "points," as well as 843 comments—was titled "So Who Else Here Left Digg for Reddit?" (ILeftDiggforReddit, 2008). The gist of the comments was that Digg was terrible and Reddit was wonderful, and Reddit had either already buried or soon would bury Digg.

The first comment read, "First digg. Then both. Then reddit. Nothing against diggers, it's the bots, having to have to randomly add so many friends to get your content on the front page." The second comment read, "The first rule of Reddit is to tell other intelligent people about Reddit. The second rule of Reddit is to tell stupid people about digg." And so on.

But Reddit's far worse Alexa ranking of 5,122, in comparison to Digg's 294, mentioned above, told a different story—a helpful reminder, though we should not need one, that democratically selected news media provide no presumptions of truth. Indeed, StumbleUpon, another Digg-like system, has an Alexa ranking of 811—much better than Reddit's—but StumbleUpon features many community applications and is as much like MySpace as it is like Digg. (See Bennett, 2009, for more on these and other alternate Digg systems.)

We turn now to two social media whose rankings in Alexa are beyond dispute, except insofar as one could be a point or two higher or lower than the rankings indicated. But both are in the top 10: MySpace at 7 and Facebook at 5.

MySpace

ALL MEDIA, NEW AND OLD, ARE INTRINSICALLY SOCIAL. EVEN ancient hieroglyphics required at least two people to work—one to write, one to read—as does all communication. A word spoken or written to oneself, unheard or unseen by anyone, may be just as real as the proverbial tree falling in a forest with no one around, but it is not communication.

New new media all heighten the crucial social aspect of communication. Wikipedia and Digg would be unworkable without groups of editors and Diggers, and a blog with no comments would technically still be a blog but much more like an online magazine or newspaper than a blog. We could say that a blog without comments is more like a new medium than a new new medium. Old media such as printed newspapers, of course, publish letters to the editor, but these enjoy a much smaller role in the daily life of a newspaper than do comments in a blog.

Some new new media, however, go beyond relying on social networks for their operation. Unlike Wikipedia, which requires groups of people to write and edit, there is a species of new new media with the very purpose of creating and developing social networks. Such media may and do offer blogging and YouTube-like storage and dissemination of videos, but their primary purpose is neither to inform nor entertain but to enable people to connect for whatever purpose.

Enter the new new media realm of social media, dominated by MySpace and Facebook.

The Irresistible Appeal of "Friends"

MySpace was launched in August 2003 by Brad Greenspan (then CEO of e-Universe) and Tom Anderson, Chris DeWolfe and Josh Berman, also with e-Universe. MySpace built upon the social dynamics of America OnLine, CompuServe, message boards, forums and computer conferencing (see Levinson, 1985 and 1997; Ryan, 2008; Vedro, 2007, for details), but Greenspan saw the key new new media value, as did Friendster (2002), of not charging for accounts. Rupert Murdoch's News Corp. purchased MySpace for $580 million in July 2005, and it currently is one of the two behemoths of online social media (along with Facebook) with more than 300 million accounts. Some number of these are different accounts used by the same people, but the number still dwarfs the populations of most countries in the world and may or may not trump Facebook, which as of February 2009 claims some 170 million "active" users (and which we will examine in the next chapter).

MySpace's tagline—the equivalent of The New York Times' "all the news that's fit to print" or Fox News' "fair and balanced"—is "a place for friends." Is that slogan any more truthful? Is it as accurate a description of MySpace as "broadcast yourself" is for YouTube, which, as we saw in Chapter 3, is accurate indeed? As we also saw earlier, The New York Times' classic blurb, on its front page since 1897, disguises the fact that what gets into its pages is not all the news that's fit to print but all the news that the editors at The New York Times deem fit to print. Fox's 1998 slogan is more subjective and thus less easy to refute—what, exactly, does "fair" mean—but no one except Fox would characterize its lineup of anchors and commentators as "balanced" between left and right, or even Democratic versus Republican points of view.

And what of "Friends" on MySpace? As we saw with "Friends" on Digg (Chapter 5), a purely online friend has only one significant thing in common with offline, in-person friends—a sharing of one or more keen interests. Otherwise, I recall the response I received shortly after I joined MySpace in 2005 and invited someone with tastes in science fiction very similar to mine to be Friends. "Uh, are we, like, going to hang out," he replied, sarcastically. I apologized, and I said I regretted that the invitation to be a "Friend" implied a connection that went far beyond a coincidence of interest in science fiction.

The problem of not really being a friend to your "Friends" on MySpace or any online system goes far deeper than whether I, in my real identity of Paul Levinson, can be online Friends with you, in your real identity. What would you do if you got a "Friend request" from Socrates, Aristotle, or "Sawyer" or "Kate" (characters on the TV series "Lost")? One advantage of such a request is that you would presumably immediately know you were not receiving a Friend request from the real Socrates. But what if you received a request from someone with a historical or fictitious name you did not recognize?

"Sierra Waters" is a lead character in my published works "The Plot to Save Socrates" (2006) and "Unburning Alexandria" (2008). I established accounts under her name on MySpace and Facebook in 2008. It was crystal clear to anyone who looked at the profile pages for Sierra that she was a character in my novels. Nonetheless, I received more than one email from men on MySpace—or accounts with male names—asking "Sierra" for sexual favors.

"Cyberbullying" on MySpace

The capacity of any user to take on a completely false identity—false not only in name but also in gender and age—opens up all kinds of possibilities for abusive and dangerous behaviors. As we will see in Chapter 11, "The Dark Side of New New Media," no medium—old or new—is immune to abusive, dangerous and criminal uses, and in that chapter we will examine some of the misuses and abuses that arise from false identities and other aspects of new new media, some seemingly innocuous, others actually very useful to users not intent on crime. But the Lori Drew "cyberbullying" case is so intrinsically an example of what can go very wrong on MySpace—how a social medium can be used to kill or can result in a "Friend's" death—that we will consider that perversion of a social medium right here.

To begin with, the Lori Drew case was not a straightforward instance of cyberstalking, in which someone, usually with a false name and picture, befriends someone else on MySpace—usually a vulnerable, young teenage girl—with the goal of arranging a meeting with this new friend, in person, for whatever nefarious purpose. The remedy for this sort of cyberstalking is to never meet a person face to face whom you know only online, unless it is in a very public, safe place.

Nor was this a typical case of cyberbullying, in which one or more people harass an individual for the purpose of embarrassing, ridiculing, or humiliating the victim (see Chapter 11).

The Lori Drew cyberbullying instance was something different, although it occurred because of the same inability of anyone to know who their online Friends really are, unless they already know them offline.

The background of the case is as follows: According to Lori Drew, a 49-year-old mother, her 13-year-old neighbor, Megan Meier, was spreading nasty rumors about Drew's daughter. Lori Drew exacted revenge. She created the false MySpace identity of "Josh Evans" on MySpace and there befriended Megan Meier. "Josh" pretended to fall in love with Megan. And when the 13-year-old was convinced of "his" love, Josh/Lori had email sent to Megan which said "the world would be a better place without you." Megan, who suffered from depression, hung herself (Masterson, 2008).

Local prosecutors were unable to get an indictment against Drew in Missouri, where she and Megan Meier lived. But federal prosecutors were able to indict her in Los Angeles (headquarters of News Corp/Fox, which owns MySpace) on three counts of illegally accessing computers (misdemeanors) and one felony count of conspiracy under the Computer Fraud and Abuse Act. The jury found her guilty of the first three, lesser charges.

As Kim Zenter pointed out in Wired.com (November 26, 2008), the prosecution was based on a "novel" equation of the use of MySpace to harass (in violation of its "terms-of-service" agreement) and "hacking" as prohibited under the federal law. Although MySpace supported the prosecution, numerous legal experts and civil libertarians objected (Zenter, May 15, 2008), and although I almost always agree with them (see my "Flouting of the First Amendment," 2005), in this case I did not. I think the verdict, even for just the misdemeanors, created an important precedent. Using false identifies for fun, role-playing and nondeceptive commercial activity is fine. But using a false identity to abuse someone—especially an adult abusing a child—would be harassment not protected under the First Amendment. (A federal judge in July 2009 announced his intention of overturning the verdict, but I still think the conviction was warranted; see Zavis, 2009.)

In terms of new new media: These systems empower us in all ways, including a parent's very wrong acting out of understandable anger at anyone, including someone else's child, who is causing any grief to her child. Therefore, we as a society need to create whatever obstacles we can to prevent, stop and punish any acting on this anger through the easy, powerful avenues of new new or whatever media.

In some ways the most disturbing part of what happened to Megan Meier is that she did not fall prey to "traditional" cyberstalking—she did not die because she foolishly met an online friend in person at some private place. Indeed, she did nothing wrong or foolish at all—other than falling in love with a "boy" on MySpace.

What can we do to protect our children from this kind of potentially deadly abuse?

Other than keeping them offline completely or forbidding them to be "Friends" with anyone they do not already know—neither of which is likely to succeed in practice—the only remedy is to hold adults accountable, as the jury did with Lori Drew.

But children can also be abusive to other children on MySpace and elsewhere online, and, in the end, there is no law or enforcement that can completely protect us from our worst instincts, expressed in new new media, old media or anyplace else.

New New Media Provide Medicine for Cyberbullying

Within a few days after I posted a blog on MySpace about Megan's awful story (Levinson, 2008), I received a message from a publicist, alerting me to a song that had just been written and released, "Shot with a Bulletless Gun" by the Truth on Earth band. The song begins, "I try to explain what it feels like when you're shot in the back of your mind with a bulletless gun by a kid that you don't even hardly know..." (written by band members Serena, Kiley and Tess).

The band put up a Web page, http://truthonearthband.com/bg, which, in addition to an MP3 of the song and its lyrics, has a link to where you can "Read Facts about Cyber Bullying." The band consists of three teenaged sisters. Their musical influences include "Crosby, Stills and Nash, Creedence Clearwater, Lynyrd Skynyrd, Jethro Tull, Eric Clapton and Santana"; their social influences include Martin Luther King, Jr., and Mahatma Gandhi.

Truth on Earth says its "main goal is to raise consciousness to a level where, over time, everyone can become part of the solutions instead of just living the experience of the problems."

I would say the band is an example of new new media providing a remedy for its own worst ills—in this case, cyberbullying. It's not a cure but a medicine that might help keep this abuse of new new media in check by alerting people to its dangers. (See "MySpace Music," below, and Chapter 10 of this book for more on the Truth on Earth band and podcasting.)

MySpace as One-Stop Social Media Cafeteria

With most new new media systems, the question of the purpose of the system— what the new new medium does—is easily answered. Wikipedia is an encyclopedia, Digg is a headline news service, YouTube shows videos and Blogspot (obviously) hosts blogs. We could say that the purpose of MySpace is to bring people together— hence its designation as a social medium—but it also serves a different purpose, profoundly different from all other new new media, with the partial exception of the other big social medium, Facebook.

That different purpose is not just one aspect or function—in fact, it is the smorgasbord multiplicity of MySpace, which gives its members a single place or platform from which to engage in a wide variety of new new media activities. These include private messages, bulletins or group messaging to all of one's MySpace Friends, blogging, posting of photographs, videos and music, IM'ing and groups devoted to common interests.

The postings of photographs, videos, music, and text of various sorts appear on the MySpace member's "Profile" page, which serves as a cyber calling card or one-stop advertisement on behalf of the user's vanity, social status, or online and offline professional pursuits. In the following sections, we examine MySpace Profiles as promoters of music and poetry.

MySpace Music and New New Media

MySpace's "music pages" are especially revolutionary. The traditional path to becoming a successful recording artist was to come to the attention of a record company's "A & R" people—"Artist and Repertoire"—which could happen at a live performance or by sending your "demos" (demonstration recordings) to the record company. The concert was usually the preferred method, because it gave the record company a way of gauging the public's interest in the potential recording artist.

The "music pages" on MySpace, initiated in 2005, offered a different approach: Set up an account on MySpace, on a special kind of page, which showcased MP3s of your music. Invite people on and off MySpace to come over and listen—for free. Build up your Friends list. And when the time was right, let a record company know about all the excitement your music page was generating.

This can now be seen as a classic new new media approach: The musician, the potential recording artist or group, need no longer rely on an agent to get into a club and on the club to book the musician for a performance, just so a record company can see what impact the artist has on the audience. The recording artist, instead, can create a club or place for performance right on MySpace and thereby eliminate several levels of middlemen or experts.

Indeed, in September 2006, this elimination of experts went even further, when MySpace teamed with "SNOCAP," an online jukebox offering free samples of your music, with a purchase option for the full recording, at the price you set (Arrington, 2006).

MySpace music pages accommodate a wide array of genres. The following recording artists all have active MySpace music pages as of December 2008. I have also played their music on my podcast, Light On Light Through, and this has given me the opportunity to get to know a little more about these artists than one might find just by reading their publicity. MySpace has figured prominently in our professional relationships.

I first heard the music of North Carolinian Ebony Moore when she contacted me in November 2006—not on MySpace—and asked me to listen to her music. I had just started my Light On Light Through podcast and thought Ebony's "Make It Count" would make a great song to play on an episode. I played it on my November 25, 2006, "Every Eye's a Camera, Every Ear's a Mike" episode (which has received more than 1,100 listens as of December 2008) and encouraged Ebony to get a MySpace music page to help promote her music. She set up a MySpace page on November 28, 2006. As of December 2008, her page has had more than 110,000 views. Ebony characterizes her music as "alternative/Christian" (I would say it is also a mix of pop and soul).

James Harris lives in Birmingham, England, and sounds a lot like Paul McCartney in the early Beatles or Gerry Marsden of Gerry and the Pacemakers' "Ferry Cross the Mersey" fame (the 1964 hit record is considered part of the "British invasion" of music in the United States—the group was managed by Brian Epstein, the Beatles' manager, and, like the Beatles, came from Liverpool). James's first and still current account on MySpace—he currently has at least six, to accommodate different mixes of his music—was established on November 26, 2006, coincidentally just two days before Ebony Moore created her MySpace page. I did not know James or his music until he later befriended me on MySpace, in January 2007. As soon as I heard his "Tonya McCreary," I knew I wanted to play it on Light On Light Through, and I included it in my February 11, 2007, episode, "How to Research Ancient History for Science Fiction" (which has received more than 4,100 listens as of December 2008). I subsequently played James's "Walking On Air" on my April 15, 2007, episode, "Four Imus Fallacies," in which I provided reasons that "Imus in the Morning," fired for racist comments on radio and television, did not belong back on the air. (As was the case with Ebony Moore's "Make It Count" and James Harris's "Tonya McCreary," the subject of the podcast had nothing to do with the lyrical theme of the song.) The "Imus Fallacies" podcast has received more than 1,200 listens as of December 2008. James recorded a "cover" version of my 1969 song "Looking for Sunsets (In the Early Morning)" (from my 1972 album "Twice Upon a Rhyme") in the fall of 2007. It appears on his "James Harris, II" page on MySpace, established September 10, 2007, and which has more than 5,500 views as of December 2008. James's main MySpace page has more than 105,000 views.

We already encountered the Truth on Earth band as an example of the Internet's self-generated medicine or antibodies for the dangers of cyberbullying. Serena, Kiley and Tess—the three sisters who comprise the band—address many other pressing, compelling problems that afflict our world, offline as well as online, including homeless people, child abuse and even the deception of mass media in their "Media Relationship" song. As mentioned previously, the band says its musical ancestors range from Crosby, Stills and Nash to Santana, but I would add, because of the topical cutting edge and relevance of their lyrics, that the band also writes and sings in the protest music tradition of Dylan, Phil Ochs, and Peter, Paul and Mary—and in the more current genre of Steve Earle and Holly Near. In Chapter 10, "Podcasting," I describe and discuss in step-by-step fashion how I produced Episode 55 of Light On Light Through about "Cyberbullying and a Remedy" in December 2008, which featured "Shot with a Bulletless Gun" by Truth on Earth and a 20-minute interview with the three sisters conducted via Skype (phone call over the Internet). Unlike the "variety show" approaches of the podcasts with Ebony Moore's and James Harris's songs—in which, as indicated above, the music was not related to the subjects of the podcasts—the music and the general topic of the "Cyberbully" Truth on Earth episode of Light On Light Through were pieces of a same theme.

Truth on Earth's MySpace page was established on April 17, 2008—some nine months before the group's publicist contacted me—and had 5,100 views as of December 2008. The band participates in just about every new new medium considered in this book, with pages and accounts on YouTube (two videos as of December 2008), Twitter, Facebook (a "Fan" page), a blog on Blogspot and several social media not discussed here, including "I Like." Their music is for sale on Amazon and iTunes—70 percent of the money they make goes to social causes. (Ebony Moore's is also available for sale on those two and many other online venues; some of James's music is on iTunes.)

Ebony Moore, James Harris and the Truth on Earth band have not, as of February 2009, broken into the mainstream. But MySpace's music pages can claim credit for several artists that made the leap from new new to old media, and, indeed, you may already know.

Kate Nash, a native of Dublin, Ireland, started her MySpace page on February 18, 2006. She then "found a manager for herself before proceeding to look for producers for her music" (Wikipedia, 2009). Her first single, produced in Iceland, had a limited 1,000-copy release in 2006. Meanwhile, her MySpace fan base grew. Her page as of February 2009 has more than 12 million views. Her songs have been listened to more than 20 million times. She has more than 200,000 "Fans" (musicians on MySpace can have "Fans" as well as "Friends"). And her "Made of Bricks" album went "platinum" (sold one million copies) and hit No. 1 in the United Kingdom in 2007.

Londoner Lily Allen "created an account on MySpace and began posting demos in November 2005" (Wikipedia, 2009). She attracted fans and mainstream press interest, notably a piece in the U.K.'s Guardian (Sawyer, 2006). Her single "Smile" was No. 1 in the United Kingdom a few months later, and her album "Alright, Still" has sold more than 3.3 million copies. She had 450,000 MySpace Friends as of February 2009.

Sean Kingston, born Kisean Anderson in Miami, Florida, raised in Kingston, Jamaica, used MySpace to ignite his musical career in a slightly different way. "I hit him up eight times a day. Kept hittin' him up eight times a day for, like, four weeks. And it worked," Kingston (2007) explained. The "him" was Jonathan J. R. Rottem, a record producer with a MySpace account, and Kingston "hit him up" with messages from his own MySpace account, started July 7, 2007. Kingston has had No. 1 songs in the U.S., Canada and Australia (Wikipedia, 2009).

The MySpace stories of Ebony Moore, James Harris and Truth on Earth—artists still struggling to break through—are far more common than those of Kate Nash, Lily Allen and Sean Kingston. More than eight million music pages competed for attention on MySpace as of January 2008 (Techradar, 2008). But the fact that Nash, Allen, Kingston and a relative handful of other singers and musicians have succeeded due to their MySpace pages is what makes all the difference and shows the mettle and potential of new new media in breaking out of the top-down old media confines of the music business. (See also Chapter 3 for YouTube music success stories.)

MySpace Poetry

I titled this section "MySpace Poetry," not as a lyrical way of describing a relationship or some kind of writing one might find on MySpace, but to call attention to a use of MySpace blogs by a self-selected group of poets (all truly new new media producers are self-selected).

Lance Strate is a colleague at Fordham University—in fact, as Chair of the Department of Communication and Media Studies in 1998, Lance first brought me to teach at Fordham. We are friends as well as colleagues—both graduates of New York University's Media Ecology Ph.D. program, where we both studied under Neil Postman at different times—and, in those capacities, we talked frequently about new new media and their impact. Indeed, as I mentioned in the Preface to this book, it was during a discussion I was having with Lance in the fall of 2007 when I was Chair, about the unsuitability of the name "new media" for one of our major tracks of study, that I realized the name "new new media" would be much better to describe blogging, YouTube, Wikipedia, MySpace, Facebook and Twitter.

Lance had joined MySpace just a few months earlier, after a year or so of casual discussion with me about the value of MySpace for promoting scholarly groups. (Lance was then also president of the Media Ecology Association, a group he and I and several others founded in 1998.) One early evening in July 2007—Lance and I were teaching graduate classes that summer—Lance walked into my office and said something along the lines of "I finally did it." He was referring to a blog he had just started, on July 4, 2007, on MySpace. Unlike another blog Lance had earlier started on Blogspot (also under my coaxing), Lance told me that this blog on MySpace was likely to consist of his poetry.

Lance had never published any poetry before. In the field of poetry, he is an epitome of the nonprofessional new new media producer. As of December 2008, Lance had published 150 poems on his MySpace blog. They had received more than 13,000 comments and more than 66,500 views from hundreds of Friends, most of whom also have poetry blogs on MySpace. Some, such as Larry Kuechlin, also have published "chap books" of their poetry—real books made of paper, which can be purchased on Amazon.

In January 2009, Lance and several of his colleague MySpace poets took another kind of step from MySpace to real space, or from the realm of new new media to the world of old media or the world at large. They announced the creation of "NeoPoiesis Press...an independent publisher whose main goal is to print and promote outstanding poets, writers, and artists whose work reflects the creative drive and spirit of the new electronic media environment" (NeoPoiesis, 2009). The NeoPoiesis page has a beautiful picture of soft long grass growing up through typewriter keys—the union of new viral media (grass spreads on its own) and old ways of producing words (the typewriter)—and lists as its partners (MySpace profile names noted in parentheses): "Erin Badough (Ciannait), David Conroy (david), Si Philbrook (Si), Amanda Pierce (Amanda), Lance Strate (Lance Strate) and Dale Winslow (Blackbird)." Lance told me that Blackbird made the picture, and he came up with the name NeoPoiesis. The dual listing of MySpace and real-life names is indicative, like the picture, of the mixing of new and old media, which typifies an increasing number of new new media activities.

The general pattern is this: (1) New new media arise as alternatives to new and old media, as blogging did to newspapers printed and online, YouTube did to television, Wikipedia did to printed encyclopedias, etc. (2) New new media create groups, businesses and products that go back to the old media, offline world and achieve success there, as Tucker Max did when he put his blog posts into a best-selling book (2006), YouTube did with its videos increasingly shown on broadcast and cable television, and perhaps NeoPoiesis Press will do for its books of poetry, writing and art.

MySpace "Bones": Cooperation Between Old Media Narratives and New New Media

The love/hate relationship between old and new new media that we first noticed in Chapter 2 about blogging frequently flares in social media. MySpace and Facebook are justifiably targeted by broadcast and print media as havens for predators—though what group of hundreds of millions of people would not have some number of psychos and criminals in their midsts—and Facebook was mentioned as an unhealthy escape from the real world on "The Sarah Connor Chronicles" (see Chapter 2). These would be examples of the hate or dislike side of the equation.

On the love or appreciation side, we have another example in the case of "The Glowing Bones in the Old Stone House," or Episode 20 in the second season of "Bones" on Fox TV in the spring of 2007. The murder victim, a chef, had a MySpace page with videos of her restaurant, and this figures in the investigation. In the special commentary on the DVD that was later released, Stephen Nathan (writer), Caleb Deschanel (father of the lead actress, Emily Deschanel, and director of this episode) and Emily explain that the producers uploaded the restaurant videos to MySpace five weeks before the episode, as a way of generating interest in the episode. This was a savvy move—what better way of creating buzz than putting elements of a fictional television story on a real social medium and in turn presenting that social medium as part of the story.

The avatar social medium of Second Life, which we will visit in Chapter 9, played an even more integral part in an old medium television story, when CBS's fictional "CSI-NY" agents entered Second Life to pursue someone who killed a Second Life denizen, in real life, in a case of cyberstalking—that is, the flesh-and-blood person who in this fictional television story was animating the Second Life avatar. Viewers were "encouraged to join Second Life and investigate the case by following a link on the CBS Web site," as Duncan Riley explains in "CSI: NY Comes To Second Life Wednesday" (2007).

MySpace and Facebook have also been enlisted by broadcast media, such as Fox and CNN, which have set up pages on both systems for their reporters as a way of hearing from the public, or at least the growing percentage of the public that spends time online. Don Lemon, a CNN reporter and weekend anchor, has accounts on both social media as well as Twitter, and regularly works responses from online "Friends" and "Followers" into his weekend news coverage.

Facebook is an especially useful place to do this, because it has developed an edge over MySpace as a vehicle for social causes.

Facebook

THE NEWS BROKE ON SEPTEMBER 29, 2008: BRITAIN'S MI6—ITS Secret Service, of James Bond fame—was using Facebook as a recruitment tool (Havenstein, 2008). Ads on Facebook stated the following, "A career in world events? Help influence world events, protect the UK. Operational officer. Roles: collecting and analyzing global intelligence."

Facebook is a logical place for such ads. It not only has more than 170 million active users—likely now more than MySpace (which does not publicly distinguish between active and inactive users) and definitely much faster growing (Nakashima, 2009)—but has roots in the college community that still shape and nurture its pages. What better place than just out of college to recruit the next real James Bond or Emma Peel?

What is the difference between Facebook and MySpace? A Friend on both systems—a purely online friend, whom I have not met in person—recently asked me which system I preferred. He said he found it "strangely displeasing" to have active accounts on both systems—answer messages, post status reports, etc.—and was thinking of leaving either MySpace or Facebook.

I told him that this was a tough question—that, a while ago, I had had the same irritation in tending to my comments, messages and Friends on both systems, but that I had now become comfortable with both and enjoyed the pursuit of both systems because they provided different services for me.

MySpace vs. Facebook: Subjective Differences

Some of these differences arise from what I call the "first love syndrome," found not only in what we most like in online systems but in movies, television shows and novels. The principle is that we most love what we first experience. People who read the "Lord of the Rings" trilogy before seeing the movies may well have enjoyed the movies but thought the novels were better, giving the definitive treatment of the epic. On the other hand, people who first saw the movies thought the novels were good but sometimes meandered. Some people who saw the movies did not even finish the novels. I have taken no formal survey, but conversations with many people over the years about which they preferred, book or movie, movie or television show of the same story, convince me that what people most prefer is what they first encountered and loved.

My Facebook account goes back to 2004. In those days, only people with .edu email addresses could get accounts on Facebook, and most of the people on Facebook were students at colleges and universities. My son was an early Facebook enthusiast; he was a student at Harvard, where Facebook was launched by Mark Zuckerberg, also a student, on February 4, 2004. I was able to join because, as a Fordham University professor, I had an .edu email address. But I rarely used my Facebook account. This was because other than my son, whom I was easily in touch with via phone and email, and my students, whom I also was in touch with via email and, if they currently were my students, in the classroom, there was no one else I was interested in communicating with on Facebook in 2004.

This brings to light a second, important subjective principle in the evaluation of online systems and communities: Whatever their objective differences and advantages, their ultimate value is the good they do for each individual user's needs. If you have 100 people you want to be in touch with in a given online community, you obviously will find that community better, or of greater value, than would I, if I had interest in only a few people in that community.

I joined MySpace in May 2005, on the recommendation of one of my students at Fordham. She had heard me lecture about how to get publicity for authors and suggested that MySpace might be a good place for me to promote my books.

But I could find no one that I knew other than her when I first logged on and did not return to MySpace until February 2006, when my science fiction novel "The Plot to Save Socrates" was published. I immediately began searching for people whose interests included "science fiction" or, better, "time travel." Within a few days, I had about 20 Friends—all people of whom I had no knowledge whatsoever in the offline, real world. Some of these people continue to be my Friends on MySpace to this day—I now have some 6,000. They comment on my MySpace blogs and my profile page, send me messages and invitations to their blogs, and wish me Happy Halloween and Thanksgiving. About 40 or 50 have purchased my books over the years, but that is no longer the main reason I value their online "friendship." Rather, I feel as if we are part of a community—one that comments on political issues, on television shows and movies we have seen—a community even though, with just a handful of exceptions, we have never met.

MySpace vs. Facebook: Objective Differences

When my MySpace Friend wrote to me—on MySpace—asking whether I preferred MySpace or Facebook, I realized that there was an objective difference, at least for me, between the two systems: Facebook has a much higher ratio of real-life friends than does MySpace.

Facebook's origins as a way for college students to "meet" each other—see what they look like, what their interests are—without having to physically meet has shaped the growth of its online communities. At first, the communities consisted of students who could easily meet in person if they wanted, because they were attending the same college. Whether the students already knew each other before meeting on Facebook, or met in person after meeting on Facebook, the result was the same: an online community directly grounded in the real world. Subsequently, as Facebook grew to be a competitor of MySpace, with 170 million active users, this real-world grounding continued even as it went far beyond students.

Currently on Facebook, I am "friends" with both of my children, all nine of my nephews and nieces, and about five other members of my extended family. I am also "friends" with at least 150 former and current students, 30 professors at Fordham and other universities that I know in person, and at least 20 other people I do real business with, as an author, guest on radio shows, etc. Add to that at least another 100 authors and podcasters whom I know moderately to very well offline—several are good friends—and at least a dozen or more old friends from various times of my life. All of these friends known in real life or offline activities and relationships account for about a quarter of my current 2,000 Friends on Facebook.

In contrast, I know at most perhaps 100 of the 6,000 Friends I have on MySpace.

MySpace has another objective difference from Facebook: MySpace allows users to decorate their profile pages with all the colors, images and sounds available through HTML (much like an independent blog page), in contrast to Facebook, which permits only plain text and links on its profile pages. But the most significant feature on both social systems is not the Profile page but the Friend.

Facebook Friends as a Knowledge-Base Resource

Facebook and MySpace both have "status bars," which, as in the case of Twitter (see next chapter) are usually used to tell the online world what you are thinking, doing or feeling. They can also be used to ask questions when you can't otherwise find the answers on the Web. The nature of the Friendship base on Facebook—in my case, as a professor, a fair number of former and current students—is especially conducive to this sort of knowledge acquisition.

Here's an example:

In the week of November 17, 2008, Keith Olbermann and Rachel Maddow were unaccountably absent from their MSNBC "Countdown" and "Rachel Maddow" shows. No explanation at all was given for Olbermann's absence; David Shuster simply said he was filling in for Olbermann. Maddow started each of her shows with an announcement that her replacements—Arianna Huffington (founder of The Huffington Post) the first night, Allison Stewart the second night—would be taking her place that night. The substitutes said at the end of each of Rachel Maddow's shows that she would be back "soon."

Not only was there was no announcement on MSNBC, but I couldn't find much about this on the Web, other than someone else (Arnold, 2008) who also was wondering what had happened to the two. I'd assumed they were on some sort of vacations, but…

I posted a question in my "Status" on Facebook, and, sure enough, Mike Plugh, one of my most brilliant and knowledgeable former students, came back with an answer (see Levinson, "Where Have Olbermann and Maddow Disappeared To?", 2008):

> Vacation. They ran straight through the election without a break and I think Rachel is on the Air America Cruise with some lucky listeners. Olbermann may be in his basement hitting rewind and play on the Ben Affleck impression at "SNL."

Mike not only answered my question with style, he also provided an important lesson in the value of new new media as sources of information. When old media fail to keep us posted, and old-fashioned searches for information on the Web fail to give us answers, the new new media and its principle of readers becoming writers and providers of information sometimes can give us the answers we seek. In this sense, Facebook and MySpace go one step further than Wikipedia, by turning the whole new new media world into one big encyclopedia, in which any one of your online Friends can write the answer to your question.

Facebook Friends as Real-Time Knowledge Resources

I am on Facebook right now, November 21, 2008, as I write this. James Winston, a Facebook Friend whom I have never met in person, asked me if he could ask me a question or two for a paper he is writing. James is a graduate student in Communication and Media Studies at Northern Illinois University.

His question was about "information overload"—did I think the Web was contributing to it, and did I think higher education was doing a good job in teaching students how to cope with it?

I replied that I do not think "overload" is the problem we face; the challenge is how to cope with "information underload," or not enough information to get the most out of new new media to successfully navigate the Web. Humans are, after all, inherently multitasking organisms. I referred him to William James' "blooming, buzzing confusion" of the world and our capacity to make sense of it (see Chapter 1 of the present volume). Updated to today's world and media, we could say that all we need is the right navigational information—that is why we do not feel too overwhelmed when we walk into a library or a bookstore, which have vastly more books than we could possibly read. We have learned, since we were children, how to navigate libraries and bookstores (see Levinson, 1997, pp. 134-135, and Levinson, "Interview by Mark Molaro," 2007, for more on information "overload" as "underload").

As for higher education, I told James I think it does a good enough job giving students some information about new new media, but the best way of learning how to use these media is to actually use them (as per John Dewey, 1925, and as we also considered in Chapter 1).

In the process of answering James, I realized that what we were doing—his asking me these questions, my answering him, on Facebook—was an excellent example of new new media as not just an interactive knowledge base but a live, real-time knowledge resource. I told him I might put this conversation in this book; he said that would be great. All of that happened just seconds before I started writing this section.

I also told James I would see that he received a complimentary copy of this book. By the time you are reading this, James will likely have already received his copy. He may be reading this section right now.

James asked me one additional question: Did I think the advantages and content of the Web were more useful to younger people—Generation Y? I told him I thought the Internet, as what I call the "medium of media" ("Digital McLuhan", 1999), had information relevant to people of all ages.

James thanked me—for answering his questions and for the "shout-out" in this book—and asked if he could ask me additional questions in the future. I said sure.

And the conversation ended. My knowledge as a resource for James was that easy. He was in Illinois, I in New York, but we could have been on opposite ends of the Earth. And the conversation could have taken place with equal ease between James and any other professor, or any other student and me, or any two people, professors, students or otherwise. The world of new new media has made knowledge easier to obtain than at any time in history.

But what if I had given James mistaken information, whether because of ignorance or malice? Had James any reason to think that, he could easily have checked my other writings available on the Web. As we saw in Chapter 4 about Wikipedia, new new media provide not only resources of knowledge but resources to check and correct any knowledge that needs revision.

Facebook Groups as Social and Political Forces

MySpace and Facebook both have "groups"—or communities of users who share and discuss links, texts, photos and videos of similar interest. Indeed, groups and similar online activities such as forums and message boards are a fundamental component of online life that goes back to the 1980s (see Levinson, 1997). But Facebook has developed the group to a fine social art and a piercing political force.

The Facebook group "Barack Obama (One Million Strong for Barack)" continued to grow even after the election on November 4, 2008, and as of May 2009 had more than a million members. Groups can be formed in a minute or two on Facebook (just as on MySpace). You come up with a topic, write a brief description, perhaps a paragraph or two about current developments, upload a picture and start inviting your Friends.

The "One Million Strong" group was created under the "Common Interests – Politics" category. Its description reads, "This is the Largest Obama Facebook Group. We started before the Campaign was official and because of all your help as volunteers, donors, and supporters." And this was added after the election: "YES WE DID..."

But Facebook is not just an American social medium, and its groups serve as vehicles of social action in countries all over the world. As Eric Shawn reported on Fox News (December 1, 2008), twelve million people "took to the streets" in 190 cities around the world in February 2008 to protest Colombia's terrorist group FARC, all in response to Oscar Morales's organization of the event in the Facebook group "One Million Voices Against FARC." Jared Cohen of the U.S. State Department explained to Shawn that, on Facebook, "you can be an activist from your bedroom."

To appreciate just how easy it is to create a Facebook group, and on whatever more narrow or arcane subject—in contrast to "One Million Strong for Obama" and "One Million Voices Against FARC," which, as the titles suggest, are directed toward mass appeal—consider the following:

I returned home late Friday of the Thanksgiving 2008 weekend, the third day of the terrorist crisis in Mumbai, India, and was looking for the latest news coverage on my favorite all-news television station, MSNBC. What I got instead was MSNBC's "doc bloc"—in this case, canned footage from several years ago, called "Caught on Camera."

I posted several blogs about this problem, such as "MSNBC Runs Canned Doc Bloc as Mumbai Burns" on Infinite Regress (Levinson, 2008), and discovered, via comments posted and email, that many other people felt the same way. We all wanted MSNBC to provide 24/7 news coverage; our day and age and world require no less. (See Chapter 11 for a discussion of how new new media Facebook and Twitter, in contrast to old medium MSNBC, provided crucially important initial coverage of the Mumbai terrorist attack and its consequences.)

MSNBC had started in the 1990s as a partnership of the best of the Internet and television, or a marriage of old (NBC) and new (Microsoft) media. I decided to see if I could harness the social power of new new media—in this case, Facebook—to influence programming on television. On December 1, 2008, I created a Facebook group called "Stop the Doc Bloc" on MSNBC, provided a description much like the above—"I returned home late Friday…"—and concluded:

> Let's see if we here on Facebook, perhaps just by joining this group, can get MSNBC to do what's best for its viewers and itself—stop the doc bloc—give us news! Tell your news junkie friends about this FB group!

I invited close to 1,500 of my then 1,600 Friends on Facebook. Users are only allowed to be in a maximum of 300 groups, which was the reason the other 100 could not receive invitations. I downloaded a public domain image of a red stop sign, used the free GIMP program (which works much like Photoshop) to write the words "DOC BLOC" under the word "STOP" on the sign, and uploaded the image to the group. Within two hours, the group had more than 50 members. Twenty-four hours later, the group had 150 members—at least 15 of whom were not on my initial invitation list. This is viral marketing in action—in this case, for a shared cause. Whenever someone on Facebook joins a group, a "notification" about that is published on the joiner's page and sent out to all of his or her Friends. If they find the group of interest, they can join, and the cycle is re-initiated.

As of May 2009, "Stop the Doc Bloc" had expanded only to a little more than 300 members, and MSNBC had not changed its weekend programming one bit. Not every group succeeds—though who knows what will happen with the group in the future (it generates a few new comments or "wall posts" each month) and what impact that might have on MSNBC programming. But the power of Facebook groups is nonetheless undeniable, so much so that the oldest media and their proponents also use Facebook groups to further their causes. Mark Hunter pointed out the irony, in his Social Media podcast (2009), of the "Don't Let Newspapers Die" cause on Facebook (a "cause" is a special kind of group), with the motto "Save a Journalist, Buy a Newspaper." Ironic, yes, to employ one of the very new new media—though it's not clear how many people get their news from Facebook—that is putting the object of your cause out of business to help promote your cause. On the other hand, it cannot hurt, and the formation of this cause-group certainly reflects an understanding, on the part of newspaper advocates, of the power of new new media. As of May 2009, "Don't Let Newspapers Die" had a little more than 80,000 members—probably not enough to stop the decline of newspapers, but they are in no immediate danger of completely dying, in any case (see Chapter 2, which discusses the continuing need in the blogosphere for old-media investigative reporting).

Facebook as Myriad Local Political Pubs

Not every group and discussion on Facebook needs to be devoted to a major cause or candidate. The ease of creating groups and discussion topics within groups means that, in addition to the huge, rally-like groups on Facebook, there also are numerous smaller groups and discussions, which, when political, feel more like the colonial pub.

What did that offline, colonial pub, feel like? In the back room of the spirited pub at the Village Pourhouse at 64 Third Avenue in the East Village of New York City, I spoke on the evening of August 28, 2007, to the NYC Ron Paul Meet-Up group about the mass media's mistreatment and miscoverage of Ron Paul in his campaign for the Republican nomination for president. I outlined the historical precedents and philosophic contexts of the mass media's behavior (see "Ron Paul and the Older Media" in Chapter 5) and what might be done about it. There were about 30 people in attendance. Over clinking glasses and happy, boisterous voices by the bar, we spoke of John Milton, Thomas Jefferson, our Founding Fathers and the ideals they set for this country (see Levinson, "YouTube Video of My Aug 28 Talk," 2007, for more).

Commenting the day after the video was posted, an observer noted on my blog, "Many a founding father of the original revolution spent hours in the local pub plotting action and debating policy. I can think of no nobler site to discuss Ron Paul and the media. Hopefully those listening were partaking (to make the bar owner happy). They should have had a small table so you could occasionally hoist the mug and wet your whistle... insensitive clods. Very nice backdrop."

One advantage of a virtual local pub on Facebook is that you don't need to rely on your hosts to wet your whistle—indeed, your whistle might not need more wetting at all, since you would be writing rather than speaking. And the meeting could take place over days, weeks, months, years, asynchronously.

The Libertarian Party group on Facebook has some 12,000 members. I joined it and started a discussion topic based on my "I'm a Progressive Libertarian" blog post (Levinson, 2008). In its original posting on my Infinite Regress blog, the 650-word essay generated 30 comments in six months, half of which were by me. Within a day after starting the topic on Facebook, I counted 60 comments, less than 10 of which were mine. As was the case with my Village Pourhouse talk, the majority of these Facebook discussants were college students. But unlike the Village Pourhouse, the Facebook participants came from universities across the country. And, more important, the conversation can continue for as long as the participants wish, and new participants can enter the conversation at any time. As in all things new new media, the political pub online makes distance and time irrelevant.

Would our Founding Fathers have been more effective, would our nation be better, if they had participated in a Facebook group rather than a local venue? That question, of course, can never be answered, short of going back in a time machine and changing history. But it will be interesting to observe what emerges in a politics nurtured and furthered on Facebook and other new new media.

Meeting Online Friends in the Real World

The twofold initial logic of Facebook—either finding out more about classmates you already knew or keeping an eye out on the physical campus for someone you did not already know but whose face you had seen on Facebook—contained an assumption, an expectation, that people might be interested in jumping from online to in-person friendships and relationships. In a campus community, safety was not a major concern. You could meet someone you first got to see or know on Facebook by going to a cafeteria or other public place with a real-life friend or two. That kind of environment was and is very different from the kinds of in-person meetings that have come to be associated with MySpace, in which two people, not part of any physical campus community, get to "know" each other online and then meet in the real world. Such meetings, as we saw in the previous chapter and will examine in more detail in Chapter 11, "The Dark Side of New New Media," are fraught with serious dangers.

But the expansion of Facebook far beyond the campus has made it more like MySpace and its inducements, whether dangerous or beneficial, for real-life meetings of online Friends. As with MySpace, the easy way to meet safely with anyone you have not met in person before is to meet in a public place or, if appropriate, in a professional environment. A restaurant would be a good example of such a public place, and a business office would be a good example of a professional environment that someone might visit for a job interview generated by an online exchange.

Leaving aside the safety considerations (but see Chapter 11), what do we know about how online relationships fare when transferred to the in-person world, when transformed from digital code to flesh and blood? As I detailed back in 1996 when I was writing "The Soft Edge: A Natural History and Future of the Information Revolution" (1997), there is a long history going back to the mid-1980s of people meeting online and falling in love (eHarmony would be a current example of a social medium devoted to initiating real-world romantic relationships) and people meeting online and progressing to successful in-person business relationships.

I have been a party, numerous times, to two kinds of business or professional in-person relationships that began online.

From 1985–1995, my wife, Tina Vozick, and I created and administered Connected Education, the first online program to offer courses for graduate credit and a complete MA in Media Studies, entirely online. Thousands of students from more than 40 states in the U.S. and 20 countries around the world registered in our courses for credit granted by the New School for Social Research, Polytechnic University, the Bath College of Higher Education (in England) and other colleges and universities (see Levinson, 1997, for details). I knew fewer than 5 percent of our students in person prior to their Connect Ed registration. I met under another 5 percent of our online students—people I had never met before in person—at conferences I attended in various cities in the U.S. and abroad during the program, or when online students came to New York City for whatever reason.

I noticed something the first time I met someone in person whom I had previously known only online, which has held true for just about every other such meeting I have had with an online student, friend or associate: After an initial jolt lasting a few minutes at most, the online persona was clearly recognizable in the person sitting across from me at a table. Indeed, in those days—from 1985 to the early 2000s—most of the online communication was in text, with no images or photographs of the people with whom you were conversing online. So meeting someone in person whom you had gotten to know online was doubly strange: You were seeing a face for the person whose written words you had come to know, as well as getting a voice and in-person personality for those words. The potential was there for concluding that this person at the table or in the room with you was very different from the person you knew online. And, yet, the result was just the opposite.

The other professional situation in which I met a fair number of people in person whom I had first come to know online—as many as 50 percent of this particular online community—arose in the early and mid-1990s, when authors and publishers of science fiction began conversing on a variety of online systems such as CompuServe and GEnie (Levinson, 1997). I had just started publishing science fiction at that time, and in 1998 I became president of the Science Fiction Writers of America. In that capacity, as well as before and after (I served from 1998–2001), I met hundreds of authors and dozens of publishers and editors in person—at conventions and smaller meetings—whom I already knew from our online exchanges. As was the case with my students, in all cases the in-person face, voice and personality were completely in accordance with what I already knew of these authors and publishers from their words online.

Reconnecting with Old Friends Online

At the opposite end of the spectrum of meeting online friends in person is the experience of reconnecting online with in-person friends and acquaintances you have not been in touch with for years. This has been happening with me for more than 10 years, mostly when old friends, classmates and former students see me on television and then contact me via email. On New Year's Day, 2000, I appeared as a panelist on Fox News' "The New Millennium: Science, Fiction, Fantasy" special. Shortly after, I received emails from Felix Poelz, a high school classmate whom I had not seen since 1963, and Peter Rosenthal, guitarist on my 1972 "Twice Upon a Rhyme" album (Peter and I had been out of touch since the mid-1970s). In the 1980s and 1990s, I received email from a handful of former students. These were early indications of the power of cyberspace, prior to 21st century social media, to vanquish the time and distance that separates us from old friends and acquaintances.

The pace picked up a bit on MySpace when I became an active member in early 2006. But Facebook, likely because of its origins as a university community, has bumped up such online reunions to a new level. Of my 2,000 Friends on Facebook, at least 100 are former students and friends I had not heard from in years. I get about one to two Friend requests per week from old acquaintances. You can easily find on Facebook many members who went to your high school and college, sorted by their graduation year. Felix's name was not among the 1963 graduates of Christopher Columbus High School (he was not a Facebook member), but of the more than 100 people listed, there were a few who were familiar.

If the dangers of meeting online "Friends" in person, when you do not already know them in person, is counted as one of the drawbacks and potential abuses of new new social media, then getting back in touch with an old, long-out-of-touch acquaintance must be considered one of its great, soul-nurturing benefits. If we agree with Carl Sagan (1978) that we are the stuff of the cosmos examining itself, then the reunification of old, in-person acquaintances via social media is the cosmos sewing itself back together.

Protection for the "Hidden Dimension": Cleaning Up Your Online Pages

The "hidden dimension" of all new new media self-productions is their endurance on the Web long after we have written or created them. I borrow the phrase from Edward T. Hall, who coined it long before the Internet, as the title of his 1966 book, about the significance of interpersonal distance and space in human relations, which we usually take for granted, even though they can powerfully shape the course and outcome of a conversation. We similarly often pay no particular attention to the longevity of our blog posts, YouTube videos, and MySpace and Facebook pages, which can be and are read by people long after we have posted the words and images and can therefore have an effect not intended or foreseen by us at the time of the initial posting.

Although I did not start blogging until 2006, words that I wrote more than a decade earlier come up in Google searches today. Fortunately for me, everything that I have written or created online—including my MySpace and Facebook pages—has been for professional not primarily personal purposes. Thus, comments by me on GEnie (the General Electric Network for Information Exchange) in the early 1990s, usually about some aspect of science fiction (see Levinson, 1997), are no more likely to be embarrassing to me now than my first published article in 1976 ("Hot and Cool Redefined for Interactive Media" in The Media Ecology Review) or, for that matter, my 1972 album "Twice Upon a Rhyme" (which was re-issued on CD in 2008 by the Big Pink record company in Korea). I am, immodestly, proud of all of that.

But most members of MySpace and Facebook see their pages as personal not professional. And the danger that must be well known now to every student with a Facebook account arises: You post photos on your Facebook page, photos taken at a party when you were drunk out of your mind or similarly indisposed. A year or two later, you apply for a job somewhere, and your would-be boss takes a look at those photos and decides not to be your boss—the drunk photos cost you that job.

In an ideal world, a potential boss would not care how you behaved at a party two years—or even two days—earlier. All that would count is how you performed in the workplace. (I made this point to Bill O'Reilly as a guest on "The O'Reilly Factor" on Fox News in 2004, when I defended the right of a local news anchor to take her clothes off in a wet T-shirt contest when on vacation; see Levinson, 2004). Or, no one other than your personal acquaintances would be able to see your photos. Facebook does provide options for allowing less than complete access to everything on your account. But re-postings by even well-meaning Friends and the easy copyability of everything online from music to videos to photos makes that second protection not very valuable, and human nature will usually get in the way of the first.

So the best remedy you can apply for embarrassing photos and other new new media creations is: do not post them in the first place. And, if you do, remember to remove them as soon as you are no longer happy with them in public view. Drunk posting need not equal drunk retention. But always remember that the viral dissemination of anything and everything online means that what you erase from your Facebook page may endure on someone else's page, Web site or personal computer. If you have to clean up a page, in other words, chances are at least some of the cleanup may be in vain.

Photos of Breastfeeding Banned on Facebook

MySpace and Facebook, for their parts, have also tried to clean up their photographic acts, or the images posted by users to their pages. But that proved more difficult than at first expected, as well.

At the end of 2008, Facebook embarked on a campaign to cleanse its pages of all pornographic photographs. Not that they were permitted in the first place, but no central system can possibly police the uploading of every single photo. The "objectionable" photographic content included women's naked breasts (MySpace has a similar policy). But, as Lisa M. Krieger detailed in the San Jose Mercury News (2008), this policy resulted in the removal from members' Facebook pages of those photographs of mothers nursing babies which were assessed as "obscene, pornographic or sexually explicit." This, in turn, resulted in online and real-world protests against Facebook, as well as a profusion of groups and causes on Facebook, for and against photos of breastfeeding on Facebook (do a search in Facebook groups, or Facebook causes, to find them).

Ironically, breastfeeding in public is allowed in 40 states. (One wonders why not in all 50. Babies should be deprived of nursing when they get hungry in public? Why? Because some prudish onlooker would rather not see that? Would not a more effective expedient be to just look the other way?) Facebook told Krieger, in its defense, that most photos of breastfeeding were not and would not be removed—only those in which the areola (darker skin around the nipple) is visible.

The moral of this story for students of new new media is that, however much we may consider the new new medium an extension of ourselves, our lives, our desires (as per McLuhan's view of all media as human "extensions," 1964), new new media are not—at least not entirely. However much we may feel that a new new media system is ours, because of the extraordinary powers of production and self-projection the new new medium provides us, the new new medium is not ours completely. In the case of Facebook, the new new medium is also and significantly Facebook's, as Wikipedia is Wikipedia's, Digg is Digg's, and so forth for every new new medium considered in this book, and any others you might name. In this profound, underlying, unalterable sense, there is no difference between old, new, and new new media. This does not mean the equally profound differences between new new and older media that we have identified and considered in this book are not real, are not profound. They are, indeed. But they are not the complete story of new new media.

And, as we have seen in this book, different new new media play out the story—the conflict between the old authoritarian and the new democratic—in their own distinct ways. Wikipedia is far less "old school" in terms of what may be removed from its pages than is Facebook and MySpace. Nonetheless, Wikipedia can still remove a phrase, an article, a photo, which you or I may write or upload, if a sufficient group of other reader/editors deem it unsuitable. Wikipedia, in other words, has to some extent replaced authoritarian, expert-driven control with democratic, group control, but it has by no means eliminated or even reduced the control over individual expression.

The new new medium that offers the most opportunity for untrammeled individual expression is Twitter.

CHAPTER 8

Twitter

Would you like everyone in the world to know what movie you just saw or are going to see, what you really think of your teacher or boss or president, what you just ate for lunch or intend to eat, whether it's raining or the police are charging where you happen to be—any and all of those things, and more, whatever you might want the world to know—just a second or so after you had the thought or experience and got the impulse to broadcast it to the world? Twitter makes it easy for you to do all of that.

You can disseminate whatever information you please, to whatever portion of the world you like, as long as the people in that portion have accounts on Twitter. That would be 32 million people in the world at large as of May 2009, with Twitter growing faster than any other social medium (Schonfeld, 2009), and the first tweet from outer space on May 12, 2009 (Van Grove, 2009).

Further, you can do that from your cellphone, BlackBerry, or any other mobile device at hand that can access the Internet.

Concerned about your privacy? Like all online systems, you can do this under a pseudonym or assumed identity. You can even adopt the name of a television star or character (see Chapter 2 for "Mad Men" characters on Twitter). Or you can be a member of Congress (see Donnelly, 2009), or a well-known public figure such as Karl Rove (Carpenter, 2009), and tweet under your real name. Rick Sanchez and Don Lemon of CNN; David Shuster, Nora O'Donnell and Tamron Hall of MSNBC; and "Meet the Press" anchor David Gregory actively use Twitter (as of February 2009) and work twitters they receive into their television news shows, in another example of old and new new media cooperation.

Welcome to the burgeoning world of "microblogging," or the publication and dissemination online of a line or two about yourself, or anything you might like to say, personally or politically, anytime you please. Twitter is the new kid on the media block, started as a project by Odeo podcasting people Jack Dorsey, Noah Glass, Biz Stone and Evan Williams in March 2006. But it has been growing so fast, not only in high-profile users but mainstream media coverage—Twitter only had a total of about six million users as of February 2009, not that many at all in comparison to Facebook and MySpace—that an article in the February 8, 2009, issue of New York Magazine (Leitch, 2009) advised, "If you're the last person in the world to not know what Twitter is, here's a simple explanation …" By June 15, 2009, Twitter was, to nobody's surprise, the cover story of Time magazine (Johnson, 2009).

But as both articles go on to explain and as we will detail below, there is much that is complex and profound about tweeting.

The Epitome of Immediacy

Instant publication—whether of text, images, sounds or videos—is one of the hallmarks of new new media. But as we have seen in our survey of new new media in this book, some new new media excel more than others in given hallmarks.

Text is usually easier to produce than sound and audio-visual recording, as we noted in Chapter 2 about blogging. A paragraph will likely take longer to write than taking a picture on your camera phone, but the text will likely be written or copied to a Web site a little faster. A line or so of text—140 characters is the limit on Twitter—moves the fastest of all.

If you're an author agonizing over every word, this very short form could take a long time to write. I was once asked to write a 200-character blurb—not 200 words, but 200 characters—about one of my novels for the Science Fiction Book Club, and this took about 15 minutes for me to write. But that was because I wanted every word, and therefore every letter or character, to count—every word to attract potential readers to my novel (the novel was "Borrowed Tides," published in 2001). If all I was writing about was how much I just enjoyed the slice of pizza I had just bought on Fordham Road, I could have dashed off that line in a few seconds.

All thoughts originate in the mind—or, if you want to be less metaphysical, in the brain. One kind of synapse or neurological pathway delivers the thought to our vocal apparatus when we speak. Another kind of synapse gets the thought to our fingers, with which we write or type. Presumably these two synapses or pathways to personal communication are the same length—the thought travels at the same speed to tongue or finger.

Prior to the advent of electronic media, immediacy of thought conveyed to the tongue only reached as far as anyone within hearing distance. Immediacy of thought conveyed to the finger was even more limited: It ended with the finger, since in order for anyone else to read what had been written, the parchment, papyrus or paper had to be passed from hand to hand. Although this nonelectronic "digital" transmission—digital as in finger to finger—could happen quickly, it was slower than the speed of sound. Thus, speech had the edge over writing in immediacy. (See Levinson, "Digital McLuhan," 1999, for handwriting as a form of "digital," or finger, communication.)

Electricity travels at the speed of light, which means that any message committed to electronic delivery—whether voice or written word—can be sent anywhere in the world instantly. Electricity travels at 186,000 miles per second, and the world is about 24,000 miles around the equator. But this did not mean that such messages would be received—heard or read—by any human being instantly. Equipment at the receiving end, whether turning on a television or walking to a ringing telephone, added seconds at the very least to the ultimate reception of information transmitted at the speed of light.

Twitter's revolution is that, more than any other old, new, or new new medium, it makes the sending and receiving of its brief messages nearly as instant as their conception and writing. Twitter's one-liners can be created, sent and received with the flick of a finger. Writing has thus become as easy and effortless to communicate over vast distance as speech has always been to people within earshot.

Further, the messages conveyed via Twitter are readable by anyone who wishes to "follow" your "twitters" or "tweets" on the system—that is the default—or they can be sent to specific groups or just one person. This means that Twitter is not only the most immediate written medium in history, but it's also the most integrated combination of interpersonal and mass communication in history.

Interpersonal + Mass Communication = Twitter

The above title is about 45 characters, so it could have easily been sent over Twitter. And it would have been sent in ways that combine these two great branches of communication.

One of the basic lessons of communication is that it comes in two kinds. Interpersonal communication consists of one person sending a message to another person, in which the second person can easily switch from being a receiver to a sender. Examples would be in-person face-to-face communication, written correspondence, IM'ing on computers, and talking and texting on the phone. Mass communication consists of one person or source sending a message to many people at the same time, with these many receivers not having the capacity to become senders. Examples would be carvings on walls, books, newspapers, motion pictures, radio, television and blogs that allow no comments. Interpersonal is thus pinpoint and two-way, whereas mass communication is broad (hence the word "broadcast," from the widespread or broad casting of seeds in planting) and one-way.

Sometimes people mistakenly say that interpersonal is nontechnological in contrast to mass media, which must be high-tech or at least use industrial technology such as a printing press. But the telephone is an example of interpersonal communication that is technological, and a poster on a wall or writing on a blackboard is an almost no-tech, or very low-tech, kind of mass communication.

Apropos of blackboards, the classroom is one of few communication settings that can and does easily switch between mass and interpersonal communication. When I lecture in a class, the students are receivers of mass communication, or my message to many people. But as soon as a student asks a question and I answer, she and I are communicating interpersonally—while for the rest of the class, who continue as listeners, the communication is still mass communication. When I finish answering the first student's question and call on another student, the first student moves back into the mass communication audience, as the second student and I now engage in interpersonal communication.

Twitter takes the classroom to a global level. Although it is not without precedent in media—chat rooms and private IM's also swing between mass and interpersonal communication—Twitter is a chat room, classroom, or gathering that goes on 24 hours a day, 7 days a week. And although the messages on Twitter can certainly be educational, it is the communication structure of the classroom, not its content, that is catapulted into a worldwide conversation on Twitter.

Twitter expands the classroom communication structure in a different way, making group-to-individual communication as easy as individual-to-group (teacher-to-class). Groups of all sizes and purposes send out tweets—old media giants such as Fox News and CNN which offer live tickers of news stories, political campaigns for president and all manner of positions, and groups devoted to a particular cause or social purpose, such as TwitterMoms, which helped mobilize opposition to Facebook's ban on photos of breastfeeding, discussed in the previous chapter. One-hundred-and-forty character messages on such subjects, with links to bigger content on the Web, reach Twitterers on the same cellphones, BlackBerrys, iPhones and laptops on which they see tweets such as "Just left my dentist's office."

Tweets also allow effortless broadcasting of professional and personal information, such as this text from Karl Rove, on February 14, 2009, "Back in Washington. Working on the book this weekend. Tune in to Fox News tomorrow AM. I'll be on Chris Wallace's 100 Day Special." Indeed, links to all of my blog posts and podcasts show up on my Twitter account and are seen by my 1,600 (as of May 2009) "Followers," as are tweets about my TV and radio appearances.

The automatic sending to Twitter (via applications or "apps") of links to anything and everything on the Web—blog posts, videos, news stories, the full gamut of new and new new media—and the instantly subsequent, automatic relay of these tweets to Facebook and "meta" new new systems such as FriendFeed ("meta" because their content consists of links from Twitter, Facebook, YouTube and other new new media activity) constitute a self-perpetuating, not entirely planned, expanding network that has much in common with living organisms and evolutionary systems (see Levinson, 1979 and 1997 for more on the organic evolution of media).

Twitter as Smart T-Shirt or Jewelry

But when Twitter functions as a statement of feeling—"I'm bored" or "I'm feeling good"—Twitter is working as a kind of virtual apparel or jewelry, something we "wear" or send out to the world, like a dark hat or a bright necklace, to indicate our emotional disposition.

When messages on Twitter get more specific, such as "I just voted for Obama," they move from jewelry to campaign pins or T-shirts with messages. Back in 1970, when the personal computer revolution was more than a decade away, Gary Gumpert wrote about "the rise of mini-comm." He was talking about how people could "broadcast" their own personal messages, or messages tailored to their views and feelings, via words printed on their T-shirts, sweatshirts and other clothing. As in all of its improvements in the printed realm, personal and political messages in the digital age—via updates on new new media such as Twitter—do the "mini-comm" one big step better, by allowing any words to be "printed" or published worldwide instantly, re-tweeted or RT'd by receivers to their Followers, and then revised or changed a split second later, with a new "tweet," if the writer so desires.

Messages on T-shirts, of course, can be commercial—promoting a given product—as well as political or personal. Twitter messages have similar diversity and can range far beyond reports of emotional states, political candidates and public demonstrations. Furthermore, since such messages are all received on media already connected to the Web, Twitter messages are well suited for creating buzz about items and activities that live on the Web, with handy URLs or links.

URLs are a frequent component of Twitter messages sent by Fox, CNN and The New York Times with links to breaking stories on their pages. In that function, Twitter becomes a type of wire service, like AP or Reuters. "Followers" receive these messages but do not usually reply. In those communications, Twitter is working as a mass rather than an interpersonal medium, though receivers of those messages can certainly communicate among themselves via Twitter. (Like Digg, Twitter allows one-way Followers, in which A gets all of B's tweets but B does not get tweets from A, and mutual Followers in which A and B each see all of each other's tweets.)

On the other hand, when Twitter works as a form of one-to-one interpersonal communication, it operates not only as a kind of jewelry but a neo-telegraph. Or as I told Ken Hudson in our November 2007 interview in Second Life, "the telegraph was much like microblogging."

Bloggers can also have links to their blog posts sent out over Twitter, either on a post-by-post basis or automatically, as mentioned previously, via free services such as TwitterFeed. In the second half of 2008, approximately 5 percent of all readers of my Infinite Regress blog arrived via links to my pages sent automatically on Twitter. To return to the jewelry and T-shirt analogy, then, Twitter messages range from store-bought (news from CNN) to hand-made (a link to a blog post by any individual). As is the case with all new new media, older media are not obliterated but subsumed and promoted on Twitter.

Speaking of blog promotion and its possibilities for monetization via advertising, there are even advertising services such as adjix.com that allow Twitterers to embed commercial links in their tweets and earn income from clicks in a way similar to Google AdSense. Twitter is not only an engine of microblogging but also a microcosm of the new new media world, in which blogging, advertising, dissemination of photos and videos, campaigns for Diggs, and seeking and maintenance of online "friendship" take place on a moment-by-moment basis.

Pownce and other Twitter-Likes

Pownce, developed by the Digg design team, was Twitter's only, and much smaller, competitor in 2007 and 2008, before it closed shop in December 2008. Its main advantage in comparison to Twitter was that files—images, music and video—could be sent along with the messages, in contrast to Twitter, which just sends links. The Pownce receiver thus was saved the step of clicking on the link and could immediately enjoy the music or video. But apparently this advantage was not enough to give Pownce a viable niche in the microblogging market, and Twitter remains the solitary titan in microblogging, as Wikipedia does for online encyclopedias—but unlike Facebook and MySpace, which continue to have joint custody of the huge social media "Friendship" arena.

Facebook and MySpace in fact compete in user self-advertising with Twitter, via their "status" boxes at the top of every user's profile, where users can indicate how they are feeling, what they are doing, etc., just as on Twitter. Facebook's "poke"—in which the receiver gets a text saying the sender "poked" you, signifying "hello" or some other kind of interest—can be considered a primitive precursor of a private tweet (or DM—"Direct Message"—which can be used for any purposes and is seen only by the Twitter receiver).

As in all aspects of the new new media universe, there is increasing convergence of systems. As more features of Facebook and MySpace become deliverable via email, and more people receive email on cellphones, iPhones, BlackBerrys and other mobile devices via which they receive twitters, the difference between a tweet and a status update on Facebook or MySpace becomes less and less. Facebook and MySpace are already offering "mobile" applications, which deliver status updates, Friend requests and other features to cellphones (see Chapter 13, "Hardware," for more about mobile devices and new new media).

At the same time, Twitter "boxes" can easily be embedded on blogs and profile pages. These boxes deliver a stream of twitters and can be tailored to receive them from anyone on Twitter you please. MySpace permits embedding of such boxes and Facebook has a slightly different application that displays tweets.

Twitter Dangers: The Congressman Who Tweeted Too Much

The dangers of telling the world what you are doing via tweets should be obvious, if what you are doing is provocative and you are in a vulnerable, publicly accessible place.

You might think the above applies to chatterbox—or, better, tweeterbox—kids, and it does. But consider the series of tweets sent by Rep. Peter Hoekstra (R-Michigan), on February 6, 2009: "Just landed in Baghdad…" And, later, "Moved into green zone by helicopter Iraqi flag now over palace. Headed to new US embassy Appears calmer less chaotic than previous here" (Donnelly, 2009). Hoekstra, a member of the House Intelligence Committee, had fallen prey to a dangerous illusion that has accompanied online communication since the 1980s and exacerbates, among other problems, "flaming," or the posting of nasty messages that are seen not only by their intended recipient (the initial "flame") but others in the online community you may not have intended. The illusion comes from mistaking the screen in front of you—whether a computer on your desk in the 1980s or a BlackBerry in your hand today—as a personal device upon which you can record your thoughts, private, angry, whatever, for delivery only to the person or people you had in mind. After all, the device in the 1980s was called a "personal computer." Twitters can be even more misleading because you may think that your tweets are seen by only your Followers. Tweets are indeed seen by your Followers but also can be seen by everyone else on Twitter, unless you chose to "protect" your Profile and make your tweets available only to your approved Followers and not the Twitter world at large.

In Hoekstra's enthusiasm for the new new medium, then, he had neglected to check out all of its features and control mechanisms. This was an understandable, albeit potentially deadly, error. Adults become children—usually in the best sense of the word—when we encounter and adopt a new mode of communication, especially one such as Twitter, which with a few keystrokes can open new vistas for our personal and professional lives. It may also be worth noting that the average age of Twitter users, according to an unscientific, sample survey conducted via Twitter in February 2009, is 37 (Weist, 2009; see also the scientific sample survey by Heil & Piskorski, 2009, and its findings of 90 percent of all tweets by the 10 percent most active users, "an average man is almost twice more likely to follow another man than a woman," and other demographics of interest). New new media in general, and Twitter as its cutting edge in particular, may not be just for kids anymore.

Far worse dangers of new new media, however, come not from their misuse but their savvy employment by people bent on bad deeds. In Chapter 11, "The Dark Side of New New Media," we will consider the use of Twitter by terrorists.

And Twitter has also been a powerful enabler of democratic expression.

Twitter vs. the Mullahs in Iran

People took to the streets in protest about what they saw as fraudulent conducting of the Presidential election in Iran in June 2009. This is an old story in dictatorial regimes—people protesting in public squares—and often has unhappy results for democracy, as was the case in Tiananmen Square in China in 1989. But people and democracy had new tools at their disposal in 2009.

The Supreme Leader of Iran, who supported the re-election of Mahmoud Ahmadinejad, moved with like-minded mullahs to ban reporting of the growing objections to the election, the call for a new one, and the fact that protesters were being beaten and killed. The news blackout worked for direct, eyewitness reporting by traditional, centralized media, such as broadcast facilities, and for professional journalists, who were easy enough to expel or otherwise prevent from directly reporting on events. But YouTube, Facebook, and, most prominently, Twitter, were not as easy to stop or even control in Iran.

Internet and cellphone service were intermittently restricted and partially shut down in Iran. But cutting off all tweets and uploads of videos to YouTube would have required all Internet and cellphone service to be severed in Iran, which the authorities were wary of doing, since that would have had ill effects for Iranian business and other essential exchanges of information. The result left protesters and citizen reporters with pipelines for their tweets and videos, which people outside of Iran could also use to send tweets back into Iran via "proxies" which appeared legitimate to the authorities.

At the same time, of course, Iranian authorities could and apparently did use Twitter to send out misleading information. When I was asked on an interview on KNX Radio out of Los Angeles on June 16, 2009, how anyone could know if tweets coming out of Iran were true or disinformation, I replied that the aggregate of Twitterers, just like the many reader/editors on Wikipedia, provided some checks and balances on the accuracy of the information (Levinson, 2009, "New New Media vs. the Mullahs"). And, indeed, tweets suspected of being planted by the government were identified and denounced (see Grossman, 2009).

As of this writing in June 2009, the outcome of the protests in Iran, and the success of Twitter and other new new media in enabling those protests, is not clear. But it is worth noting that a new medium of the late 1970s, the audio cassette, was instrumental in the Iranian revolution of 1979 (Zunes, 2009), cellphones helped organize the successful Second People Power Revolution in the Philippines in 2001 (see Rheingold, 2003; Popkin, 2009), and the U.S. State Department thought Twitter was so crucial in the early days of the 2009 protest that it asked Twitter to delay a scheduled shutdown for maintenance until a time when most of Iran was likely asleep (Grossman, 2009).

Here is a timeline of some of the major clashes of new media with dictatorial governments in the twentieth and twenty-first centuries:

1942–43: The White Rose uses photocopying to tell the truth to Germans about the Nazi government. Fails to dislodge the Nazis.

1979: Audio cassettes of Ayatollah Khomeini distributed in Iran. Succeeds in fomenting successful revolution against Shah.

1980s: Samizdat video in the Soviet Union criticizes Soviet government. May have helped pave the way for Gorbachev's perestroika and glasnost, and end of Soviet rule.

1989: Email gets word out to the world about Tiananmen Square protests. Fails to dislodge Chinese government.

2001:   Cellphones help mobilize peaceful opposition to President Estrada in Philippines. The Second People Power Revolution succeeds.

2009:   Twitter and YouTube get word out to the world about Iranian opposition to reported election outcome. Result: not yet clear as of this writing.

McLuhan as Microblogger

The short form of Twitter is not only a politically efficient and personally cool necessity; it had already been developed, long before Twitter, into a well-known literary form. Marshall McLuhan died on the last day of 1980—not only years before there was microblogging and blogging but a few years before email and more than a decade before easily accessible Web pages. But he was twittering or microblogging in one of his most important books, "The Gutenberg Galaxy" (1962), with chapter titles or "glosses" such as "Schizophrenia may be a necessary consequence of literacy" and "The new electronic interdependence recreates the world in the image of a global village." There were 107 such "twitters" in that book.

I first recognized the digital affinity of McLuhan's writing two decades prior to Twitter. In 1986, I wrote a piece for the IEEE Transactions of Professional Communications titled "Marshall McLuhan and Computer Conferencing," in which I suggested that the pithy, aphoristic bursts that characterized his writing—his great works from the 1960s consisted of chapters often not more than a page or two in length—were actually a form of Web writing ("computer conferencing"), or what we today call blogs, decades before the Web and online communication had emerged.

Fast-forward 21 years … I was browsing through the Twitter public page, a few months after I had joined in the summer of 2007, and was struck that the tweets bore a strong resemblance to the titles of those short chapters in McLuhan's books. If the contents of his chapters were blogs, a page or two of thoughts, with no necessary connection between one chapter and the next, no fixed order, then the titles of those chapters were twitters, an arresting phrase or two, at most. McLuhan's chapter "glosses," in other words, were twitters before their time (Levinson, October 2007). Of course, titles such as "Nobody ever made a grammatical error in a non-literate society" in "The Gutenberg Galaxy" were far better than most of the tweets on Twitter. So McLuhan's titles not only presaged Twitter, they also presaged the best that Twitter could be. (Indeed, there are several Twitter accounts under McLuhan's name which tweet his aphorisms.)

But how did the real Marshall McLuhan see the digital age? It was not that he had access to some sort of crystal ball that provided glimpses of the future. McLuhan owned no fantastical speculum across time. It was rather that, for some reason, McLuhan's mind worked in a way that our digital age, and new new media in particular, have captured and projected on our screens and lives. This in turn suggests that such a short form of writing was always part of our human capability, but our culture and education served to limit or rule out. McLuhan was able to break through those expectations, which are now becoming the norm in texting, IM'ing, status reporting and tweeting.

This also points to a more general historical dynamic between old and new new media. We always desired to write as well as read our reference sources and to select as well as receive our news. But our cultural heritage, our education and training, taught us to be spoon-fed. Yet, just as with the short form of writing, we never lost those human productive urges, and they have been retrieved with Twitter, Wikipedia, Digg and the new new media we have been examining in this book.

Retrieval of earlier communication forms by new technologies is also an important part of McLuhan's media schema and was most developed in his "tetrad" or four-part model of what he referred to as media "effects." Every new medium "amplifies" aspects of our communication (radio, for example, amplifies sound across distance), "obsolesces" a currently widespread form (radio took the place of some reading), "retrieves" an earlier form (radio brought back the spoken word), and eventually reverses into something else (radio becomes audio-visual television). "Digital McLuhan" (Levinson, 1999) provides more details and examples of tetrads, but, regarding Twitter, we could say it amplifies the short written phrase, obsolesces long blogs and phone calls, retrieves poetic phrases and McLuhan's writing, and reverses into ... well, that's yet to be seen.

McLuhan's work thus clearly can be very helpful not only in understanding media (the title of his 1964 master work) but in understanding new new media. Another one of his notions is "total immersion"—to use a medium is to become fully engulfed in it, whatever we may otherwise think we are doing (see McLuhan & Fiore, 1967). Mobile media, to the contrary, work against this immersion. If we're looking at Wikipedia or YouTube or writing a blog from a mobile device, we are usually more in touch with the outside world, and with people around us, than if we are engaging those media from a desktop computer.

But one new new medium—in fact, the final specific system we will consider in this book—goes to great lengths to give us the illusion of total immersion. We turn in the next chapter to Second Life.

CHAPTER 9

Second Life

IT WAS COLD AND RAINING IN NEW YORK CITY, EARLY ON A SUNDAY evening in December 2007. I did a reading from my novel "The Plot to Save Socrates", to an international audience—people from Romania and other places overseas, as well as the U.S.—and not a raindrop hit me as I traveled to the reading. That's because I did not do it in this world but in Second Life.

In Second Life, avatars not only read aloud from their books to audiences of avatars, but they also do lots of other things we ordinarily do in our flesh-and-blood lives. Avatars get their hair styled, buy clothes and land, dance, make love, do all manner of business and run shops. I had just opened a "virtual" bookstore, the "Soft Edge Book Shop" on Book Island in Second Life. My rent was paid in "Linden dollars," which were purchased by real U.S. dollars and came to about $5 per month. My store was stocked with covers of all of my books—some 15 of them—which visitors could click upon and see reviews of the books, as well as links through which they could read more about the books and buy them on Amazon. I did my reading to a crowd of about 40 avatars, standing right in front of the bookstore, as my avatar sat in a rocking chair on the porch of the store.

I have since closed my shop—I could no longer afford the time to tend it—but if it were still open, it would no doubt have a cover of this very book, "New New Media," on one of its walls. (See Kremer, 2008, for a summary of authors who have given readings, established two-dimensional offices and bookstores and conducted other professional writerly activities in Second Life.)

Everything in life has precedents, and Second Life is no different. People have been chatting online now for decades—back before anyone even talked about new media, let alone new new media—ever since the French Minitel system in the 1980s (Levinson, 1997). Texting is still essential to communication in Second Life, as blogging is to most new new media (even videos on YouTube have written titles and descriptions), but Second Life in 2007 added voice chat capabilities. You can find an avatar to dance with and select a script—you can waltz or boogie or whatever—and you chat either via text or voice and watch your avatars dance on the screen.

Second Life residents use Linden dollars to purchase land, objects, skin, and scripts that animate the avatars. Linden dollars (named after Linden Labs, which created and continues to develop and administer Second Life) can either be purchased with real dollars, via PayPal, or earned from other residents in Second Life. In December 2008, $5 U.S. purchased 1,310 L (Linden) dollars. I decided to make my books available only for purchase on Amazon via U.S. dollars, in part because I was interested in the Second Life/real-life interface—how permeable was the boundary between the two, how could success in Second Life translate into success in real life—and in part because it is always better for an author if his or her books sell through a bookstore and money goes back to the publisher, from whom the author receives royalties. In that way, your advance from the publisher can be repaid, and the publisher can be impressed with the sales of your book, which make additional printings and contracts for subsequent books more likely.

About a week before my first Second Life reading at the bookstore, I did a Sunday afternoon reading as a guest on Adele Ward's Second Life "Meet the Author" series. This reading was "televised" live in Second Life on SLCN.tv—Second Life Cable Network—and is now available to everyone on the Web at the SLCN.tv Web site. (I also embedded copies and excerpts of this video on my blogs and posted excerpts on YouTube; see Levinson, Reading from "The Plot to Save Socrates," 2007.)

The availability of Second Life "off world"—or on computer screens in real life, or RL, as the residents say—is part of the growing intermingling of Second Life and the rest of the Internet. I was also interviewed by Esther DeCuir in a Second Life newspaper for an article about my Soft Edge bookshop. Like the SLCN.tv interview, the article in SLNN—Second Life News Network—is available to everyone on the Web (DeCuir, 2007). Like my Amazon book links, these news and television operations show the extent to which Second Life works with the rest of the online world.

Selling books from a virtual bookshop, with chairs and tables and photos on the walls, however, feels more like selling books at an author's reading in a real bookstore than IM'ing from a Web page with images of my books. One night, my avatar was standing in front of my shop. Another avatar was walking by and stopped to look at the big book cover of "The Plot to Save Socrates" that was slowly spinning on the first step in front of the shop. We chatted for a few minutes about the book, and then the customer clicked on the Amazon link and purchased it. I told him where he could mail my novel, if he wanted me to autograph it. This felt so close to being in a real bookstore, I could almost feel the texture of the book in my hand.

More than any of the other new new media we have examined in this book, the avatars and animation and sounds of Second Life make it seem more like an alternative than adjunct to our lives—a third place, different from our lives away from computers, yet also different from the work we pursue and the fun we have via our computers and cellphones. But, of course, Second Life is nonetheless a part of our real lives, exists in the same online matrix as all the other new new media, and ultimately proves its mettle to the extent that it can make a difference in our real-life activities of fun, love, politics and business.

History and Workings of Second Life

Second Life commenced on June 23, 2003, and was brought into being by Linden Labs (more formally Linden Research, Inc.) under the supervision of Philip Rosedale. It had as of September 2008 about 15 million users, making it less than a tenth as populated as Facebook and about half as populated as Twitter as of May 2009. As on Facebook and MySpace, the 15 million no doubt includes a large number of multiple accounts by individual users as well as inactive accounts.

Like Facebook, MySpace, Twitter and all successful new new media, joining Second Life—becoming a member or "resident"—is free. But unlike the other new new media, spending money in the form of Linden dollars is an essential part of Second Life.

Here's how that works: After joining Second Life, you can choose a male or female avatar and then select a body type, precise facial attributes ranging from plumpness of lips to facial hair, and clothes. All of this is free. But the nature of the free clothing, and even the facial attributes and hairstyles, mark the new resident as a "newbie." This is where the spending starts. Residents can purchase just about anything, ranging from a kick-ass earring to a great looking backside, for modest to large amounts of Linden dollars.

In one sense, Linden dollars are play money—like Monopoly game money— and residents indeed frequently refer to their experiences as "playing" Second Life. But Linden dollars can be purchased by real U.S. dollars and many international currencies and converted at the going rate back into dollars or the international currencies, which means that spending Linden dollars in Second Life can quickly become serious and even big business. Business Week reported that Ailin Graef (avatar name Anshe Chung) made more than a quarter of a million U.S. dollars in Second Life as of May 2006 (Hof, 2006), and Reuters' Second Life bureau said Chung had announced Second Life "real estate" assets worth $1 million U.S. at the end of November of that year (Reuters, 2006). Reuters also indicated that 58 Second Life residents "were earning more than $5,000"—a "surge in high-end Second Life business profits"—but by April 2008, The Alphaville Herald (a Second Life newspaper, unaffiliated with Linden Labs) reported the "lowest profit per capita growth ever in Q1 2008" in Second Life (Holyoke, 2008). It will be very interesting to see how commerce in Second Life fares in the worldwide economic crisis of 2008–2009, and however long it lasts.

But this much is clear: Given the easy exchange via PayPal of Linden dollars and non-Second Life currencies (i.e., "real" currencies, associated with real countries), what is the difference between Linden dollars and Australian or Canadian dollars, from the standpoint of an American, or the difference between Linden dollars and American and Canadian dollars, from the standpoint of an Australian? From the point of view of a person in any country, Linden dollars are no different than any other foreign currency—or, the only difference is that Linden dollars work in a virtual realm, easily and nearly instantly accessible from just about any country in the world, via desktop, laptop or iPhone.

Second Life and Real-Life Interface

Real life—what we do in the physical world when we're not interacting on a computer or cellphone—figures in, or lurks behind, everything we do online. Did mybarackobama.com result in more votes for Barack Obama? There is no way we can conduct a controlled experiment and restage the election of 2008 without Obama's Web sites and all the other new new media, but they undoubtedly played a role in his election to the presidency (see Chapter 12, "New New Media and the Election of 2008"). And this would be an example of an online or new new media series of activities having a profound effect in the real world.

Second Life, apropos its development by Linden Labs, can be considered an ongoing laboratory for such online/real-world impacts. Every time someone clicked on a link in my Soft Edge bookshop in Second Life and then bought one of my novels on Amazon, that Second Life denizen was moving from the new new medium of Second Life to the new medium of Amazon, on which an interaction— a purchase, in this case, with real, not Linden, dollars—resulted in a hardcover or paperback copy of my novel shipped to the Second Life buyer's real-world home or place of business.

But if business is the most easily quantifiable kind of Second Life interaction with real life, it is by no means the only one. We consider several other Second Life activities with real-world impact in the sections below, ranging from educational seminars to sex.

A Seminar in Second Life

Given the voice capabilities of Second Life, we could say that any time an avatar talks to a group of other, assembled avatars, the first avatar is conducting a live-streaming audio seminar, or webinar.

But some Second Life events are more explicitly seminars or webinars than others. In a typical reading from one of my science fiction novels that I conducted in Second Life, announcements were sent to various communities on Second Life, as well as to my Friends on Second Life. They received those announcements in their message boxes on Second Life, and/or via their real-life email, if they had enabled that option. In reality, these flesh-and-blood people were invited to attend my reading via their avatars on Second Life. The "game" or experience of Second Life, however, is so realistic that it could also be reasonably said that avatars and personas received the invitation.

I also announced the reading in my "off-world" online communities—on Facebook, MySpace and on my blogs—and invited off-world friends in these social media, and via Gmail, to the reading. The invitation included instructions on how to get a free Second Life account and the location—or "coordinates"—of the reading and details on how to get there, from any point of entry in Second Life.

The last names of every avatar or denizen on Second Life are provided by Second Life. Aeon, Latte and Freenote are examples of the many possible last names. If someone wishes to disguise totally a true, offline identity on Second Life, this can easily be accomplished by creating a first name that has no connection to your real-life name—Star Aeon or Tasty Latte. This, indeed, is by far the most common way that names are created on Second Life and underscores the fact that, of all the social media considered in this book, Second Life is by far the most anonymous. In the cases of Facebook, MySpace and Twitter, you can create an account under a fictional name if you wish. In the case of Second Life, you have to go out of your way to have an avatar name that has a connection to your real-life name. The way to do that is to create a Second Life first name that consists of your real-life names. If you ever run into a PaulLevinson Freenote on Second Life, that would be me.

A fine assemblage of avatars convened for my appearance at Adele Ward's "Meet the Author" event on Sunday, December 9, 2007, at 2 p.m. SLT (Second Life Time, which is the same as Pacific time). It was held in a beautiful venue—the Town Center in a sim (or virtual place) by the name of Cookie. I and the invitees were given the "coordinates" of the Town Center, which enabled us either to log on directly to that virtual place or "teleport" there from some place else in Second Life. "Teleporting" is an instant way to move from one place to another in Second Life. Other, slower options are flying and walking. Members of my audience arrived in all three ways.

Before I began the reading, attendees chatted among themselves, via text or voice, as they arrived. There were seats upon which the avatars could sit, and they were encouraged to do so—not only out of courtesy to the avatars but because standing required more computing power from Second Life to keep the simulacrum intact (you can see the seated audience a few minutes into the interview in Levinson, Reading from "The Plot to Save Socrates," 2007). A week before the reading, Adele had explained to me—via her Jilly Kidd avatar (Adele Ward is her real name, and she is a real poet who lives in London)—that the Town Center venue could only support a maximum of 45 to 50 avatars. (Other venues can support as many as several hundred avatars. "Support" is the Second Life computing power needed to maintain the "sim" or virtual imagery, which can crash if the number of avatars exceeds Second Life bandwidth required for the sim.) I had estimated, based on the number of invitations distributed and the number of attendees I had attracted to other online events not in Second Life, that my reading would attract a maximum of 30 avatars. I thus was very happy with the 36 avatars I counted in the audience as I took my place on the stage—more is always better for an author, as long as the event is not in Second Life, and the number of attendees shuts down the system (not Second Life as a whole but the specific audio-visual part of the system or sim where the reading is conducted). Of course, an in-person bookstore can attract an audience that exceeds its seating, but that's what standing room is for, and overflow audiences do not shut down the bookstore.

Arton Tripsa (a historical fiction writer from Australia in real life), aurel Miles (a writer from Vancouver, Canada, in real life), Kenny Hubble (a professor in real life, also from Canada—more about Kenny below), iodache Gumbo (an author from Romania, in real life), Kelsey Mertel (an American author living in Greece, in real life) and Dreame Destiny (a publisher in real life from Australia), as well as Polaris Snook, Tinkerer Melville, Edward Russell, Toria Mumford and Zeropoint Thielt—virtual beings whose real names and real-life locations I still do not know—were some of the avatars who walked, flew or teleported in to my reading, in a pageantry of color, feathers and costumes that exceeded anything you might find even at a Star Trek convention. But one thing that readings in Second Life and real life do have in common—they are likely to be well attended by other authors and, if the author giving the reading is a professor, by another professor and student or two as well.

As indicated above, Starr Sonic and her crew at SLCN.tv videotaped the reading. As of May 2009—18 months after the reading in Second Life—the video clips of the reading I posted on YouTube and Blip.tv have received more than 4,500 views. Thirty-six avatars at the live reading in Second Life, and more than 4,500 views on YouTube and Blip.tv a year and a half later, gives a good indication of the power of the Web outside of Second Life, and YouTube in particular, in comparison: An event on Second Life put on YouTube has drawn more than a hundred times the number of original virtual attendees or viewers.

Kenny Hubble, Second Life Astronomer

In real life, Ken Hudson heads the Strategic Innovation Lab at the Virtual World Design Centre for the Loyalist College in Canada. Not surprisingly, Ken has a keen interest in Second Life; it was his invitation to interview me about new new media in his Second Life Media Ecology symposium (Levinson, Interview by Ken Hudson, 2007) that brought me to Second Life in the first place in November 2007 and resulted in the "birth" of PaulLevinson Freenote.

One of Ken Hudson's other keen interests has always been astronomy. Hence his Second Life name, "Kenny Hubble." In 2008, Kenny created the Caledon Astrotorium and The Caledon Astronomical Society in Second Life. Caledon is a virtual place or sim—like Cookie Town Center and Book Island—but constructed to look and feel like a Victorian corner of the city, the kind of place that Charles

Dickens or Charles Darwin might have strolled through on a sparkly wintry evening. Kenny told me he not only loved astronomy and looking at the heavens, but looking at it with the sense of wonderment that he associates with Victorian eyes and minds, their belief in the progress of science and the joy of new discovery. (I share his admiration of this aspect of Victorian culture.) The CAS's explanatory text says that it "operates the planetarium as a public service to the citizens of Caledon and of Second Life. The Society holds regular events including readings, lectures, discussions, demonstrations, social events, and other astronomically related activities" (Hudson/Hubble, 2008; see also Merlot, 2008).

A planetarium, if you think about it, is an ideal real-world place to build in Second Life. The images you see at the Hayden Planetarium, in New York City, are just that—images, brilliantly constructed, to give you the illusion that you are looking at this or that part of the night sky. We might even say, looking at the Hayden or any real-world planetarium through retro eyes, that we are seeing the stuff of Second Life, created decades—or in the case of the Hayden Planetarium, which opened in 1935, almost 75 years—before Second Life was possible on our little computer screens. Unlike what we see through the Hubble Telescope, including raw photographs of what the Hubble sees—which is the cosmos as it is—what Kenny Hubble's Caledon Astrotorium and planetariums in the real-world show are artists' renderings of the cosmos. A photograph, of course, may be part of a Second Life, or a planetarium's, presentation. But the milieu in both environments is always more than photographic.

Ken Hudson told me (via Facebook message, December 26, 2008) that his Caledon Astrotorium "gets over 100 visitors per week—many just use the space to relax in the stars...." Not relax "looking or gazing at" the stars but relax "in" the stars. This is the "total immersion" in the medium McLuhan was speaking of—without ever knowing Second Life—which I mentioned regarding McLuhan and media at the end of the previous chapter.

And if you want more immersion in the stars in Second Life, you can teleport over to the Van Gogh Museum in Second Life, walk out on the terrace, and see the night sky cool and ablazed with Van Gogh's "The Starry Night." And if not just Van Gogh but Don McLean's "Starry Starry Night" is now in your head, you can go over to Robbie Dingo's off-world page and look at "A Second Life Machinima" (Dingo, 2007). You do not need to be on Second Life to see this. "Shot on location in Second Life then post-produced," Dingo explains. "Ever looked at your favorite painting and wished you could wander inside?" That's what Dingo, Second Life, and Blip.tv (Dingo removed the video from YouTube) have done for "The Starry Night." (See Au, 2007, for further details about the creation of the video.)

Sex in Second Life

Not everything in Second Life is astronomy and Impressionism. As is the case in real life, sex flourishes in all of its forms in Second Life.

Whether an assignation with a prostitute, a pick-up in a bar, or making love at home next to the fireplace with your Second Life spouse, sex in the virtual realm always requires two components: body parts and scripts.

The body parts are just what you would expect. You purchase breasts, derrieres, pudenda, which are available in all shapes, colors and sizes. You "wear" them—that is, make them part of your avatar—as you would an article of jewelry or a piece of clothing. "That's a nice ass you're wearing" can be a literal compliment, more than a metaphor, in Second Life.

You can purchase body parts for yourself or give them to your lover. A woman avatar I interviewed in Second Life told me that she brought a man home to her Second Life bedroom, gave him a "script" for sex (see next paragraph) and was unhappy to see when the man took off his clothes that he had a "Louisville Slugger"-sized penis. "I gave him something more suitable," she said.

But body parts, as they are in real life, are just the beginning or prerequisite for sex in Second Life. All unusual movement of avatars in Second Life, any motion beyond walking, waving, flying and teleporting (flying and teleporting are intrinsic to Second Life), are made possible by "scripts" of special programs to control or guide the avatar. Some scripts come in objects. If you see a chair and you want your avatar to be seated, you click on the "sit" option or script that is programmed in the image of the chair, and, voila, your avatar is seated. Other scripts can be purchased or given to you by other avatars. If your avatar goes to a nightclub, you may well be offered scripts to do all kinds of dances. Your avatar and your avatar partner can rumba, waltz or twist the virtual night away.

Sex scripts sometimes come packaged in bed or other "love furniture," or they can be offered by a potential partner. They vary as to length and the specific sexual activity desired. The specific moves programmed in these scripts represent the limit of your choice and control of the sexual act in Second Life. You can choose the script. But once you and your partner are in the script, you can't decide to shift positions or even hold a kiss a little longer. Spontaneity, in other words, is scripted.

How much would such body parts and scripts cost a Second Lifer looking for love? In December 2008, Animation Sensations placed a classified ad that invited shoppers to "Come and check out our HUGE selection of menu driven BEDS, RUGS, HOT TUBS, POOLS, GAZEBOS and MORE!!!! Up to 206 ANIMATIONS!!!! Group Sofas too! Best prices in Second Life—why pay more? Prices as low as L$550!!! Kisses and cuddles to every loving position you can imagine." Henmations advertised "SEXY DANCES, LOVE FURNITURE & HUDS—MOTION CAPTURED ANIMATIONS. High Quality motion captured Dance and Love Animations. The biggest choice of animated Furniture like Bedrooms, Bathrooms, Livingrooms, Saunas, Dining etc… Photorealistic Skins and lots of HUDs, Club Equipment and scripted Products to make your SecondLife more Authentic. Sex bed, sex bed, sexbeds, sex beds, sex rug, sex rugs" for L$230,002 in a package for someone who wanted to set up shop and retail all of the above. Five-hundred and fifty Linden dollars cost about $20 U.S.

As is the case with all cyber sex—going back to the French Minitel system in the 1980s and its origin of sex via texting (see Levinson, 1992)—sex in Second Life has the advantage of not conveying sexually-transmitted disease or resulting in pregnancy. But it also is prone to the drawback of all virtual or online social activity, sexual or otherwise: Unless you already know the real-life person running the avatar, you have no way of knowing the gender and age of that real-life person.

"Lost" in Second Life

The relationship between real, off-world life (life either offline or on systems other than Second Life) and Second Life flows both ways. Not only do denizens of Second Life make money, or try to make money, which can be converted into real currencies, but they bring into Second Life all manner of media and issues from real life, ranging from what I did with my books, to supporters of Barack Obama meeting via their avatars to discuss how to promote their candidate in both Second Life and the real world, to groups on Second Life devoted to the appreciation of television shows seen in the real world.

"'Lost' in Second Life" refers to a group of devotees of the "Lost" television show in Second Life and not to being lost in Second Life, though one might say that some of the inhabitants of Second Life are lost in it, even though they may feel they have really found their truest lives in the game of Second Life. In May 2007, around the time of the extraordinary Season 3 finale (which I have described as one of the best hours ever on television, see Levinson, "'Lost' Season 3 Finale," 2007), several "Lost" fans began construction of a virtual "Lost" island in Second Life. Their goal was to create a place, similar to the island on the television program, where their avatars could meet and discuss the program. They later also created a Web site off of Second Life, sl-LOST.com, where they tell the story of their Second Life group and island. It is a story—a true story—of surprises and heartbreaks and redemptions, including a disappearing island, which almost rivals the story in the television series.

One of the deepest realities of Second Life, as we have seen, is that everything costs money. This means that, whether you want to set up a bookshop to sell your books or create an island to talk about "Lost," someone has to pay Linden dollars, either in rental or purchase of the property, or someone in Second Life has to be willing to give you use of such property for free. My first bookstore, on Book Island, off of Pulitzer Square in Second Life, cost me about $5 U.S. a month rental. I was later offered a free bookstore in another place in Second Life, The Artists' Village, so I closed the first one and opened the second version of The Soft Edge bookshop. After about four months, the landlord disappeared and with it all the stores on her island, including my bookshop. Although I could have reopened it elsewhere in Second Life—and may still do so, someday—I decided I was too busy (in part, with writing this book) to reopen the store at that time.

The "Lost" group in Second Life encountered a similar problem of the rug—or island—being pulled out from under them. As they explain on their Web site, one day in "October 2007 the original financial owner of the island disappeared without giving his group any warning or explanation." The island was reopened in November 2007—not by the long-gone owner but by the administration of Second Life—"for 24 hours in order for members of the group to collect the items they made." The homeless-in-Second-Life group eventually found new backers and new headquarters, giving this true saga a happy ending. But the value of having a Web site, off of Second Life, was amply demonstrated. Before their second "Lost" island was created in Second Life, the Web site served as a way of keeping the group together. I got to know the group when it published an interview with me in January 2008, about "Lost," conducted by one of the group's leaders (which, however, ironically vanished from the group's off-world Web site). I also visited the new headquarters in Second Life in 2008. (See the end of chapter 6 for another kind of television series involvement in Second Life, "CSI-NY's" staging of an episode in that virtual realm.)

But why was it so important for this "Lost" group to meet via their avatars in Second Life, when they already had a Web page and could easily have IM'd about "Lost," out of Second Life, as much as they liked? The answer gets, again, at the immersive appeal of Second Life versus the rest of the Web for all things in Second Life: When you're in Second Life, you feel, much more than on other nonsimulation sites on the Web, as if you are really in this community. The combination of the moving graphics and voices, the way you can move your avatar through this environment, creates a powerful illusion that you are actually in, rather than looking at, listening to or reading it.

Second Life thus represents the epitome of total involvement in a new new medium. You can pause a video on YouTube, stop editing on Wikipedia, leave your profile page on the screen and grab a bite to eat without missing too much on Facebook or MySpace, but to leave the screen when you are connected to Second Life is, literally, to leave your avatar frozen or sleeping—that is what you through your avatar will look like to all the other avatars in your vicinity—and, of course, your avatar will neither see nor hear anything they say or do.

In contrast, a podcast, as is the case with all acoustic media, is designed to be listened to when you are doing something else. We examine this archetypal multitasking new new medium in the next chapter.

CHAPTER 10

Podcasting

Historically, the recording and dissemination of images preceded the same for sound. Photography was developed by Daguerre in the 1830s, in contrast to the phonograph invented by Edison in 1876. Motion pictures, also invented by Edison—as well as the Lumière Brothers in France and William Friese-Greene in England, more or less independently—also preceded Marconi's radio in 1901 by more than a decade (see Levinson, 1997, for further details). Indeed, if we take cave paintings as a form of recording images, we have this visual medium preceding anything acoustic, as far as we know, by at least some 30,000 years.

On the other hand, radio in 1901 certainly preceded the invention of television in 1927, and the commercial success of radio in the 1920s presaged the commercial success of television by at least 20 years.

And at this current stage—the year 2009—of the digital age, recording and dissemination of sound programs is still a bit easier than webcasting, YouTube, and the new new media recording and dissemination of audio-visual content.

The recording and dissemination of sound—music, interviews, soliloquies—is known as podcasting. The "casting" part comes from broadcasting, or the widespread casting or dissemination of first sound by radio and then images and sound via television. The "pod" comes from iPod, which was the device via which podcasts were first intended to be heard.

But podcasts are now easily available on any computer and indeed in cars, via Bluetooth connections to phone banks that play podcasts. Since radio, available in automobiles since Transitone in the late 1920s, and more recently just a click away on the Web, presents the same kinds of programs as found on podcasts, we could say that podcasts and radio are becoming one and the same.

Except for the important fact that radio programs are professionally produced whereas podcasts—like all new new media—can be made and disseminated by anyone.

In December 2008, a new member of Podcastalley.com, a social site for podcasters and listeners, asked if "anyone here can explain what a podcast is? What are the benefits?" I replied as follows, "It's an audio or audio-visual program you can get, for free, over the Web. Its advantage is that the podcast comes straight from the podcaster and does not have to meet whatever the requirements of radio and television broadcast producers. This means that the podcast can be more original and idiosyncratic, and the podcast does not have to attract x number of listeners or viewers in order to continue—that is completely up to the podcaster" (Levinson, "Response to 'What Is A Podcast'", 2009).

How Is a Podcast Made?

You need a microphone and a sound-recording program to produce a podcast. Like most new new media software, sound-recording programs can be purchased (such as Sound Forge, which I use) or found for free on the Web (Audacity would be an example). The commercial programs usually have a few more bells and whistles than the freebies, but the free programs certainly do the job.

Recording a podcast that sounds good takes a little talent, as well as a decent-sounding voice. But mistakes, coughs and other acoustic errors can usually be edited out with ease, and professional and free programs (the Levelator would be an example) can be used to improve the voice quality and reduce undo fluctuations in loudness and softness.

Podcasts vary in length from a few minutes to a few hours long. The longer the podcast, the bigger the file required to store it and the more bandwidth required to disseminate the podcast on the Web. Recordings can be stored in a variety of acoustic formats, ranging from uncompressed WAV files to highly compressed MP3s. The MP3s, in turn, can range from 64 kbs compression, which has the sound quality of talk you might hear on the radio, to 320 kbs, which provides crystal clear CD-quality sound. The greater or more detailed the kbs compression of the sound file, the more space will be needed to store the file and the more bandwidth to disseminate it.

Once recorded, the podcast has to be uploaded someplace on the Web, from which it can be disseminated to the world—or to anyone with a computer, iPod or a phone connection in a car.

Blueprint for a Podcast

Although a podcast requires more production than writing a blog, it shares the blog's and all new new media's advantage of being doable, capable of being made, without needing anyone else's permission. Unlike the "showrunner" of a television series, or person who first came up with the idea for the television show, the podcaster can move from conception to production in hours or days, and sometimes minutes.

Here's an example of a new podcast I am producing today: a new episode of Light On Light Through about cyberbullying. As I mentioned in Chapter 6 about MySpace, I was contacted by the publicist for a band, Truth on Earth, shortly after I had posted a blog on MySpace in late November 2008 about cyberbullying. The band wanted me to know about its new song "Shot With a Bulletless Gun," which I immediately realized was an example of the Internet's musical medicine for the new new media abuse of cyberbullying.

After I heard the song, I was thinking about what I could do to help promote it and asked the band members if they would like to be interviewed on Light On Light Through. They agreed. I called the band via Skype—my Skype connection to theirs—on what is known as VOIP, or voice over IP connection. It sounded fine and cost nothing. I had a microphone and earphones—my standard podcasting gear. The band, which consists of three young women, Serena, Kiley and Tess, used the built-in microphone and speaker system of their Mac. I used another free program, "Hot Recorder for VOIP" to record the program. (But I needed an "Audio Conversion for Hot Recorder" program, which I had purchased the year before for $15, to translate the Hot Recorder file into a WAV file I could use to make the podcast.)

The interview took 15 minutes and included a live performance of a new song by the band about homeless people. The band had emailed an MP3 of "Bulletless Gun" to be included in the podcast. I have just confirmed that the recording of the interview came out fine. The entire process, at this point, including the recording, has taken about 45 minutes.

At some point in the next few days, I will record an introduction and brief discussion of the problem of cyberbullying, an oral rendition of my written blog. I will put in my "bumper" music, at the very beginning and end of the podcast. It is a riff taken from "Looking for Sunsets (in the Early Morning)," the lead song from my 1972 album, "Twice Upon a Rhyme". I will spice up the podcast with sound effects here and there and will add a few commercials—either for my novels, "The Silk Code" and "The Plot to Save Socrates", or a commercial I might receive payment for playing (see "Advertising on Podcasts" later in this chapter). I haven't decided yet, but given the topic of the podcast, I probably will not go the paid commercial route. I will, however, also likely add several "promos," or free ads for other podcasts, at the end of my podcast. After the podcast is totally assembled, I will run it through another free program, the "Levelator," which as I mentioned earlier equalizes, or gives equivalent tone and volume, to all the pieces of the podcast. This is especially important when the podcast consists of different parts, recorded in different ways, as is the case with this episode of Light On Light Through, which consists of just my voice (at the beginning); my interview with Serena, Kiley and Tess; a studio-recorded MP3 of "Shot With a Bulletless Gun"; and their live performance of "Where You Sleep Tonight."

It will take me a little longer to do all of that than it just took me to write about it, but, all in all, not much longer—likely less than an hour. And then the podcast will be ready for distribution.

Podcast Storage and Distribution: Players, iTunes and RSS Feeds

Before a podcast can be disseminated—or listened to on laptops, iPods and phones—it has to be uploaded from the producer's computer to a storage site on the Web. Such sites function much like blog sites, except the "posts" are acoustic podcasts. Blog posts sometimes accompany the podcasts on such sites and can be read before, after or during the playing of the podcasts. If the podcast is also delivered via a "feed" to iTunes or some other system from which the podcast can be downloaded for free for listening via an iPod, the blog posts can be "coded" to accompany the podcast, so as to be readable on the iPod's screen. Podcast storage sites usually do that automatically.

As is the case with blog sites, podcast storage sites are either free or "rentable" under a variety of options. My Levinson News Clips podcast, which started as brief 5 to 6-minute commentaries on media and political news but soon developed into brief reviews of television shows, is housed on Mevio.com, for free. My AskLev podcast, which provides 5 to 10 minutes of advice for writers, is hosted on TalkShoe.com, also for free. Mevio and TalkShoe on occasion insert their own ads at the beginning and/or end of the podcasts they host, and they offer some of the podcasters on their sites opportunities to earn advertising income (see "Advertising on Podcasts," later in this chapter). There are also ads on their Web sites that house your podcast—that is one of the ways those sites earn revenue. My Light On Light Through podcast, usually about 30 minutes in length and devoted to various aspects of popular culture and politics, can be found at Libsyn.com, which charges me $5 per month and costs as much as $60 per month depending upon how many podcasts and what length and compression you want to store on the system. (I switch from $5 to $12 per month, depending upon how many podcasts I produce.) There are dozens of other podcast hosts available, free or for hire.

Why would a podcast producer pay for storage rather than use a free site? Libsyn offers highly detailed, much better statistics on podcast dissemination than do the free sites. A podcaster is interested not only in how many times a podcast has been listened to but also via what means of dissemination, and the podcaster prefers such information updated on an immediate or close-to-immediate basis. Libsyn does both, as well as provide a blog environment for posts about the podcasts that is available on the HTML design level to the podcaster, which gives the podcaster more control over the look and feel of the blog.

Once the podcast is housed on a site, the most straightforward way of attracting listeners is by posting links to the podcasts, in all possible places on the Web, just as a blogger would for a blog. In 2008, my Light On Light Through podcasts attracted more than 75,000 listeners and Levinson News Clips more than 125,000 listeners. Nearly 90 percent of them heard the podcast via a link to the podcast page, where the podcast could be played on any one of several "podcast players" I have on the page.

A podcast player is in effect a kind of widget that contains links to the MP3s of each podcast episode stored on your podcast-hosting service. Libsyn, Mevio and Talkshoe automatically provide their own links to every blog post on their pages with a podcast. They also provide players that can be put on other blog pages and Web sites. At the same time, Big Contact offers "feed players" that can be put on any blog pages and Web sites, including Libysn's. I have both kinds of podcast players, and several others, on my Libsyn podcast pages and on my blogs.

Of the other 10 percent of my listeners in 2008, nearly 9 percent heard the podcasts via iTunes, and the other 1 percent on smaller "aggregation" or distribution systems including Juice, Zune and iPodder. Thus, nearly 99 percent of my listeners either heard my podcast by direct link (90 percent) or via iTunes (9 percent).

In all cases, the podcast was free to the listener—which, unsurprisingly, is one of its appeals. Indeed, iTunes, which functions as an old medium, or an old medium in the new medium of the Web, when it charges for its music, performs much more like a new new medium when it provides podcasts (and vidcasts, which are podcasts with not just sound but video) for free. These can be heard either by logging directly onto iTunes and searching for the podcast or by subscribing to the podcast on iTunes.

But how does the podcast get from the producer's host site (Libsyn) to iTunes? RSS, an acronym for Real Simple Syndication, does the heavy lifting. Podcast hosts provide easy ways of getting a podcast series onto iTunes. The host sends out a feed—an RSS feed—which iTunes or in fact any RSS receiver can pick up. In the case of iTunes, the podcast producer has to first submit a description of the podcast, with its unique RSS feed (provided by the hosting service), to iTunes. Once accepted by iTunes—and I don't know of any podcast producer whose podcast was ever rejected—each episode of the podcast automatically appears on iTunes, brought there by the RSS feed. "Juice" and other podcast distributors work the same way, although podcasts do not have to go through a formal submission process.

Case Study of Podcast Success: Grammar Girl

Mignon Fogarty started her Grammar Girl podcast—more formally, Grammar Girl's Quick and Dirty Tips for Better Writing—in July 2006, the year in which podcasting first emerged as an important new new medium. Four months later, in November 2006, Grammar Girl had received more than one million listens and downloads (Lewin, 2006). The number had grown to seven million by December 2007, and Mignon had appeared on CNN and the "Oprah Winfrey Show" (Wikipedia, 2009). Grammar Girl is often in the top five most-listened-to podcasts on iTunes, and Fogarty's paperback book based on the podcast, "Grammar Girl's Quick and Dirty Tips for Better Writing" (2008), was No. 9 on The New York Times' best-seller listing in August 2008. These accomplishments are another example of the power of new new media to call the shots in traditional modes of public presentation. Fogarty was a science writer before she started the podcast, and the success of Grammar Girl made her a star.

But how did a show about split infinitives and the difference between "affect" and "effect" become so popular? Bloggers such as Tucker Max (2006) have had best-selling books, understandable due to the raw sexual nature of the content, in Max's case, but a show about grammatical subtleties? We might think that just about everyone is interested in improving his or her grammar, so the show had a big potential audience, but that's probably not the reason for Grammar Girl's success and not even true in the first place. Indeed, had Fogarty presented her podcast idea to a radio station, it is unlikely that the show would have been given a broadcast spot—I don't know of any show on radio about grammar. The enormous success of Grammar Girl thus can likely be explained by something else: the capacity of podcast listeners to receive useful lessons in grammar, in a way that seems like fun because it is still so new. (See Levinson, 1977, for more on the debut of technologies as toys.) It's both valuable and enjoyable, in other words, not just to hear a witty show about grammar but to hear it on your iPod or computer at a time of your choosing. And podcasts are now beginning to be heard on older media, such as telephones and car radios.

Podcasts on Phones and in Cars

RSS feeds can also bring podcasts to sites that disseminate sound in ways very different from iTunes. Podlinez.net, for example, assigns each podcast series a telephone number. When one calls that number, the most recent episode of the podcast is played. (The service is, as of May 2009, free to the podcaster and the listener.)

Availability via phone opens up all sorts of additional possibilities for podcast dissemination and reception. My Prius has a Bluetooth connection for my cellphone, which plays the voice of the person I'm talking to right out of the radio speakers. I can call the Podlinez phone number and the podcast will play on the radio. Thousands of podcasts are available in this way.

Stepping back and looking at the larger picture of this media environment, what we have with podcasts that can be heard through car radios is a co-option or merging of the digital (podcast) and broadcast (radio) ages—or yet another integration of old media (radio) and new new media (podcast).

The result is a very different kind of "radio" in the car. The traditional broadcast radio comes into the car via a professional production, broadcast from a huge central facility, at a specified time. The podcast on the car radio can be produced from a rocking chair—mine often are—and is uploaded to a Web site that produces an RSS feed. It then becomes available to the listener any time he or she chooses to call the Podlinez number. In both the production and the reception end, the sound program has been greatly democratized. This is likely the beginning of a much larger co-option of old by new new media, which will include YouTube on televisions in living rooms (Orlando, 2009) and podcasts on car radios without cellphones.

Traditional broadcast radio and podcasts do have a very significant characteristic in common: both are free. But podcasting also provides free-of-charge acoustic programs which otherwise would have to be paid for by the listener.

Podiobooks

Audiobooks are still a small part of the book publishing industry, but their sales have been growing. May 2008 statistics reported about $425 million in domestic sales for hardcover and paperback books (not including textbooks) versus $12 million for audio books (Jordan, 2008). But audio book sales have increased by more than 12 percent in the past two years, and 28 percent of Americans reportedly have listened to them at one time or another (Sharp, 2008). If a driver wants to enjoy a book while driving, certainly an audiobook is preferable, and far safer, than opening a book and reading it.

Audiobooks come in various configurations: just narrated or the parts more performed; with sound effects and music, or not; abridged or complete. Depending upon the length and production, audiobooks cost more or less the same as a hardcover or expensive trade paper book, usually between $15 and $30.

Tee Morris and Evo Terra came up with an alternative a few years ago: "podiobooks," or audiobooks available in sequential episodes, a chapter or two per episode. Like all podcasts, these podiobooks are free. Readers, however, are encouraged to make donations to the authors and/or narrators, via PayPal, with the Podiobook.com site keeping 25 percent of the proceeds. (See also "Podcasting for Dummies," 2nd edition, 2008, by Tee Morris, Chuck Tomasi, and Evo Terra for more on their approach to podcasting.)

Shaun Farrell produced and narrated a podiobook of my 1999 science fiction novel, "The Silk Code," in 2007. The novel was already well known—it had won the Locus award for best first science fiction novel—but there's nothing as appealing as something for free, especially when alternative versions cost. It placed in the top 20 podiobooks downloaded in 2007 (Podiobooks did not provide exact rankings for the top 20).

Poor economies make free content even more appealing. In January 2009, Time magazine wondered if podiobooks were "publishing's next wave," noting that "book sales are down; MacMillan has laid off employees, as have Random House and Simon & Schuster; and Houghton Mifflin Harcourt has suspended the purchase of most new manuscripts." Evo Terra told Time that 45,000 episodes from podiobooks were being downloaded daily (Florin, 2009).

Podcasts and Copyright: Podsafe Music

But providing content for free to the audience—whether podcasts or blogs—can be difficult if the producer has to pay for part of that content. This problem usually does not arise in blogging, where quotes from other sources can be worked into the blog, without payment, under Fair Use, and it certainly doesn't arise when a podcast consists of just the podcaster talking. But what if the podcaster wants to play some music?

The problem first arose and was dealt with almost a century ago in the dawn of radio. ASCAP (American Society of Composers, Authors and Publishers, created in 1914) licensed music for live performances and expanded to radio. BMI (Broadcast Music, Inc., created in 1940) did the same for radio, and now ASCAP and BMI both license music for broadcast on radio and television. I am a member of both organizations, as a songwriter. In the 1970s, I received thousands of dollars from ASCAP, for broadcast of my song, "Merri-Goes-'Round" (co-written with Ed Fox) on the "Wonderama" television show. In 2007, ASCAP distributed $741.6 million to its members (ASCAP, 2008), and BMI distributed $732 million (BMI, 2007).

ASCAP and BMI collect such monies as "performance rights" fees, payable by radio and television stations and networks. Given the billions of dollars of profit earned by television and radio every year, payments to ASCAP and BMI are relatively small potatoes.

Where does this leave podcasters? They can earn money from advertising (see "Advertising on Podcasts," later in this chapter) which could pay for music performance rights, but what if a podcaster wants to play music but runs no advertising? Should these podcasters violate the copyright of recording artists and songwriters, and play their music without compensation?

This problem of copyright and compensation is the podcasting equivalent of what I called the "Achilles' Heel of YouTube" in Chapter 3—the violation of copyright in posting of numerous videos on YouTube. My solution to YouTube's problem was that copyright should be relaxed, to allow posting of any content online that does not remove the creator's attribution or earn money for the poster without the creator's permission (much the same as what Creative Commons advocates).

Podcasting has come up with another, partial solution. Adam Curry, whose pioneering championship of podcasting in 2004, after a career as an MTV "veejay," earned him the moniker of "Podfather" (Jardin, 2005), created the "Podsafe music" network in 2005 (Sharma, 2005). Its idea is that artists and songwriters upload their music to the Podsafe network, where they are made available, free of charge and without giving up the copyright, to podcasters, for the sole purpose of being played on a podcast. The artists get publicity and the podcasters free music in this symbiotic relationship. (Yes, I have about half a dozen of my recordings in the Podsafe network. I was pleased when one of my least-known songs, "Snow Flurries," Levinson and Krondes, 1969, was played on Erin Kane and Kristin Brandt's popular Manic Mommies podcast in February 2007.)

But the Podsafe solution is partial because podcasters might well still want to play a Beatles recording, or music by anyone who wants a performance fee for a podcast play. At present, such podcasters have a choice of playing the music in violation of copyright or earning enough via advertising revenues to pay a performance fee.

Advertising on Podcasts

Advertising on podcasts—or podcasters making money from ads placed in their podcasts—is more like the traditional television and radio approach to advertising than Google AdSense, Amazon Affiliate and similar kinds of advertising on blogs that we examined in Chapter 2.

The way most podcasts obtain paid advertising on their podcasts is via affiliation with a monetizing podcasting community, or, in more old-fashioned terms, an organization that acts as a broker or middleman between advertisers and podcasters. These can be podcast hosting sites such as Mevio, or services devoted purely or mostly to advertising deals, such as the "Blubrry" community, run by Raw Voice. Both offer a variety of advertising deals to its podcasters. These come in two varieties.

1. GoDaddy.com—the place where most domain names are registered and well known to the general public through its saucy Superbowl ads—and many other well known companies ranging from car rental to selling footwear offer commission ad deals. The podcaster is given talking points and asked to talk in his or her own voice for 30 to 60 seconds about the sponsor. The pitch ends with a unique code, "xxx Levin" or "podcast xxx," that the listener is told to use when ordering anything from the sponsor in response to the special deals offered in the ad. The podcaster is paid a flat fee for every sale made in response to the ad—$10 or $20 or whatever number of dollars, or a flat percentage, depending upon the nature of the promotion. Such ad campaigns can generate thousands of dollars for podcasters.

This commission approach also can work with ads that are recorded by the advertiser and given to the podcaster, or with ads that the podcaster reads verbatim from specific scripts provided by the advertiser. Many advertisers, however, prefer the podcaster to deliver the ad with his or her own words and style, because that endows the ad with a more personal quality and can be more effective with the podcaster's loyal listeners. Late-night radio, such as the "Long John Nebel Show" in New York City, used that kind of personal rendition of ads for years. But most current radio shows, such as the Bob Shannon show on WCBS-FM Radio in New York City, play ads in which the disc jockey, in this case Bob Shannon, reads from a script verbatim.

2. A very different kind of ad buy, based not on commissions for actual sales but on the number of people who hear the ad, is also offered by Mevio and by Raw Voice to podcasters. The ad itself can be prerecorded, spoken verbatim from a script or ad-libbed by the podcaster from talking points provided by the advertiser—just as with the commission ads—but, unlike the commission approach, the podcaster needs to report the number of people who heard the podcast. As is the case with advertising in old media newspapers and broadcast media, the podcaster is paid on a cost-per-thousand basis. Mevio keeps its own tally of these statistics.

Blubrry (Raw Voice) provides its own "counter" for numbers of listens—sometimes also referred to as downloads, even though the podcast also can be listened to live, and live listens count the same as downloads. Blubrry also accepts stat reports from podcasting hosts such as Libsyn. (Note that number of listens is not the same thing as number of people who have listened, because one person, of course, can listen to a podcast more than once, but I am using these measures here interchangeably, because the best that any stat counter can do is keep track of the IP addresses from which a podcast is accessed. One person, if he or she wants, can obviously listen to the same podcast more than once from different IP addresses.) Five thousand listens or downloads in a given period of time can earn more than $500 from ads paid for on a cost-per-thousand basis.

This payment for number of listens—which is equivalent, in blogging, to payment for impressions or views of ads, in contrast to payment for clicks or clicks with purchases—is clearly a more reliable source of revenue than payment for actual sales, or commissions. Why, then, would any podcaster choose the commission method?

Part of the answer is that the podcaster usually has no choice. An advertiser is not likely to want to waste time on a podcast with just a handful of listeners, not the time needed to plan the ad campaign but the accounting time required to determine the negligible payment for the small number of listeners. In contrast, commission payment requires no accounting, no reports, other than keeping track of the special promotion codes that accompany online sales made in response to the ads.

But part of the answer is also that a small audience of listeners, highly responsive to a commission advertising campaign, can generate far more income for the podcaster than an ad campaign for a larger audience with a payout based on the number of listeners. For example, 30 listeners out of an audience of 1,000 purchasing a product or service with a $20 commission would yield the podcaster $600, in contrast to a $10 payment for every thousand listeners and an audience of 3000, which would net the podcaster only $30. In other words, the commission podcaster would earn twenty times as much as the cost-per-thousand colleague, even though the commission podcast had only one-third the audience. Of course, the commission mode of payment is nonetheless more of a gamble, since the commission podcaster's audience might not make even a single purchase.

This brings into play another question, the answer to which can also help explain why a podcaster goes with either a commission or a CPM (cost per thousand) approach, and indeed, why podcasters with small numbers of listeners can still take on ads on a CPM basis. The question is why would a podcaster go with an ad broker or an ad-providing site rather than working with advertisers directly?

First, ad brokers take a substantial portion—as much as 30 percent or more—from all ad revenues earned by podcasters who play ads that come from their deals. That might be reason enough for any podcaster to want instead to work directly with the advertiser—except, most podcasters have little or no knowledge about whom to contact for ad deals.

Even if the podcasters did, the ad broker helps in an additional way, of special benefit to the podcaster with a small number of listeners. The ad broker or ad-providing podcast host negotiates deals with advertisers who want, for example, 10,000 listens, by people listening to a podcast on a topic of value to the advertiser, say, movies and television for Blockbuster. The advertiser does not care if these 10,000 listens come from one podcast or a thousand podcasts—all that counts are the statistics which accurately show that the ad was listened to or downloaded 10,000 times (or via 10,000 IPs). Thus, a podcaster with just 100 listeners in the period of time covered by the deal (could be a week, a month, or several months) can get a piece of this action. If $1,000 is earned from the 10,000 listens, the podcaster with just 100 listens would earn $10 for participation in this deal (or, actually, $7, after deduction of the ad broker's cut).

Podcast ad brokers and ad-providing hosts usually require the podcaster to agree not to work directly with an advertiser who has come to the podcaster through the broker's service. This seems only fair, to protect the broker, and is another reason why direct deals with advertisers are rare for most podcasters. Some ad brokers also insist that their podcasters take on no ads other than those provided by the broker. But should a podcaster be fortunate enough to be solicited directly by an advertiser, in a way that does not conflict with any agreements between podcaster and ad broker, the podcaster would be wise to consider it.

There is just about no downside to running advertising on your podcast, other than the amount of time it might take to report the statistics. This is usually just a few minutes, and even this is not needed if the ad broker or ad-providing podcast host provide their own statistics.

But there is one other, less tangible aspect to running ads on your podcasts that some listeners and podcasters might see as a drawback. The ad, unless it is a public service ad, makes the podcast "commercial." The podcast, of course, would still be available free of charge and, in that very important sense, would be noncommercial, whether it included ads or not. But for some people, myself not included, who regard noncommerciality, not making money from a creative work, as an ideal in itself, an ad on a totally free podcast could be seen as a betrayal.

Free promo exchanges—advertisements for podcasts that podcasters exchange and play on their respective podcasts at no charge—can be an attractive option for those who eschew any kind of commercial advertising. Or they can be and are often played along with paid-for ads. The MikeThinksNews podcast plays both, as do my Light On Light Through, Levinson News Clips and Ask Lev podcasts. The free promo exchange in podcasting works the same as link exchanges in blogging. Podcasters would like their promos to be on as many other podcasts as possible. But since every promo for your podcast played on another podcast requires you to play a promo for the other podcast on your podcast, you need to make sure the promos do not dominate your podcast show.

Live Streaming

Podcasts can be considered a form of publishing—sound rather than text and, in the case of vidcasts (podcasts with video, which we will examine in the next section), publishing of audio-visual productions. But sound can also be "streamed" live on the Web, in which case the podcast becomes a form of broadcasting, or Internet radio.

Indeed, traditional broadcast radio has been live streaming online for at least five years. WCBS Radio in New York City, which commenced broadcasting (as WAHG) in September 1924, began "simulcasting" online at the end of 2004. You could not ask for a better example of an old medium joining the new media world, much as traditional print newspapers such as The New York Times now have online venues. When I was interviewed every Sunday morning from 2006–2008 about media, politics and popular culture on KNX Radio (see Levinson, "The KNX 1070 Interviews," 2007)—the CBS all-news station in Los Angeles—the broadcast was simulcast online, and the majority of email I received was from listeners nowhere near Los Angeles. This globalization, one of the key features of new media, and thus new new media, is one of the main advantages of an old medium simulcasting online. The other would be that you can hear it on your computer, which can make listening easier and more discreet than turning on a radio in your office. But unlike true new new media, a radio broadcast simulcast on the Web is subject to the same top-down control as radio broadcast the old-fashioned way. When KNX decided in 2008 that it wanted to feature CBS news people and commentators rather than outside professors, my weekly interviews on KNX concluded. In contrast, a podcast series, whether recorded or simulcast, ends when the podcaster decides—there is no boss other than the creator in the realm of new new media. (Of course, a podcast that is a copy or adjunct of a cable TV or traditional mass-media show—such as by CNN's Larry King or MSNBC's Rachel Maddow, both of whom do podcasts—can be terminated if and when the network so decides.)

BlogTalk Radio, launched in August 2006, offers live streaming and podcast archiving, and features anyone who comes forward with an idea, a microphone and a computer connection. As the BlogTalk Radio Web site correctly notes, "Finally, a 16-year-old expressing her views and passions from Jacksonburg, Ohio, could secure quality air time alongside famous personalities." David Levine (2008) said it was the "newest form of new media; the audio version of the Internet blog." And, indeed, BlogTalk Radio is five months younger than Twitter and its March 2006 debut and certainly is an "audio version" of a blog. But so is podcasting, and the most distinctive characteristic of BlogTalk Radio is that it is live streaming, not of an old broadcast medium such as WCBS Radio online, but of a new new medium with all the quintessential characteristics of consumers becoming producers we have been considering in this book.

Talkshoe is BlogTalk Radio's main competition. It has roots that go back to April 2005 but was launched in its current form in June 2006, or two months before

BlogTalk Radio. The main difference between the two is that Talkshoe paid its producers a small amount for every listener and download (in the case of its podcasts), though Talkshoe "paused" this "Cash" program in June 2008, and as of February 2009 this "pause" has been permanent. In contrast, BlogTalk Radio started an advertising revenue-sharing program for its producers in January 2008, which pays on both audio ads inserted in the live streams and podcasts, and on banner ads placed on the Web pages for the radio programs. (Talkshoe also offers ad deals for its podcasts similar to Blubrry's.) The bottom line, financially, is that Talkshoe's per-listener/download fees were a more reliable source of revenue. (See Talkshoe, 2009, for more details.)

Talkshoe hosts my recorded Ask Lev podcast, which provides advice to writers. Unlike BlogTalk Radio, which only offers podcasts as recordings of its live-streamed shows, Talkshoe also offers the option of a standalone, recorded podcast with no live streaming (as is the case with podcasts on Libsyn and Mevio). Ask Lev was brought to Talkshoe by the 10-Minute Lesson network, which received a percentage of my Ask Lev earnings for the first year.

This points at a significant limitation of all new new media, regarding monetization possibilities. As a consumer-producer, you may have complete control over what goes into the podcast or live-stream radio, including how long you want to continue the series. But you have no control over the host and its payment policies and no control over the advertising rates and therefore revenue you might receive (unless you are able to secure a direct advertising deal), other than making a decision to run advertising on your show, or on your show's Web site, or not, if you decide to be part of the host's advertising deals. You, of course, also have no control over whether your podcast or radio host charges you for use of its system, other than your decision to work with a host that requires payment or not. As indicated above, Talkshoe, like Mevio, is a free host. Libsyn charges and thus can raise its price whenever it pleases. For that matter, a free host can change its policy and become a host that charges, at any time. The upshot for both the podcaster and live streamer is that costs and payment, whether from hosts or advertisers, is a fluid situation and must be carefully monitored if the podcaster is interested in making a profit or at least not being out-of-pocket for the podcast.

As of February 2009, I have not hosted any live radio shows on BlogTalk Radio or Talkshoe. (I did participate as a guest on Shaun OMac's BlogTalk Radio show about "Journeyman" in the fall of 2007, on the Gypsy Poet's BlogTalk Radio show in May 2009, and on Máia Whitaker's show on Talkshoe in February 2008.) The reason I have not hosted a live show is that I do not want to be locked into a specific time; I value the podcaster's power to record the podcast at times of the podcaster's choosing. This highlights one of the prime decisions of all new new media producers—live blogging vs. "regular" blogging, live conversations on Twitter vs. posting of one-liners for later reading, and live streaming of audio (and visual) vs. podcasting and vidcasting. The choice goes back more than a decade, to the first expression of new media in the late 1980s and early 1990s, and the advantages of IM'ing, or instant messaging, and chatting versus email. They, of course, both have their advantages—just as did live conversation versus letter writing in a world before email—which is why social media such as Facebook and MySpace provide both IM'ing and email-like messaging. The producer of a new new medium live show on BlogTalk Radio and Talkshoe can have the show recorded and saved as a podcast with no additional work needed. But the podcast recording of a live show might lack some of the sound effects and production values of a podcast recorded from scratch—just as a film of a theatrical performance will be different from a film made as a film in the first place. This means someone who is weighing whether to produce a live-stream show or a podcast still needs to decide which is more important, or consonant with what the producer wishes to create.

Similar issues arise with live, interactive streaming for education, or webinars.

Webinars and Vidcasts

A live-streamed radio show need not be interactive—the show could be streamed without any callers or input from anyone other than the producer—but every live-streamed new new media show I've ever heard has featured callers, who connect to the show online, via VOIP (voice over Internet protocol, or through your computer connection) or via telephone. In contrast, although broadcast radio can and does integrate callers into its simulcast programming, these calls come in to the radio station, that is, into the source of the broadcast in the offline world, not via the Internet (unless the caller is using a VOIP phone to reach the radio station's control room). Thus, another difference between new new media live streaming and old media streaming on the Web is that the new new media live streaming can easily feature call-ins from people anywhere in the world, at no charge to them.

Call-ins via computer are the essence of webinars—seminars conducted on the Web—which can be distinguished from live-streaming lectures in which the call-in is not crucial to the presentation. A typical webinar, conducted via Go To Meeting, ReadyTalk or any number of similar organizations, begins with a preparatory email sent to one or more participants, with a specific time and link to click to get to the webinar. As is the case with podcasts, the webinar can be conducted via the computer's speakers and microphone, but the sound exchange is more clear and private when the caller has earphones or earbuds and uses a more professional microphone. The moderator or webinar leader can see who has logged on to the webinar site and can test the connections.

In a typical webinar, the moderator controls who can talk—the same as in a call-in show on BlogTalk Radio. But unlike BlogTalk Radio and Talkshoe, where the Web page is secondary and the talk is primary, the Web page in the case of the webinar is just as important as the talk. In a full multimedia webinar, the moderator will in effect conduct a tour of the Web page, play videos, show graphics and demonstrate programs. The participants will see all of this on their computer screens, will hear the moderator describe what is happening in the videos and other multimedia, and will be able to ask and answer questions. Text chat boxes are usually available, in case the audio fails or if the moderator or participants want to communicate something more easily written than spoken, such as a URL. If the moderator and user have webcams, the webinar can be video, but this is not essential to the webinar, unless some visual characteristic such as what the webinar participants are wearing is germane to the subject of the webinar.

Podcasts, as indicated above, can have video with sound rather than sound only. Usage varies as to what they are then called—vidcasts or just podcasts. The "podcast" appellation probably makes more sense, since the "pod" is neither intrinsically audio or video but derives from iPod. The most logical designations would therefore seem to be that podcasts can be either vidcasts or audiocasts, but terminology that catches on may not necessarily be the most precisely logical. Vidcasts or podcasts with video are stored and disseminated on audio podcast hosts, but they are also hosted by video-only sites such as Blip.tv, which, in the same way as podcast hosts such as Mevio and Libsyn, can easily route the vidcast to iTunes (which offers free vidcasts in the same way as podcasts). YouTube can be considered a vidcast host.

Webinars, whether audio or video, can be conducted for business, education or fun. If the user's computer has a big enough memory, email and other regular functions of the computer can be accessed during the webinar. But the power of user's and moderator's laptops or desktop computers is the weak link of webinars. In the dozens of webinars I have attended (the majority of which have been on Second Life—see the previous chapter), there has rarely been a time in which one or more of the participants has not gone silent and needed to log back on to resume participation. Webinar software also limits the number of participants.

Webinars and their educational uses can be seen as one of the loftier applications of new new media. Of course, a webinar can be conducted on any topic—including a planned criminal activity. In the next chapter, we turn to "The Dark Side of New New Media."

The Dark Side of New New Media

I HAVE FOR DECADES BEEN DELIVERING A LECTURE TO MY CLASSES, and at conferences and symposia, titled "Guns, Knives, and Pillows." The lecture seeks to answer the question of whether some technologies are inherently good and bad in their use and impact on people.

I start with guns—they kill and wound people and are implements of crime. Indeed, they help make some violent crimes possible. So the gun is bad, right? It is a weapon, which we would be better off without. But what if someone uses a gun as a weapon to stop or prevent a crime? Or not as a weapon against humans at all but as a way of getting food? Or as a technology of sport? Or, again as a weapon, but to defend our nation against violent attack? These cases make it clear that, although we might argue that the world as a whole would be better off without guns, we cannot consider them only or exclusively devices of evil.

OK, then, what about the other side—can we think of a technology that is consistently, solely good? Is there a device with no ill effects? How about a pillow? It is soft, comfortable and helps us sleep. So far, so good. But a pillow can also be used to murder someone via suffocation. This means that the pillow can be used to accomplish something that is not so good. Just as the gun cannot be considered solely a "bad" technology, neither can the pillow be considered solely good. Guns and pillows are actually a lot alike, in that they can each be used for good or bad.

Perhaps the problem is that we are looking at weak examples. How about stronger, more powerful technologies? Nuclear weapons, atomic power, started off with a pretty bad reputation—atom bombs and nuclear weapons. Even that, however, had a morally ambiguous component; historians are still arguing about whether President Harry Truman was right to drop the atom bomb, twice, on Japan. On the one hand, it soon brought the world, in the Cold War that followed, to the brink of atomic destruction. And it killed many innocent civilians in Japan. On the other hand, the Japanese government was insisting on continuing the war, which would have meant the death of some number of American soldiers, had the bomb not been dropped. And Japan did attack the United States to start the war in the first place, not vice versa. Further, in addition to those ethical controversies, nuclear energy has been put to indisputably good use as a source of energy to generate electrical power and in medicine via radiation therapy. Nuclear energy thus turns out to be like guns and pillows, too, with both good and bad results for humanity.

Can we think about any stronger example of a good technology? How about medicine, which cures or reduces the damage of illness? Unfortunately, that same technology can and has been turned into a weapon arguably as dangerous as nuclear weapons—germ warfare. This was used in World War I and by Saddam Hussein against Iran and his people in Iraq, but even Adolf Hitler, fearing it could be used against German troops, refrained from using it in World War II. So medical technology ends up in the same category as guns, pillows and nuclear energy: All can be used for good and bad purposes.

All technologies indeed are best described, in their capacity for good or bad, as knives. A knife can be used to cut food, which is good, and to stab an innocent person, which is bad. The determining factor in whether the knife—or whatever the technology—is used for good or bad turns out not to be the technology but the human being or group of humans using the technology.

In this chapter, we look at how the knives of new new media, which up until this point we have examined mostly with an eye to their advantages, can be used in the wrong hands for bad. Unfortunately but not surprisingly, the evidence is that they can. We thus consider how the very advantages of new new media, when understood by people with evil intentions, can be used to hurt us.

Pre-New New Media Abuses: Bullying, Flaming, and Trolling

Some misuses and abuses of Web life predate new new media and were already part of the older new media constellation from which new new media arose.

Email, as is the case with any kind of communication, can be used to harass and cyberbully. Lori Drew used MySpace's message system to send her deceptive "the world would be better off without you" note but it just as easily could have been sent via email. And, indeed, email is used to convey all manner of spam and scams, ranging from easy ways to increase your sexual assets; to offers to entrust millions of dollars in your safekeeping by some desperate widow on the other side of the world, in order to get your bank account information; to messages urging you to immediately log on to your PayPal account, designed to get you to unknowingly give up your password to someone who would clean out your account. Confidence games of course predate the Internet. There were probably Cro-Magnons who charmed the prehistorically naïve out of their best shells and furs. But the absence of a face and voice in email has long made it especially well suited for all kinds of swindles.

There was probably bullying going on in Cro-Magnon circles as well—it certainly has long been a distressing feature of our schoolyards. Faceless, voiceless names on the Web have made bullying easier to mete out, too.

But bullying in a schoolyard or any physical place is usually more dangerous than cyberbullying, since physical intimidation is involved and can escalate into a "beat down." And, as we saw in Chapter 3, YouTube, unfortunately, has given physical bullies an additional inducement, by providing a worldwide audience for videos uploaded of the beatings. Victoria Lindsay, a 16-year-old girl in Lakeland, Florida, was hospitalized in March 2008 after receiving a severe beating from six teenage girls, who videotaped it and told police they were responding to "trash" that the victim had posted about them on MySpace. "Police say the teens planned to post the video on YouTube," Rich Phillips reported on CNN.com (2008). He noted that "the idea of girls administering a vicious beating so they can post the video online may seem shocking, but it's becoming an increasingly common scenario, according to experts and news reports." The suspects were offered plea bargains in November 2008 (Geary, 2008).

The new new medium of YouTube thus can act as an accelerant for the ancient abuse of bullying. The one drawback of bullying in person—disadvantage for the bullies, benefit for potential and actual victims and the world at large—is that the bullies can usually be clearly identified. This, obviously, does not stop bullies who want to see themselves on YouTube, but it does help police catch them (and, as Manjoo, 2008, suggests, potential bullies could even be deterred by the thought that the police might see them on a YouTube video made by some onlooker—see Chapter 3 for more on such possible beneficial effects of YouTube). Physical bullying, cyberbullying, flaming and all abuses that not only end up online as a YouTube video but are perpetrated online in the first place flourish in anonymity or under cover of false names.

Flaming goes back to the very origin of online communication in the 1980s; I noticed it in the first online class I taught for the Western Behavioral Sciences Institute in September 2004. The students were CEOs in business and public service, along with several Army generals, and we all used Kaypro II CP/M computers and 300 to 1200 bps modems to communicate. In this case, people did use their real names—we had met several months earlier in an in-person seminar, and the lack of pseudonymic cover likely restrained the flaming. But it was there, nonetheless, in comments entered late at night, when one student would be far harsher in criticism of another student than these business and public service executives had ever been as in-person students years earlier, or as business executives at the time of the online course. I realized back then that the synapse between anger and the expression of it was a lot shorter and quicker when it went to fingers over a keyboard than to tongues in in-person conversation (see Levinson, 1997, for more).

The synapse only gets shorter and more grievous when real names and identities are unknown. Here is a user's assessment of the flaming she witnessed of another user on a popular conspiracy theory site in November 2008: "You hide your mediocrity and spew your rancor from behind your anonymity and attack/

accuse/berate someone who could surely tear your ass up if he were similarly cloaked." This analysis of flaming accords double importance to the incendiary nature of anonymity: It emboldens the flamers and restrains the victim (who is not "similarly cloaked") from responding in kind. And this makes perfect, unfortunate sense. Although the flamers and targets are similarly out of any in-person, physical range, and the flamers are encouraged by that distance to give vent to their anger or grievance, the target, using his or her real name, takes heightened care in commenting and responding, because those comments will leave a record directly traceable to the real-life commenter.

Trolling, which also goes back to the origins of online communication in the 1980s, is usually anonymous for much the same reason. But users can troll under their real names as well, as when a political troller writes comments for the purpose of inflaming and angering those with different or opposite political opinions. In comments on my numerous blogs in support of Barack Obama in the 2008 presidential campaign, I encountered many Republican or conservative trollers who were proud to use their real names.

But what constitutes a comment made by a troll versus a comment made by someone with a genuinely different opinion, political or otherwise? Sometimes it is difficult to tell the difference, but the defining characteristic of a troll's comment is that it is intended to evoke an angry reaction, not to promote dialogue. "Obama will work with those who share his Islamic terrorist religion to destroy the United States" is what a troll's comment looks like. (Mattathias Schwartz notes in "The Trolls Among Us," 2008, that a troll has long been defined as "someone who intentionally disrupts online communities.") In contrast, "Obama's insistence that the surge in Iraq did not work makes him utterly unsuitable to be president" could well be an example of an attempt to make a point in a dialogue.

Genuine attempts at dialogue invite rational response—or a reply that employs some kind of logic or offers evidence in support of its view—and suggests a response to inauthentic trolling. "Do not feed the troll" is the advice offered by many an online discussant in an attempt to silence or mute a disruptive commenter. Since the goal of the troller is to disrupt an online conversation by directing attention away from the conversation and toward the troll, starving the troll for attention makes sense.

Ironically, flaming can arise from a genuine attempt at dialogue, when one or more people in the conversation lose their temper. In contrast, trolling is a deliberate attempt to bury or disrupt a dialog. Trollers may be more incorrigible than flamers, who I have seen apologize and sometimes leave an online forum completely after regretting their initiation and pursuit of a flame.

Online Gossiping and Cyberbullying

Online gossiping also has roots in earlier digital and offline media but brings us more fully into the realm of social new new media. Cyberbullying, which usually entails a group of online users "ganging up" on another user and talking "trash" or otherwise ridiculing and embarrassing the target, feeds on online gossip and can be fanned by flaming. (The Megan Meier case, which we considered in Chapter 6 about MySpace, is not really an example of cyberbullying, even though it was extensively reported as cyberbullying in the media, which is why I have used the term in connection with that case in this book and online. But it is, rather, an example of cyberstalking—by an adult of a teenager. See "Cyberstalking" below.)

Online gossiping has colorful roots in newspapers, which reach back at least as far as Walter Winchell in the 1920s. As in all things new new media, the difference between Walter Winchell's columns in the New York Daily Graphic (and later in the New York Mirror) and online gossip leading to cyberbullying is that Winchell, Ed Sullivan and Louella Parsons dished gossip about celebrities, whereas online gossip is often about the kid sitting next to you in class. JuicyCampus.com, which began in August 2007, brags that its "posts are totally, 100% anonymous" and inveighs its users to "give us the juice"—that is, juicy tidbits about people on campus, which may or may not be true. For example, when I logged on to the site on December 22, 2008, I found this on the front page about a student at a major university: "really loose girl." Searching on another university, I found this bit of gossip from a few days earlier: "What do you think about this girl? I heard she has a tattoo of a pussy cat right below her panty line." Forty-three percent of the seven people who voted on this entry agreed that it was true. Another entry said someone was "ugly"— 100 percent of the two people who voted on this agreed.

Online gossiping hardens into cyberbullying when the nasty messages are directed at the target, so the target sees them, and the people sending the messages work intentionally or unintentionally not as disparate individuals but as a group. I-Safe (2009), reported for the 2003–2004 school year that "42% of kids have been bullied while online," a figure that held constant through 2007–2008, with the National Crime Prevention Center indicating that "40% of all teenagers with Internet access have reported being bullied online" during that year (Cyberbully Alert, 2008). Since MySpace did not go online until August 2003, and Facebook not until February 2004, the stability of the 40 percent number between 2003–04 and 2007–08 suggests that MySpace and Facebook inherited cyberbullying from earlier social media such as instant messaging and chat rooms. Indeed, I-Safe indicated with its 2004 survey that "savvy students are using Instant Messaging, e-mails, chat rooms and websites they create to humiliate a peer." And Cyberbully Alert in 2008 included MySpace: "Chat rooms, MySpace, email, instant messaging and other online tools have all helped create the cyber bullying epidemic." The remedies advised by I-Safe are the same as those for traditional schoolyard bullying: A victim should let school officials and/or parents or a trusted adult know about the bullying and contact the police if physical harm is threatened—with the additional advice especially appropriate to targets of cyberbullying to block the bullies' accounts and keep copies of all harassing messages.

In terms of a ranking of possible new new media abuses, one of the goals of responding to cyberbullying is to stop it before it escalates into cyberstalking, which can take the abuse out of the virtual schoolyard, into someplace much more dangerous. Kathy Sierra received harassing comments on her Creating Passionate Users blog, initially ranging from "banal putdowns to crude sexual garbage," which then turned violent, with posts such as "…i hope someone slits your throat…" (Walsh, 2007). Sierra stopped writing her blog, "cancelled all speaking engagements" and added that "I am afraid to leave my yard" (BBC, 2007). Creative Passionate Users continues as a comment-only public record of Sierra's earlier blogging (Sierra, 2007). Her case serves as a disquieting example not only of the dregs of bullying humanity but that cyberbullying can target adults and professionals and veer into a kind of cyberstalking that makes the victim afraid to leave her own yard.

Cyberstalking

If cyberbullying is usually a group activity, cyberstalking is usually solitary, just as is stalking by a psycho or some other kind of obsessed or maladjusted individual in the real world. NetLingo (2009) says cyberstalking "refers to contacting a person online persistently, especially out of obsession or derangement." And just as stalking in the real world can be much more dangerous than traditional schoolyard bullying, so can cyberstalking have much worse impact than cyberbullying. Lori Drew in effect stalked Megan Meier—first with feigned affection, then a vicious comment—and Megan Meier took her own life (see Chapter 6, MySpace).

More common examples of cyberstalking entail a stalker with real, unrequited affection or obsession for the target. A U.S. Bureau of Justice Statistics advisory in 2009 reported that "3.4 million persons identified themselves as victims of stalking during a 12-month period in 2005 and 2006." Further, "more than one in four stalking victims reported that some form of cyberstalking was used, such as email (83 percent of all cyberstalking victims) or instant messaging (35 percent)." MySpace and Facebook were still but a year or two old when those people fell prey to cyberstalking. As with cyberbullying, cyberstalking has migrated from IM'ing and chat rooms to the specific, highly publicized venues of social media.

"Enhancing Child Safety & Online Technologies: Final Report" (Internet Safety Technical Task Force. 2008)—a task force of which Facebook, MySpace, Linden Labs (Second Life), Google, Yahoo and 25 other major cyber players were members—highlights the conduciveness of social media for cyberstalking: "Contrary to popular assumptions, posting personally identifying information does not appear to increase risk in and of itself. Rather, risk is associated with interactive behavior" (p. 20). The recourse for targets of cyberstalking is the same as for victims of cyberbullying: Let responsible, trusted people know, including police if any physical threats are made.

Google Earth unfortunately can provide an ideal tool for those who want to take their cyberstalking to the real world. Many an address typed into the system yields a photograph literally of a house on a street, replete with yard signs and cars parked in the driveway. Fortunately, for some people, not every address has a corresponding photograph on Google maps, but those that do can have the whole world see when their lawn is not mowed.

And Google maps can also be used by terrorists...

Twittering and Terrorism

Let's begin by looking at how new new media can assist not terrorists but the combating of terrorists and the reporting of terrorism and its aftermaths in the real world.

New new media helped, and even played a crucial role, in the initial reporting of the Mumbai massacre on November 26, 2008. Adrian Finnigan on CNN International early the next day said how he had heard on his Facebook account from a friend in Mumbai, with word that he was OK and details on what he was seeing. James Winston, a Facebook Friend (see Chapter 7), IM'd me on November 28, 2008, that his "best friend just moved to Mumbai a couple of weeks ago. He lives about two miles from the Taj Hotel. Facebook let me know he was safe." Meanwhile, Finnigan also reported that Twitter was buzzing with brief messages from people near the hotels that were under attack in Mumbai.

John Ribeiro (2008) provided similar news that the "Micro-blogging site Twitter is also being used to pass on information, or to just express feelings about the terrorist attack, and sometimes about the inadequate coverage of the crises by some Indian TV channels"—more evidence of new new media providing a dimension not available via old broadcast media, in this case, providing direct, personal information about a terrorist massacre. Just as students sent email from the Tiananmen Square massacre of 1989, letting the world and the mass media know what was happening, so Twitter and Facebook provided much needed windows onto what had happened in Mumbai.

At times during the three-day crisis, in fact, the old media of television provided no coverage at all. On the final night of November 28, 2008, as the Taj Mahal Hotel still burned and Indian commandos were readying their final assault, MSNBC ran canned programming—its "Doc Bloc" with unrelated footage several years old—and Fox interspersed its coverage of Mumbai with reruns of "The O'Reilly Factor" and Greta Van Susteren's "On the Record." Only CNN provided live, continuing coverage (see my "MSNBC Runs Canned 'Doc Bloc,'" November 28, 2008, for further details; see also the discussion of the "Stop the Doc Bloc" Facebook group in Chapter 7.) Fortunately, people interested in learning what was happening in Mumbai could consult Twitter, where updates were posted more often than once a minute from onlookers in Mumbai.

These are some of the tweets I noticed, just seconds apart, in the early morning, New York time, of November 28, 2008: "Indian officials are big on bulllshit, weak on results"..."What guns are our commandos using???"..."100 trapped at

Trident"…"this whole thing stinks, our govt have left us as sitting ducks, throw UPA [political party in power in India] out"…"Japan had terrorist strike in past, China is blessed to have neighbors like us, we are not that fortunate." Twitter advised that 216 new tweets on this subject had arrived in the 30 seconds it took me to capture the above tweets. Of course, there is no guarantee that those microblogs all came from Mumbai—though Twitter would have a record of the IP addresses.

But no system is perfect. As Stephanie Busari pointed out on CNN.com/asia (2008), "Someone tweets a news headline, their friends see it and retweet, prompting an endless circle of recycled information" on Twitter.

And Twitter, to return to the evil use of new new media that is the subject of this chapter, can also be an effective tool for terrorists. Busari notes that "it was suggested via Twitter that terrorists were using the medium to gain information about what Indian security forces were doing." And this does not address the possibility, even likelihood, that Twitter and other social new new media could have been used by the terrorists in the planning and coordination of their attacks.

Indeed, a U.S. Army report of October 16, 2008, expresses the concern that Twitter "could theoretically be combined with targeting" by terrorists (Musil, 2008). The Army report does not point out, however, that Twitter offers no digital communication that could not already be accomplished by group email, IMs and chatrooms. But Twitter and its facility for rapidly creating de facto groups of "Followers" undeniably makes the mobilization and deployment of any group easier—including groups of terrorists. The upside for civilization is not only that law enforcement and security can similarly twitter, but, in the event that Twitter is used by terrorists or criminals, Twitter would have a record of those communications, for subsequent pursuit and conviction of the terrorists.

New new media thus can be employed for abusive social activities ranging from virtual school bullying to worldwide terrorism. We look next at how new new media can abet a more conventional kind of crime.

The Craigslist Bank Heist

Almost sounds like the name of a movie, doesn't it? But it's real, and, even if Craig's didn't quite rob the bank, it was used to hire "a dozen unsuspecting decoys" (see King5.com, 2008) to help the real bank robber get away in a heist that took place on September 30, 2008, at a Bank of America branch in Monroe, Washington.

Now, my wife and I frequently use Craigslist to do good things. Just last week, we used it to purchase a nice La-Z-Boy loveseat for $75. But like the knives of all media, the no-cost ads sell just about anything people want to buy and sell, including not only loveseats but, until recently, prostitutes (see Lambert, 2007; Abelson, 2009) and, in the case of the Bank of America in Monroe, accomplices in a robbery.

The robber's plan was quite ingenious. Have a dozen people, dressed just like you, standing in front of the bank. This would dilute the value of what eyewitnesses told the police. "I came across the ad that was for a prevailing wage job for $28.50 an hour," one of the decoys explained to King5.com. He was instructed to wear a "yellow vest, safety goggles, a respirator mask…and, if possible, a blue shirt"—the same outfit as the robber, who made good his escape through a nearby creek.

He was, however, arrested a few weeks later—DNA did him in (see Cheng, 2008, for details). I guess this shows that biological code is still more powerful than digital code. Or, as my character, NYPD forensic detective Dr. Phil D'Amato says in my 1999 science fiction novel, "The Silk Code," "DNA is the ultimate dossier" (The New York Times liked this line so much, it was quoted in Gerald Jonas's review, 1999).

It's fun to take a break in this dark chapter with such an amusing, true story. But the unyielding, grim reality is that the criminal use of new new media can facilitate death and destruction. The accused "Craigslist Killer" Philip Markoff, arrested in April 2009 on charges of murdering a masseuse obtained through Craigslist, brings home the perilous, frightening side of new new media. Yet, as Leslie Harris (2009) notes, "What if the criminal in question had lured his victims using newspaper classifieds? Would we be calling this the *Boston Globe* Killer?" Her apt point is that killers trolling the media for victims are hardly an invention or unique consequence of new social media. Still, their abuses, whether unique or in common with older media, must be studied, understood and protected against, where possible.

Spam

We conclude our tour of the dark side of new new media with the least destructive but most prevalent despoilers of online systems: conveyors of spam. In its most common form—comments about gold jewelry or something else utterly irrelevant to the subject of the blog post—spam is like an online mosquito bite, digital graffiti, which distracts from the reading of the blog and may annoy the reader but otherwise does no harm.

Indeed, the main ill effect of spam is the extra work it imposes on bloggers and Web administrators who want to eliminate it and the impediment protective measures installed by bloggers can have upon nonspamming commenters. As we saw in Chapter 2, CAPTCHAs are a common defense against spammers, but these make legitimate commenters go through an additional hoop to enter their comments. A blogger interested in a no-holds-barred political discussion might choose to leave a blog unmoderated, to encourage immediate entry of comments and rapid response, but this would also leave the blog open to spam having no connection to the blog.

MySpace, Facebook and all social media suffer from similar annoyances, in blogs and items posted on the systems or, in the case of MySpace, on the member's profile comment section. One vulnerability that spammers have on these systems, but not when they post spam on individual blogs not situated on some central social system, is that MySpace or Facebook can and do cancel the accounts of spammers. New accounts can be created easily enough, but the spammer is at least slowed down a little.

"Blog spam" is a phrase that applies to something a little different from the above. In general, "blog spam" is a derogatory assessment of the worth of a blog post, and it sometimes refers to a blog post whose only goal—as least as perceived by the person who calls it "blog spam"—is to lure readers for the purpose of earning Google AdSense revenue, or clicking on some other ad or link associated with the blog. Digg has yet an additional usage of the "blog spam" appellation, which refers to a news article that has taken a story from a previously posted article, with an eye toward drawing readers to the new post. This might also be called plagiarism, except the new post might even give credit to the earlier source of the story.

Stepping back a little and looking at new new media as part of the larger constellation of all human communication, we can see that spam is just the digital equivalent of noise, or the most common example of noise, that afflicts all media. In the case of older media such as newspapers, noise occurs every time the newspaper prints something that is false. Noise can occur when the ink smears or when we get distortion on our television screens. Similar kinds of noise can occur with false information on blogs and Wikipedia, or when any online system or laptop encounters technical difficulties. But the power that new new media gives all consumers to become producers creates a new kind of noise—a noise deliberately created and posted by a user. In the old media world, and indeed in the physical world as well, noise has long been recognized as never totally reducible or capable of elimination. You introduce a new system for improving storage and transmission of music—MP3s—and this creates new intellectual property problems. Every remedy for one kind of noise opens up the system for a new kind of noise. As a form of new new media noise, spam is likely also impossible to eliminate entirely, at least not without incurring a new form of new new media noise. Fortunately, the price of spam on blogs is usually not too high to pay.

Or, put otherwise, one form of noise that new new media are especially not likely to eliminate, or even effectively control, is the digital trespass of spam—because, to truly and effectively eliminate spam, the new new medium would have to be so heavily controlled as to no longer be a new new medium. (See also Chapter 4, Wikipedia, for intrinsic new new media capabilities of identifying and removing noise.)

Old Media Overreaction to New New Abuses: The Library vs. the Blogger

We have been tracing throughout this book the antagonism (as well as the mutual dependence) of various old media to new new media—antagonism that looks at new new media as unworthy competition and alternatives to old media. Critiques of bloggers by press and broadcast media—not the content of given blogs, which is fair game, but the process of blogging itself—is the seminal example. Denunciations of "bloggers in pajamas" discussed in Chapter 2 are indicative of the ridicule and scapegoating, going beyond rational criticism, that bloggers have been subjected to. New new media have not been above wielding similar attacks on themselves, as we saw in Chapter 7, when Facebook banned photos of women nursing their babies.

But the underlying tension is greatest between old and new new media, and it comes to the surface whenever any real wrongdoing on or by new new media is involved. Cyberbullying and cyberstalking are justifiably big stories in all news media—old, new, and new new—because they can lead to real life-and-death situations, and therefore need to be known by everyone. But the tension also erupts when there is no real wrongdoing in the new new media, only the incorrect perception of it.

Twanna A. Hines writes in "I'm a Writer, Not a Child Pornographer" (2008) that she showed up for "a hard day's work" with her laptop at the Mid-Manhattan branch of the New York Public Library, where she liked to do her writing, to find that access to her blog had been banned. The reason? She writes in her blog about "dating, sex and relationships…about men who wear thongs, technology and sex." The library advisory indicated that sites that depict obscenity, child abuse and materials "harmful to minors" could be blocked.

None of these were depicted on Hines's site, and, indeed, after someone contacted the library and complained that access to her site was blocked, the library removed the block. But what does the fact that her site had been blocked at all say about the role of libraries in our new new media world?

A frequent critique of personal computers, going back to the 1980s (see Levinson, 1997), is that people who spend time on them are cutting themselves off from "real," i.e., in-person, interactions with other human beings. This argument might claim today, for example, that shopping in a Barnes and Noble would be better or healthier than buying books on Amazon, because in a Barnes and Noble you deal with real people not pixels. MySpace and Facebook would be seen as exacerbating this perceived problem, by offering digital social alternatives for a variety of in-person interactions. (And, indeed, as we saw in Chapter 3 in the Vatican's statement accompanying the Pope's new YouTube channel, the Vatican has expressed this concern about social media.)

Looking at the case of Hines in this context of virtual vs. in-person interactions, we can see that she sought to be out among real people, in a public library, when she was practicing her new new media craft of blogging. And this made the New York Public Library uncomfortable, because of the content of her blog. To be clear, she was not using a library computer, just its Wi-Fi Internet connection. If we agreed with the library that the materials on Hines's blog were not suitable for children, would not a better method of protecting them from the site, but not blocking out everyone else, including adults and the author herself, have been to require some special code to access sites like that, given only to people showing proof of age?

One hopes that these will be the kinds of solutions that libraries use in the future. But in the present age of misunderstanding and suspicion of new new media, including not only by old media but their repositories in venerable institutions of free societies such as libraries, the simple banning or blocking of the new new media access is, unfortunately, the easy remedy.

For her part, Twanna Hines says she continues to love the New York Public Library and quotes T. S. Eliot that "the very existence of libraries affords the best evidence that we may yet have hope for the future of man." That future will be a little better assured when libraries show a little better comprehension of media that are increasingly rivaling and supplanting the books on their shelves as the library's intellectual stock and trade.

As with going out to the movies rather than watching television, or dining in a restaurant rather than at home, the eventual future of libraries will reside in providing places that offer social advantages not found at home, along with all the informative avenues available at home, to lure people out of their homes with their laptops and iPhones.

In the next chapter, we see how Barack Obama's campaign for president in 2007 and 2008 combined both the best of new new media and their inextricable interaction with the offline world.

New New Media and the Election of 2008

Eric SCHMIDT, CHAIRMAN AND CEO OF GOOGLE, IMMEDIATELY agreed with Arianna Huffington—founder and continuing chief of The Huffington Post—when she said Barack Obama won the presidency because of the Internet. Schmidt was a guest on "The Rachel Maddow Show" on MSNBC on November 17, 2008, 13 days after the election, where Huffington was filling in for Maddow.

The perspective of "New New Media" is, of course, that Huffington and Schmidt are completely right. But more than the general Internet, the new new media that have so recently become the major players of the Internet were essential to Obama's successful presidential campaign and continue to play a central role in his relationship as president to the American people—and, indeed, the people of the world.

Blogging, the oldest of the new new media, was well established in 2004. But YouTube, Digg, Facebook and Twitter did not even exist then. Nor did Barack Obama's campaign Web site, which played a crucial role in his election by empowering its members, as did no other prior political Web sites.

I registered at mybarackobama.com early in 2008. I occasionally posted a blog on that site and from time to time logged on to keep apprised of various developments in the campaign. In the two days prior to Election Day on November 4, 2008, and Election Day itself, my wife and I logged on to do something else.

The site provided names and phone numbers of Obama supporters. You could locate supporters in many states via a map on the site. We chose Pennsylvania, since the McCain campaign had been saying it was its "last stand"—i.e., a state crucial to any chance of a McCain victory.

It took about an hour for each of us to call about 50 different Obama supporters. We encountered some wrong numbers and left voicemail for many people who were not at home. But we managed to speak to dozens of supporters, from Philadelphia to the other side of the state—all from the convenience of our living room, a little north of New York City. After each phone call, we filled out a brief form on the site, where we indicated if we had made contact and what was the result—was the supporter still planning on voting for Obama, did he or she know where the polling place was located, etc.

Keith Goodman of the Obama campaign sent out the following email on November 6, 2008, to everyone who had made calls for Obama: "I wanted to thank you for helping us make an astounding 1,053,791 calls on Election Day. I know it wasn't easy, and many of you kept calling long after you were tired and your voice had grown hoarse, but your calls to get our supporters out to the polls helped tip the scales in key battleground states like Florida and Ohio. Together we did it!"

Through the combination of the new medium of the Web and the old medium of the telephone, mybarackobama.com had created a truly new new medium in which the reader became even more than a writer. In making those calls two days prior to and on the day of the election, I had been transformed from an occasional reader and writer into an active campaign worker.

Obama "Married the Internet to Community Organizing"

"He married the Internet to community organizing," David Gergen observed on CNN, close to 7 p.m. Eastern Time on the evening of November 4, 2008, a few minutes before the election returns began coming in on television. Gergen was talking about Barack Obama and his campaign, in comparison to Howard Dean's unsuccessful 2004 campaign for the Democratic nomination, which was the first to harness the Internet.

Howard Dean, who went on after his loss in the 2004 Democratic primary to head the Democratic National Committee, was responsible for Obama's triumphant "50 state" strategy in 2008—campaigning aggressively in every state of the nation, not conceding a single state to the opposition. And, indeed, Obama's win in Ohio—a "red state" won by George W. Bush in 2004—was the first clear sign on the evening of November 4, 2008, that Obama would be the new president.

New New Media VP Announcement Misstep

Before we go too far down the misty road of hindsight that Obama did everything right, at least regarding new new media in the 2008 campaign, we need to note that his campaign was not infallible in its use of new new media. The single biggest misstep was likely its announcement in July 2008 that it intended to let the world know about Obama's choice of VP running mate, not only by email, but only via email to people on Obama's mailing list, to the explicit initial exclusion of media such as television, radio and newspapers—or the old media press.

This announcement was ill-advised for at least two reasons. First, there were, obviously, many members of the traditional press on this email list, and they could easily have transmitted Obama's choice to their old media channels instantly. Second, the telegraphing of anything to be done on new new media, any new new media strategy, runs contrary to the viral new new media principle of making the event seem as if it happened spontaneously, not via high-level, top-down strategy.

I posted a blog with these thoughts on the Daily Kos (Levinson, "Announcing Obama's Choice Through Email Not Good Idea," 2008). The responses ranged from annoyance to outright anger—at me, not the campaign—that I failed to understand that the Obama campaign was rewarding the segment of the population that was most responsible, at least in their view, for getting Obama the nomination: the new new media or Web 2.0 Internet generation.

As it was, word of Obama's choice of Joe Biden first broke on the old medium of CNN. But few if any devotees of Obama and new new media obviously held that against him on Election Day, when he won by the most impressive margin in two decades.

Inauguration and After on the Internet

CNN reported a four-fold increase in the number of live-streamed videos viewed on Barack Obama's January 20, 2009, Inauguration Day in comparison to Election Day November 4, 2008, viewing—some 21.3 million in a nine-hour period through mid-afternoon on Inauguration Day versus 5.3 million all day on Election Day. The New York Times also reported that "Internet traffic in the United States hit a record peak at the start of President Obama's speech as people watched, read about and commented on the inauguration, according to Bill Woodcock, the research director at the Packet Clearing House, a nonprofit organization that analyzes online traffic" (Vance, 2009, which also provides details on CNN video viewing; Internet traffic and viewing of online videos exceeded those numbers for the Michael Jackson memorial in July 2009, see Hibberd, 2009).

Unsurprisingly, a lot of this traffic and viewing got stalled, as the Web and its carriers struggled to meet the demand. But such problems are healthy growing pains and the best stimulus for improving the hardware infrastructure on which all new new media depend (see the next chapter).

Obama's new administration took control of whitehouse.gov—the official president's Web site—right after the noon hour of the Inauguration. The change not only in president but approach is a textbook example of the difference between new and new new media. Under the George W. Bush administration, the site provided information— in the words of one obsever, mainly "links to press releases, speeches, and propaganda documents" (Manjoo, 2009). The new rendition of the site will no doubt be no less propagandistic but much more interactive. Its first blog post, on January 20, 2009, proclaimed that "One significant addition to whitehouse.gov reflects a campaign promise from the president: we will publish all nonemergency legislation to the website for five days, and allow the public to review and comment before the President signs it."

Unstated and unknown was to what degree the president would be apprised of such comments and, if apprised, how seriously he would take them. At its best, such a system would allow the president to make more informed decisions. At its most propagandistic, such comments on whitehouse.gov would provide only the illusion of a president being so informed.

Regarding the propaganda of presenting a president as open to communication from the public, I'm reminded of the response my wife received when she mailed a letter to Richard Nixon in 1970, protesting the U.S. incursion into Cambodia. She received a response from the White House, warmly thanking her for her support.

At the very least, we can say that whitehouse.gov is providing a new avenue for communicating with the president and his staff, which will make the sending of the communication much easier. What impact it will have, and what the receiver will do with that communication, is yet to be seen.

There is also an argument that, in a democracy, elected officials should do what they think best—follow their intellects and their consciences—and let the people demonstrate their approval or not in the next election. ("A leader's relevant decision makers should be his heart and mind, not his political consultants and Gallup polls readouts," Messerli, 2006). In our day and age of constant consultation of polls, this ideal, to the extent that it was ever held, has been mostly abandoned. New new media may well have the effect, for better or worse, of pushing that principle ever further out of play.

The President and the BlackBerry

Not everyone in government is happy about new new media. The story broke 11 days after the election that prospects did not look good for Barack Obama to continue sending and receiving email once he got into the White House (Zeleny, 2008). The problem of hacking into the president's email was raised, as well as the Presidential Records Act, which requires all presidential communications to be eventually available for public review.

I blogged at the time that I thought depriving the president of email, especially in this day and age, was a bad idea (Levinson, "Keeping Obama with His Email," 2008).

The president and the BlackBerry turned out to be a story in four parts, with a happy ending.

1. Surely a system could be devised that would automatically record all email that the president sends and receives. Come to think of it, isn't that what happens on every Gmail or Yahoo mail account right now?

More important, should not a president be able to communicate in whatever way is most effective for him? A person in his position needs to devote maximum attention to thinking and communication, without having to be handicapped by using old-fashioned paper, telephone and other systems. Email has grown astronomically in the past decade for good reason: It has all the advantages of writing—permanence—and yet it is as immediate as speech. Plus, it is global and easily searchable. (See Levinson, 1997, for more on the evolution and advantages of email.)

And then there is the question of mindset: Should not a president be able, if at all possible, to continue to use a communications system with which he is already very comfortable and accustomed to?

This raises an issue fundamental to the evolution and adoption of all media. As we begin and continue to employ any new—or new new—medium, we come to rely upon it as we would our eyes, ears, mouths and fingers. As Marshall McLuhan (1964) famously put it, media act as our "extensions"—as surrogates for the communicating parts of our bodies and brains.

Taking email away from anyone so accustomed to using it would thus be the equivalent of a psychological or communicative amputation. The president should be the last person we would want to undergo such draconian and counterproductive treatment.

2. Barack Obama himself offered a very new new media savvy argument in favor of keeping his BlackBerry—short for unfiltered email contact with the world—in an interview as president-elect with Barbara Walters on November 26, 2008. "I'm negotiating to figure out how can I get information from outside of the 10 or 12 people who surround my office in the White House," Obama told Walters. "Because one of the worst things I think that could happen to a president is losing touch with what people are going through day to day" (Obama, November 26, 2008). In a January 7, 2009, interview with John Harwood on CNBC-TV, Obama said the same thing, adding, in Charlton Heston-and-gun fashion, that "they would have to pry" the BlackBerry out of his hands. In other words, at the same time as the president-elect was assembling not just a team of rivals but a team of the best experts in foreign and domestic policy he could find, he was also fighting to keep his lines of communication open to the world at large of nonexperts—or open to the logic of blogging, Wikipedia, Twitter, and the revolution of nonexpert opinion—which is the democratizing hallmark of new new media ("every consumer a producer"), the logic that helped elect him, and the focus of this book.

Or, as Mike Allen, chief political correspondent for Politico.com told Norah O'Donnell on MSNBC on November 26, 2008, "people [read: appointed experts] are reluctant to tell the truth to their boss...let alone a President of the United States." President Obama will need new new media to get him beyond the informational bubble that contributed to the poor response of the Bush administration to Hurricane Katrina. Whether president of the United States, like Barack Obama, or town supervisor of Greenburgh, N.Y., like Paul Feiner—who, as we saw in Chapter 2, relies upon anonymous comments in his blog to keep informed—our leaders and representatives will find new new media connections to the people increasingly indispensable. Note that this is significantly different from following polls, on the one hand, and the advice of expert advisers, on the other. A BlackBerry connection to a given person not in the government could conceivably provide an insight, an off-the-radar idea, which could save the world.

3. Norah O'Donnell reported on MSNBC at 1:45 p.m., January 18, 2009, two days before Obama's inauguration, that the "lawyers" had informed Obama and his team that they would be able to keep their BlackBerrys but not their instant messaging. The lawyers thought that IM'ing could make "embarrassing" messages available to hackers. If the concern, however, is salty language, such as that spoken by White House Chief of Staff Rahm Emanuel, chances are it will become known to the public sooner or later (see rahmfacts.com for many examples).

4. And on January 21, 2009, at 11:50 a.m., Marc Ambinder reported in The Atlantic online that "Obama Will Get His BlackBerry," albeit with "a super-encryption package," but nonetheless for "routine and personal messages." An excellent example of human beings—in this case, the president—running our technologies, rather than letting concerns about their possible problems run us.

White House Moves from Web 2.0 "Dark Ages" to New New Media

Meanwhile, as President Obama successfully struggled against the forces of legal caution and inertia to keep his BlackBerry, his staff discovered upon moving into the White House that its telecom was stuck in a "technological dark ages" (Kornblut, 2009; Patterson, 2009), with no Facebook or Twitter, not even Gmail.

Law has always been among the slowest elements of society to embrace new media. Verbal contracts were considered more binding than written documents until the printing press standardized writing. Digital contracts have been a problem for decades, with questions arising over what constitutes a valid and binding signature if it is not produced by pen on paper (see Wright and Winn, 1998, for some early details).

But law sooner or later does catch up to technology. As of February 2009, new new media were breaking out all over, especially in our political sphere. Republicans twitter during meetings with President Obama (Goddard, 2009). Sens. John McCain (R-Ariz.), Claire McCaskill (D-Mo.) and Mark Warner (D-Va.) have Twitter accounts, and who knows how many more by the time you are reading this—likely just about everyone in the House and Senate by the end of 2009. "One Million Strong for Barack," the Facebook group that served Obama so well during the campaign, continues to grow—with more than 1,027,000 members in May 2009.

As the nation and the world combat the ongoing economic crisis that hit in the fall of 2008, new new media will become more appealing than ever, to everyone. Being free is never more appealing than when money is tight.

But there is one crucial aspect of new new media recalcitrant in its cost and unlikely to ever be free. It is, indeed, an aspect without which new new media would not be possible.

In our final chapter, we briefly look at the hardware via which new new media operate.

13 CHAPTER

Hardware

THE FOCUS OF THIS BOOK HAS BEEN ON THE SYSTEMS—OR software, to use that now almost old-fashioned term—that make new new media possible, or through which they work. Blogspot, Wikipedia, Digg, Facebook, MySpace, Twitter and the rest are all computer programs, which organize information, each in its distinct and complex way. The option to allow comments or not on a blog, the capacity to embed a YouTube video on a Web page, the ability of any reader of a Wikipedia entry to edit or write more or less in the entry, the "Friending" feature on Digg, the profile pages on MySpace and Facebook, the one-liners with and without links on Twitter, the avatar world of Second Life and the delivery of podcasts—all of these features of new new media are made possible by specific code and designs in the software or system.

Hardware, of course, is also essential, and it plays its crucial role at two points of the new new media process. First, the system or software has to live on some central computer. Since such hardware is invisible to the user, who sees and hears only the "interface"—or the blogging, Wikipedia or Facebook system—there is no need to address that hardware in this book. Interested readers can consult numerous sources—for example, Wikipedia servers (2009), Justin Smith (2008), Layton and Brothers (2007)—that examine the complex "servers" that make not only new new media but also old media and many other things, such as banking, run in our world today.

At the other end of the spectrum, however, we have the technologies that people use to read, write, see, hear and produce new new media—the devices, in other words, that we hold in our hands when we work and play with new new media. A desktop, laptop, or cellphone or cellphone-like device is engaged any time someone reads or writes a blog, views a video on YouTube or sends and receives a tweet.

All of those devices existed before the advent of new new media. But the portable devices—laptops and cellphones—play an especially important role in new new media (see Levinson, "Cellphone: The Story of the World's Most Mobile

Medium", 2004, for the evolution of mobile media up until that time). Whether you're messaging a friend on Facebook, looking something up or editing on Wikipedia, or commenting about an article on Digg, the capacity to do this at any time and from any place of your choosing is one of the cardinal features of new new media.

The introduction of the first iPhone in July 2007, when the engines of new new media were already well under way, captured and catapulted this marriage of mobility and user control. We could say that, with the iPhone, for the first time, we had a technology specifically designed to enable not just new media but new new media literally at the user's disposal, any place the user happened to be.

Twitter is, of course, intrinsically mobile—the capacity to tweet from cellphones and BlackBerrys is a defining characteristic of the system. Wikipedia started to "go mobile" on August 20, 2008—meaning a free "application" became available for iPhone, which enabled fast browsing online of Wikipedia (Pash, August 20, 2008). This was prelude to "Wikipedia Officially Launches Mobile Version" on December 15, 2008 (Pash), when Wikipedia put up a version of itself especially suited to iPhone and mobile access. Blogspot has offered "Blogger on the Go" since May 2005 and Google an "AdSense for Mobile Content" since September 2007. MySpace has had mobile applications since 2006, as has Facebook since 2007. YouTube was a highlighted application of the very first iPhone released in July 2007.

Mobile new new media applications and mobile devices spur each other in an obvious, powerful mutually catalytic relationship: The better the mobile application, the more incentive to have a cool mobile device, and the better the mobile device, the greater the incentive for new new media to develop cool new mobile applications. But one mobile device more than any other ignited and now typifies new new media in everyone's hands and pockets: the iPhone.

The Inevitability of iPhone and Mobile Media

I wrote in my doctoral dissertation way back in 1979—"Human Replay: A Theory of the Evolution of Media"—that "the wireless, portable evolution of media should continue to the point of providing any individual with access to all the information of the planet, from any place on the planet, indoors and outdoors, and, of course, even beyond the planet itself as communication extends into the solar system and cosmos beyond" (p. 275). And I added on the next page that this " 'systemless' system...will eventually give the individual the same unrestrained access to information on the global basis that the individual has always enjoyed to information in the immediate physical environment."

This inevitability of what in 2007 would be called the iPhone flowed from the "anthropotropic" theory of media evolution I devised, developed and named in "Human Replay" back in the late 1970s, and mentioned briefly in Chapter 2 of the present book. As in "anthro" meaning human and "tropic" meaning toward (like plants growing toward the sun, or being "heliotropic"), I discovered that as media evolve—as we invent successive media—they eventually become increasingly human in their performance. Initially still, black-and-white, silent photography changed to talking motion pictures with color, and still photographs that we could send and receive about as easily as we could speak on the phone. The original telephone itself was an anthropotropic update of the telegraph, which used Morse code, an abstraction of writing, which itself is an abstract—or unnatural representation—of speech. More details about this "anthropotropic" theory are in "The Soft Edge: A Natural History and Future of the Information Revolution" (Levinson, 1997).

The iPhone starts to satisfy the longstanding human need to have any and all information, anytime we may want it, wherever we and the information we seek may happen to be. Like all anthropotropic media, the iPhone makes real what we envision in our mind's eye—brings to the little screen in our hand the newspapers, video clips, Web pages, Friends on MySpace and Facebook, twitters and blogs that previously we only had been able to think about, to imagine, until we arrived home or in our office or another place that housed a computer. The Rolling Stones' "You Can't Always Get What You Want" may still and always be true for life in general, but the iPhone has made it much less so for information.

The Price of Mobility

But the iPhone costs money—and, at several hundred dollars per phone, is certainly not cheap. This has always been the drawback, the burden of electronic media—going back to radio and television—and the monetary tradeoff of electronic with print media. The music and talk we hear on radio, the programs we watch on network (noncable or DirecTV) television are free—unlike books and newspapers—but we are obliged to pay far more for the television receiver than for most books or any newspaper.

New new media continue this electronic tradition, but are losing a great piggybacking advantage of operating on equipment that consumers already owned and were using for older new media such as email. When someone uses a desktop to blog, access YouTube, Wikipedia, or Facebook, or send and receive tweets, all aspects of these new new media activities are free, including the hardware, if the user already owns the desktop. In contrast, the move to mobile applications on mobile media works against this no-cost and its advantages, if the mobile medium has to be purchased and if its use requires a monthly subscription.

Are iPhones, BlackBerrys and similar enlivened cellphone media on a collision course with what one observer aptly called "this freaky land of free...the Web" (Anderson, 2008)? Cellphone sales did drop more than 12 percent in the last quarter of 2008, but sales of "smartphones," including iPhones, were up by as much as 70 percent in North America (Reardon, 2009), which suggests that the appeal of new new media via mobile applications is so strong as to be counteracting the reduction of disposable income that the financial crisis of 2008–2009 has brought.

But the length and severity of the economic recession, as of this writing in May 2009, is far from clear. If it continues and worsens, we may see a decline in sales of new smartphones, a reliance on older mobile devices that people already own or are willing to buy secondhand, and a focus on mobile applications that work well with these older devices. Highly unlikely to change is the public's taste for the freedom iPhones, BlackBerrys and other smartphones give them from, on the one hand, conventional places of communication such as the home and the office, and, on the other hand, the many other places in our daily lives which, prior to cellphones and smartphones, were useless for communication.

The New New Media Exile of Useless Places

I was in an elevator yesterday afternoon. It almost got stuck. It stopped for a split second in between floors, shuddered and then resumed its upward journey.

But it got me to thinking about how mobile media have made every place more useful than it used to be. A stalled elevator, a car stuck in a traffic jam, a seat in a doctor's office when you're waiting endlessly for an appointment—a wireless device, whether cellphone, BlackBerry or iPhone, makes all of those formerly useless places useful.

The result is that we are enjoying increasing discretion and control over our lives and our activities. The investment of portable devices with new new media means that we have a vast array of options when we happen to be in a useless physical place—read or write a blog, promote it, look at a video on YouTube, read or write on Wikipedia, etc. (Second Life, because of the greater bandwidth it requires, has been the least successfully grafted into mobile media—see Talamasca, 2008).

Increasingly, we do nothing when we want to do nothing, not when circumstances dictate that we do nothing.

Smartphones in the Car, in the Park, and in Bed

When I wrote "Cellphone" (2004), I discussed and analyzed in detail the way that the mobile phone cut the umbilical cord of the landline phone in our homes and places of business and allowed us to roam in the outside world, on foot or in cars, and stay in touch, via voice or text, with anyone we pleased. The general principle was that the cellphone liberated us from the home or office, and the specific consequence I explored was how this freedom moved us outdoors.

The new new media available on smartphones are, of course, available outside of the home or office, but given the YouTube videos, podcasts, blogs, and MySpace and Facebook Friends we might wish to access, and the blogs and tweets we might wish to write, the bed has also become one of our prime new new media locations. And, indeed, the bed and the park are almost equidistant from the desk, as powerfully different from the desk, in different directions. Smartphones have made the circumstances in which we engage new new media more private (the bed) and more public (the park).

The car has been a popular place for use of electronic media outside of the home and the office since Transitone introduced the first car radio in 1929 (Levinson, 2004). But radio turns out to be a special case, at least for the driver, because it can be listened to while the listener is looking at and concentrating on something else. In contrast, watching a television show or a YouTube video on an iPhone while driving a car would be a quick way to end that ride in the worst possible way: Our eyes cannot be in two places, cannot look carefully at two or more things at the same time. Neither, for the same reasons, can a driver safely read a newspaper online or a blog or consult Wikipedia, let alone write and edit. For this reason, as we saw in Chapter 10 about podcasting, about the only new new medium that we can safely appreciate while behind the wheel of a car would be a podcast. Car passengers, on the other hand, can safely read, write, view or otherwise interact with all new new media via smartphones.

To what extent will this increasing availability to new new media outside of the home and office lead to their actual use in cars, beds, parks and the like? Reading books and newspapers on park benches is a time-honored tradition, which certainly suggests that reading, writing and viewing new new media in public has a bright future. Since none of the new new media, except recording a podcast, require talking, new new media on smartphones have an advantage over cellphones in not disturbing anyone in the vicinity (see Levinson, 2004, for cellphone etiquette). Internet cafes and wi-fi in Starbucks can be seen as the first step of new new media in public—a step in a short journey that will move from the laptops in Starbucks to smartphones anywhere and everywhere.

Batteries as the Weak Spot

The weak spot of all mobile electronic media, as far back as the transistor radio in the 1950s, is the battery. iPhones, for example, have batteries that last only 30 minutes and need recharging from an electrical outlet or desktop. Laptops have notoriously short battery charges, and cellphones are chronic in going silent due to an exhausted battery.

The solution resides in what I said about the enduring advantage of reading paper rather than screens in Chapter 2—paper requires only the light of the sun, or any artificial source in the vicinity, to be readable. Ultimately, smartphones and laptops—which are already in the process of converging with smartphones—will have "batteries" that can be recharged by sun or any ambient light. As is usually the case with new technologies that free us from less convenient earlier technologies, such "smart batteries" will likely cost a lot more than our current "dumb" ones. But once they become standard, the battery will no longer be the weak link of mobile media.

iPhones, BlackBerrys, Bluetooth and Brains

Media convergence—one or fewer media doing more and more, different things— has been recognized for decades as an important principle of media evolution (see Levinson, 1997). BlackBerrys, which began as mobile email devices, have had cellphone capabilities for several years and are offering increasing access to the new new media of the Web. iPhones from their beginning had both new new media and email capabilities. The two devices, along with other smartphones, will increasingly become the same.

The next step, already well under way for all mobile media, will be for new new media devices to become even smaller and lighter than they are now. Buckminster Fuller's (1938) "dymaxion principle," which holds that new technologies get ever smaller and more powerful—more from less, in terms of power (more) and size (less)—has never been as well borne out as with 21st century mobile media.

The adult human brain, after all, at just over a kilogram in mass, is the ultimate new new medium. Our brains read, write, view and hear—receive and produce all the content of new new media—not to mention think, feel, believe, dream, imagine and much more. And, as I indicated in my 2007 interview on The Alcove with Mark Molaro (where I first spoke publicly about "new new media"), that triumph of multitasking which is our brain is likely, at some point in the future, to be where at least some of us initiate via digital embeds in the brain what we produce for new new media. And it will also be the place where some of us directly receive the words and images and sounds of new new media, without that content first being processed by our eyes and ears. Bluetooth, hands-free technology, is but the first step in that direction.

Over on YouTube, where that interview now can be found, one commenter said, "I don't think people will be too accepting of implants...."

No problem, I replied. The essence of new new media is choice.

bibliography

Note: URLs listed in this Bibliography were confirmed as working as of February 2009.

Aasen, Adam (2009) "ABC's 'Lost' is Required Viewing for Students in UNF Course," Florida Times-Union, May 12.   http://www.jacksonville.com/lifestyles/ 2009-05-11/story/abcs_lost_is_required_viewing_for_students_in_unf_course

Abelson, Jenn (2009) "Craigslist Drops Erotic Services Ads," Boston Globe, May 14. http://www.boston.com/business/technology/articles/2009/05/14/craigslist_ drops_erotic_services_ads/

Ahmed, Mural (2008) "Apple Threatens to Shut Down iTunes Over Royalty Hike," (London) Times Online, Oct. 1.   http://technology.timesonline.co.uk/tol/news/ tech_and_web/article4859885.ece

Allen, Lily (2005) MySpace music page, Nov 7.   http://www.myspace.com/lilymusic

Allen, Mike (2008) Interviewed by Norah O'Donnell, MSNBC-TV, Nov. 26.

Alter, Jonathan (2008) Conversation with Keith Olbermann on "Countdown," about YouTube, MSNBC, June 9.

Ambinder, Marc (2009) "Obama Will Get His Blackberry," The Atlantic, Jan. 21. http://marcambinder.theatlantic.com/archives/2009/01/obama_will_get_his_ blackberry.php

Anderson, Chris (2008) "Free! Why $0.00 Is the Future of Business," Wired, Feb. 25. http://www.wired.com/techbiz/it/magazine/16-03/ff_free

Angle, Jim (2008) Report about the impact of blogging on presidential appoint- ments, "Brit Hume's Special Report," Fox News, Dec. 22.

Armstrong, Jennifer (2009) "Super Bowl: With 95.4 Mil Viewers, Game Was Second Most Watched Ever," Hollywood Insider, Feb. 2.   http://hollywoodinsider .ew.com/2009/02/ratings-super-1.html

Arnold, Gin (2008) "Missing in Action—Olbermann and Maddow," Op-Ed News, Nov. 17.   http://www.opednews.com/maxwrite/diarypage.php?did=10837

Arrington, Michael (2006) "MySpace to Sell Music Through Snocap," TechCrunch, Sept. 2.   http://www.techcrunch.com/2006/09/02/myspace-gets-into-music-biz

Arthur, Charles (2008) "Censor Lifts UK Wikipedia Ban," The Guardian, Dec. 9. http://www.guardian.co.uk/technology/2008/dec/09/wikipedia-iwf-ban-lifted

ASCAP (American Society of Composers, Authors, and Publishers) (2008) "2007 Annual Report". New York: ASCAP.   http://ascap.com/about/annualReport/ annual_2007.pdf

Associated Press (2005) "Wikipedia, Britannica: A Toss-Up," Dec 15.
http://www.wired.com/culture/lifestyle/news/2005/12/69844

——— (2008) "Network Television Viewership Plunges by 2.5 Million People, Data
Shows," May 9.   http://www.foxnews.com/story/0,2933,270965,00.html

——— (2008) "Thomson Reuters Reports Lower Profit on Costs of a Merger," The
New York Times, Aug. 12.   http://www.nytimes.com/2008/08/13/business/
13thomson.html

Au, Wagner James (2007) "Remake the Stars," New World Notes blog, July 18.
http://nwn.blogs.com/nwn/2007/07/remake-the-star.html#more

Baez, Joan (1966) Performance of Bob Dylan's "With God on Our Side," in Stockholm,
Sweden, video.   http://www.youtube.com/watch?v=Pih1hVdflnQ

Baird, Derek E. (2008) "Youth Vote 2008: How Obama Hooked Gen Y," Barking
Robot blog, Dec. 1.   http://www.debaird.net/blendededunet/2008/12/youth-
vote-2008-how-obama-hooked-gen-y.html

Barack Obama (One Million Strong for Barack) (2007) Facebook group.
http://www.facebook.com/group.php?gid=2231653698

"Barbara Walters Special: Interview with Barack Obama" (2008) ABC-TV, Nov. 26.

Barlow, Perry (1955) "Another Radio to the Attic," The New Yorker, cover, Oct. 22.
http://www.tvhistory.tv/1955_Oct_22_NEW_YORKER.JPG

Bennett, Chris (2009) "Beyond DIGG and StumbleUpon," Sociable Blog, Feb. 13.
http://www.sociableblog.com/2009/02/13/beyond-digg-and-stumbleupon

"Big Love" (2009) Season 3, Episode 6, HBO TV series, Feb. 22.

BlogTalkRadio (2009) "About BlogTalkRadio."   http://www.blogtalkradio.com/
about.aspx

BMI (Broadcast Music, Inc.) (2007) "Broadcast Music Inc. Announces Record-
Setting Royalty Distributions," Sept 4.   http://www.bmi.com/press/releases/
BMI_revenues_release_2007_final_9_4_07.doc

British Broadcasting Company (BBC) (2007) "Blog Death Threats Spark Debate,"
March 27.   http://news.bbc.co.uk/1/hi/technology/6499095.stm

——— (2009) "Pope Launches Vatican on YouTube," Jan 23.   http://news.bbc.co.uk/
2/hi/europe/7846446.stm

Brown, Stephen E. F. (2009) "Amazon Sells Blogs on Kindle," New Mexico Business
Weekly, May 15.   http://www.bizjournals.com/albuquerque/stories/2009/05/11/
daily59.html

Buggles, The (1979) "Video Killed the Radio Star," recording, Island Records.

Bureau of Justice Statistics (2009) "3.4 Million People Report Being Stalked in the
United States," U.S. Department of Justice, Jan. 13.   http://www.ojp.usdoj
.gov/bjs/pub/press/svuspr.htm

Busari, Stephanie (2008) "Tweeting the Terror: How Social Media Reacted to Mumbai," CNN.com/Asia, Nov. 27.   http://edition.cnn.com/2008/WORLD/asiapcf/11/27/mumbai.twitter/index.html

Butler, Samuel (1878/1910) "Life and Habit." New York: Dutton.

Carpenter, Hutch (2009) "Karl Rove Is on Twitter," I'm Not Actually a Geek blog, Jan. 9. http://bhc3.wordpress.com/2009/01/10/karl-rove-is-on-twitter

Carr, David (2005) "Why You Should Pay to Read This Newspaper?" The New York Times, Oct. 24.   http://www.nytimes.com/2005/10/24/business/24carr.html

"Casino Royale" (2006) Directed by Martin Campbell, written by Neal Purvis & Robert Wade and Paul Haggis, MGM.

Catch Up Lady blog (2007) "Dick in a Box Grabs Emmy Nod, NBC's YouTube Mea Culpa Complete," July 23.   http://catchupblog.typepad.com/catch_up_blog/2007/07/dick-in-a-box-g.html

Cheng, Jacqui (2008) "For the Young, TV's Passivity Is Passé Next to the Internet," ars technica, March 24.   http://arstechnica.com/news.ars/post/20080324-report-kids-use-internet-to-enhance-tv-experience.html

Cohen, David (2007) "Hunting Down Digg's Bury Brigade," Wired, March 1. http://www.wired.com/techbiz/people/news/2007/03/72835

Cohen, Noam (2008) "Delaying News in the Era of the Internet," The New York Times, June 23.   http://www.nytimes.com/2008/06/23/business/media/23link.html

Collins, Barry (2008) "Web Censor Lifts Wikipedia Ban," Computer Buyer, Dec. 11. http://www.computerbuyer.co.uk/news/242253/web-censor-lifts-wikipedia-ban.html

Comenius, Johann Amos (1649/1896) "Didactica Magna." Translated by M. W. Keatinge as "The Great Didactic." London: Adam and Charles Black.

Comscore (2008) "Social Networking Explodes Worldwide as Sites Increase Their Focus on Cultural Relevance," Aug. 12.   http://www.comscore.com/press/release.asp?press=2396

Crocker, Chris (2007) "Britney Fan Crying (Leave Britney Alone)," video, Sept. 11. http://www.youtube.com/watch?v=LWSjUeoFyxQ

Cyberbully Alert (2008) "Cyber Bullying Statistics That May Shock You!" Aug. 27. http://www.cyberbullyalert.com/blog/2008/08/cyber-bullying-statistics-that-may-shock-you

Dahl, Melissa (2008) "Youth Vote May Have Been Key in Obama's Win," MSNBC.com, Nov. 5.   http://www.msnbc.msn.com/id/27525497/

Dawkins, Richard (1976) "The Selfish Gene." New York: Oxford University Press.

——— (1991) "Viruses of the Mind" in "Dennett and His Critics: Demystifying Mind," ed. Bo Dahlbom. Cambridge, MA: Blackwell, 1993.   http://modox.blogspot.com/2007/12/memes-viruses-of-mind-or-root-of.html

DeCuir, Esther (2007) "Soft Edge Bookstore to Showcase Works of Paul Levinson," Second Life News Network, Dec. 4.   http://www.slnn.com/index.php?SCREEN=print-article&sid=CIyx6K2BPbc3rPez&articleID=1015

Dewey, John (1925) "Experience and Nature." Chicago: Open Court.

"Dick in a Box" (2006) Video featuring Justin Timberlake and Andy Samberg; written by Andy Samberg, Akiva Schaffer, Jorma Taccone, Asa Taccone, Justin Timberlake, Katreese Barnes; produced by The Lonely Island for "Saturday Night Live"; Dec. 16.   http://www.youtube.com/watch?v=WhwbxEfy7fg

Dickinson, Tim (2006) "The First YouTube Election: George Allen and 'Macaca,'" Rolling Stone, Aug. 15.   http://www.rollingstone.com/nationalaffairs/?p=426   video: www.youtube.com/watch?v=r9ozoPMnKwI

"Digg Terms of Use" (2009).   http://digg.com/tou

Dingo, Robbie (2007) "A Second Life Machinima," My Digital Double blog, July 16. http://digitaldouble.blogspot.com/2007/07/watch-worlds.html   and video: http://blip.tv/file/get/RobbieDingo-WatchTheWorlds570.mov

Donnelly, John M. (2009) "Congressman Twitters an Iraq Security Breach," CQ Politics, Feb. 6.   http://www.cqpolitics.com/wmspage.cfm?docID=news-000003026945

Dumbach, Annette E., and Newborn, Judd (1986) "Shattering the German Night." Boston: Little, Brown.

Dunlop, Orrin E., Jr. (1951) "Radio & Television Almanac." New York: Harper & Bros.

Eisenstein, Elizabeth (1979) "The Printing Press as an Agent of Change." New York: Cambridge University Press.

Elba, Idris (2006) Private messages to Paul Levinson, on MySpace, Oct. 28 and Nov. 7.

Fark (2009) "Increase the Chances of Your Submission Being Posted on Fark." http://www.fark.com/farq/submit.shtml#Increase_the_chances_of_your_submission_being_posted_on_Fark

Feiner, Paul (2009) Interview with Paul Levinson, "The Greenburgh Report," WVOX Radio, Jan. 9. Also included in Levinson, Paul (2009), "Conversation with Greenburgh NY Town Supervisor Paul Feiner About Blogging, Obama, and Caroline Kennedy," Light On Light Through podcast, Jan. 16. http://paullev.libsyn.com/index.php?post_id=423351

Finnegan, Adrian (2008) "Report on November 2008 Mumbai Massacre and Facebook," CNN International, Nov. 27.

Fleetwoods, The (1959, 2007) "Come Softly To Me" and "Mr. Blue," originally released in 1959 on Dolphin Records, performance on "American Bandstand" 1959, live performance 2007.   video: http://www.youtube.com/watch?v=DgJwm9erBaQ   and   video: http://www.youtube.com/watch?v=vclkm6nsnWY   and   video: http://www.youtube.com/watch?v=AgQl6Rxk_uM

Florin, Hector (2009) "Podcasting Your Novel: Publishing's Next Wave?" Time, Jan. 31. http://www.time.com/time/arts/article/0,8599,1872381,00.html

Fogarty, Mignon (2008) "Grammar Girl's Quick and Dirty Tips for Better Writing." New York: Holt.

Fouhy, Beth (2008) "Obama to Pioneer Web Outreach as President," USA Today, Nov. 12. http://www.usatoday.com/news/topstories/2008-11-12-1697755942_x.htm

Friedman, Josh (2007) "Blogging for Dollars Raises Questions of Online Ethics," Los Angeles Times, March 9.   http://articles.latimes.com/2007/mar/09/ business/fi-bloggers9

Frith, Holden (2008) "So iTunes Won't Be Closing After All," Tech Central, (London) Times Online, Oct. 3.   http://timesonline.typepad.com/technology/2008/10/ itunes-wont-clo.html

Fuller, Buckminster (1938) "Nine Chains to the Moon." Carbondale, IL: Carbondale University Press.

Fund, John (2004) "I'd Rather Be Blogging," The Wall Street Journal, Sept. 13. http://www.opinionjournal.com/diary/?id=110005611

Geary, Jason (2008) "Plea Deals Offered in Video Beating Case," The Ledger, Nov. 18. http://www.theledger.com/article/20081118/NEWS/811180269

Gergen, David (2008) Guest on CNN, election night coverage, Nov. 4.

Giles, Jim (2005) "Special Report: Internet Encyclopaedias Go Head to Head," Nature, Dec. 14.   http://www.nature.com/nature/journal/v438/n7070/full/438900a.html

——— (2008) "Do We Need an Open Britannica?" guardian.co.uk, June 20. http://www.guardian.co.uk/technology/2008/jun/20/wikipedia

Gill, Andy (2007) "Famous Five: Why the Traveling Wilburys Are the Ultimate Supergroup," The Independent, June 19.   http://www.independent.co.uk/ arts-entertainment/music/features/famous-five-why-the-traveling-wilburys- are-the-ulimate-supergroup-453788.html

Gladkova, Svetlana (2008) "Barack Obama Uses the Power of Social Media Noticed by Mainstream Media," profy, Aug. 25.   http://profy.com/2008/08/25/barack- obama-uses-power-of-social-media/

Glater, Jonathan D. (2008) "At the Uneasy Intersection of Bloggers and the Law," The New York Times, July 15.   http://www.nytimes.com/2008/07/15/ technology/15law.htm

Goddard, Taegan (2009) "Republicans Twitter Meeting with Obama," Political Wire blog, Jan. 28.   http://politicalwire.com/archives/2009/01/28/republicans_ twitter_meeting_with_obama.html

Gold, Matea (2008) "Obama's 30-minute Ad Attracts 33 Million Viewers," Los Angeles Times, Oct. 31.   http://articles.latimes.com/2008/oct/31/entertainment/ et-obama31

Golobokova, Yulia (2008) "YouTube as an Alternative Medium of Political Communication," final paper for "Media Research Methods," Graduate School of Arts and Sciences, Fordham University, Paul Levinson, professor, Dec. 17. http://sites.google.com/site/ygolobokova/youtube-research-proposal-paper

Greider, William, (2005) "A New New Deal," The Nation, Sept. 16.

Grimes, Sara (2008) "Campus Watch: Statistics Support Youth Vote Turnout," The Daily blog, Nov. 12. http://dailyuw.com/2008/11/12/campus-watch-statistics-support-youth-vote-turnout/

Grossman, Lev (2006) "Time's Person of the Year: You," Time magazine, Dec. 13. http://www.time.com/time/magazine/article/0,9171,1569514,00.html

_____ (2009) "Iran Protests: Twitter, the Medium of Movement," Time magazine, June 17. http://www.time.com/time/world/article/0,8599,1905125,00.html

Gumpert, Gary (1970) "The Rise of Mini Comm," Journal of Communication, 20, pp. 280-290.

Hall, Edward T. (1966) "The Hidden Dimension." New York: Doubleday.

Hancock, Georganna (2007) "PageRank Promotes Blogicide!" A Writer's Edge blog, Nov. 28. http://www.writers-edge.info/2007/11/pagerank-promotes-blogicide.htm

Hannity, Sean and Colmes, Alan (2007) Different interpretations of Ron Paul's first-place finish in post-debate poll, Fox News, Oct. 22. video: http://www.youtube.com/v/hDwDIj5ahuY&rel=1

Harris, James (2007) "Tonya MacCreary," "Walking on Air," recordings. http://www.myspace.com/jamesharrismusic and http://www.myspace.com/jamesharrismusic2

Harris, Leslie (2009) "Because 'Classified Ad Killer' Doesn't Have the Same Ring," The Huffington Post, April 24. http://www.huffingtonpost.com/leslie-harris/because-classified-ad-kil_b_190965.html

Harrison, George (1971, 2002, 2006) Performances of George Harrison's "While My Guitar Gently Weeps," at Concert for Bangladesh, 1971, George Harrison, Eric Clapton; at Memorial Concert for George, 2002, Eric Clapton, Paul McCartney, Ringo Starr, Dhani Harrison; at Rock 'n' Roll Hall of Fame Induction (Posthumous) of George Harrison, 2006, Tom Petty, Jeff Lynne, Prince. (See also McCartney, Paul.) video: http://www.youtube.com/watch?v=T7qpfGVUd8c and video: http://www.youtube.com/watch?v=zNp45m92e1M and video: http://www.youtube.com/watch?v=cYl942_I3W0

Harwood, John (2009) Interview with Barack Obama, CNBC-TV, Jan. 7.

Havenstein, Heather (2008) "Britain's MI6 Recruiting Spies on Facebook, Report Says," Computer World, Sept. 29. http://www.itworld.com/career/55450/britains-mi6-recruiting-spies-facebook-report-says

Hawthorne, Nathaniel (1851/1962) "The House of the Seven Gables" (novel). New York: Collier.

Heil, Bill and Piskorski, Mikolaj Jan (2009) "New Twitter Research: Men Follow Men and Nobody Tweets," Conversation Starter, Harvard Business Publishing, June 1.   http://blogs.harvardbusiness.org/cs/2009/06/new_twitter_research_men_follo.html

Hibberd, James (2009) "MSN Gets Record Traffic During Jackson Memorial," the live feed, July 7.   http://www.thrfeed.com/2009/07/jackson-memorial-web-traffic.html

Hines, Twanna A. (2008) "I'm a Writer, Not a Child Pornographer," The Huffington Post, Dec. 31.   http://www.huffingtonpost.com/twanna-a-hines/im-a-writer-not-a-child-p_b_154584.html

Hof, Robert D. (2006) "My Virtual Life," Business Week, May 1.   http://www.businessweek.com/magazine/content/06_18/b3982001.htm

Hoffman, Auren (2008) "It Takes Tech to Elect a President," Business Week, Aug. 25.   http://www.businessweek.com/technology/content/aug2008/tc20080822_700775.htm?campaign_id=rss_tech

Holyoke, Jessica (2008) "Lowest Profit per Capita Growth Ever in Q1 2008," The Alphaville Herald, April 29.   http://foo.secondlifeherald.com/slh/2008/04/state-of-the-ec.html

Hudson, Ken (Hubble, Kenny) (2008) "Caledon Astronomical Society."   http://agni.sl.marvulous.co.uk/group/Caledon%20Astronomical%20Society

——— (2008) Facebook message to Paul Levinson, Dec. 26.

Huffington Post, The, Editors of (2008) "The Huffington Post Complete Guide to Blogging." New York: Simon & Schuster.

Hunter, Mark (2009) Podcastmatters Social Media podcast, Feb. 6.   http://socialmediapodcast.tumblr.com/post/76150739/edition-2-twestival-swearing-and-cameron-reilly

ILeftDiggforReddit (2008) "So Who Else Here Left Digg for Reddit?" Dec. 25.   http://www.reddit.com/r/reddit.com/comments/7ll45/so_who_else_here_left_digg_for_reddit/

Innis, Harold (1951) "The Bias of Communication." Toronto: University of Toronto Press.

Internet Safety Technical Task Force (2008) "Enhancing Child Safety & Online Technologies: Final Report," Berkman Center for Internet & Safety at Harvard University, Dec. 31.   http://www.wiredsafety.org/resources/pdf/2009_isttf_final_report.pdf

Ironic Pentameter (2006) "How Old Is Digg's Median User?" Sept. 14.   http://ironic-pentameter.blogspot.com/2006/09/how-old-is-diggs-median-user.html

I-Safe (2009) "Cyber Bullying: Statistics and Tips." http://www.isafe.org/channels/
sub.php?ch=op&sub_id=media_cyber_bullying

"I've Got a Crush on Obama" (2007) Video featuring Amber Lee Ettinger, produced
by Ben Relles for BarelyPolitical.com, song written and sung by Leah Kauffman,
June 13. http://www.youtube.com/watch?v=wKsoXHYICqU

James, William (1890) "The Principles of Psychology." New York: Henry Holt.

Jardin, Xeni (2005) "Audience With the Podfather," Wired, May 14. http://www.wired
.com/culture/lifestyle/news/2005/05/67525

Jarvis, Jeff (2008) Interview about investigative journalism in peril,
"On the Media," National Public Radio (NPR), Aug. 15.
transcript: http://www.onthemedia.org/transcripts/2008/08/15/01

Johnson, Peter (2005) "'Times' Report: Miller Called Her Own Shots," USA Today,
Oct. 16. http://www.usatoday.com/life/columnist/mediamix/2005-10-16-
media-mix_x.htm

Johnson, Steven (2009) "How Twitter Will Change the Way We Live," Time magazine, June 15, pp. 32-37.

Jonas, Gerald (1999) Review of "The Silk Code" by Paul Levinson, The New York Times,
Nov. 28. http://www.nytimes.com/books/99/11/28/reviews/991128.28scifit.html

Jones, Alex (2007) "Ron Paul Beats Digg Bury Brigade," Prison Planet, May 21.
http://www.prisonplanet.com/articles/may2007/210507paulbeats.htm

Jordan, Tina (2008) "Domestic Book Sales See Slight Decline in May," AAP (The
Association of American Publishers), July 11. http://www.publishers.org/
main/PressCenter/Press_Issues/May2008SalesStats.htm

Kane, Erin and Brandt, Kristin (2007) "Welcome to Hollywood," Manic Mommies podcast, Feb. 18. http://www.manicmommies.com/2007/02/welcome-to-hollywood/

Kaplan, Benjamin (1966) "An Unhurried View of Copyright." New York: Columbia
University Press.

Kells, Tina (2009) "Wikipedia Ponders Editorial Reviews After Kennedy Death Post,"
Now Public, Jan. 26. http://www.nowpublic.com/tech-biz/wikipedia-ponders-
editorial-reviews-after-kennedy-death-post

Kerry, John (2008) Speech at Democratic National Convention, Denver, Co., Aug.
27. video: http://www.youtube.com/watch?v=dO2PAm4iCtE

King5.com (2008) "Armored Truck Robber Uses Craigslist to Make Getaway," Oct. 1.
http://www.king5.com/topstories/stories/NW_100108WAB_monroe_robber_
floating_escape_TP.ce3930c1.html

Kingston, Sean (2006) MySpace music page, July 7. http://www.myspace.com/
seankingston

——— (2007) "Kingston's MySpace Success," contactmusic.com, Sept. 6. http://www
.contactmusic.com/news.nsf/article/kingstons%20myspace%20success_1042855

Kirk, Jeremy (2008) "Wikipedia Article Censored in UK for the First Time," PC World, Dec. 8.   http://www.pcworld.com/article/155112/wikipedia_article_censored_in_uk_for_the_first_time.html

Kornblut, Anne E. (2009) "Staff Finds White House in the Technological Dark Ages," The Washington Post, Jan. 22.   http://www.washingtonpost.com/wp-dyn/content/article/2009/01/21/AR2009012104249.html

Kreiger, Lisa M. (2008) "Protesters to Facebook: Breast-Feeding Does Not Equal Obscenity," San Jose Mercury News, Dec. 26.

Kremer, Joan (2008) "The Start of a Central Information Source for Writers in Second Life," Writers in the Virtual Sky blog, Dec. 31.   http://www.writersinthevirtualsky.com/the-start-of-a-central-information-source-for-writers-in-second-life/

Krupp, Elysha (2008) "Wikipedia, Britannica Battle over Credibility," examiner.com, Aug. 10.   http://www.examiner.com/a-1529791~Wikipedia__Britannica_battle_over_credibility.html

Kurtz, Howard (2007) "Jailed Man Is a Videographer and a Blogger but Is He a Journalist?" The Washington Post, March 8, p. C01.   http://www.washingtonpost.com/wp-dyn/content/article/2007/03/07/AR2007030702454.html

———— (2009) "Online, Sarah Palin Has Unkind Words for the Press," The Washington Post, Jan. 9, p. C01.   http://www.washingtonpost.com/wp-dyn/content/article/2009/01/08/AR2009010803620.html

Laipply, Judson (2006) "Evolution of Dance," video, April 6.   http://www.youtube.com/watch?v=LWSjUeoFyxQ

Lambert, Bruce (2007) "As Prostitutes Turn to Craigslist, Law Takes Notice," The New York Times, Sept. 4.   http://www.nytimes.com/2007/09/05/nyregion/05craigslist.html

Lavigne, Avril (2007) "Girlfriend," video, RCA Records, Feb. 27.   http://www.youtube.com/watch?v=cQ25-glGRzI

Layton, Julia, and Brothers, Patrick (2007) "How MySpace Works," HowStuffWorks.   http://computer.howstuffworks.com/myspace.htm

Leibovich, Mark (2008) "McCain, the Analog Candidate," The New York Times, Aug. 3.   http://www.nytimes.com/2008/08/03/weekinreview/03leibovich.html

Leitch, Will (2009) "How Tweet It Is," New York Magazine, Feb. 8.   http://nymag.com/news/media/54069/

Let Joe Stay (2008) blog.   http://letjoestay.blogspot.com/

Levine, David (2008) "All Talk," Conde Nast Portfolio.com, Feb. 26.   http://www.portfolio.com/culture-lifestyle/goods/gadgets/2008/02/26/Internet-Talk-Radio

Levinson, Paul (1972) "Twice Upon a Rhyme", music recording, LP, HappySad Records; CD reissue, Seoul, South Korea: Beatball Music, 2008. reviews: http://rateyourmusic.com/release/album/paul_levinson/twice_upon_a_rhyme/

————— (1977) "Toy, Mirror, and Art: The Metamorphosis of Technological Culture," Et Cetera journal, June. Reprinted in "Technology and Human Affairs," ed. L. Hickman & A. al-Hibris, St. Louis, MO: Mosby, 1981; "Philosophy, Technology, and Human Affairs," ed. L. Hickman, College Station, TX: Ibis, 1985; "Technology As a Human Affair," ed. L. Hickman, New York: McGraw-Hill, 1990; Levinson, Paul, "Learning Cyberspace: Essays on the Evolution of Media and the New Education," San Francisco: Anamnesis Press, 1995.

————— (1979) "Human Replay: A Theory of the Evolution of Media," PhD dissertation, New York University.

————— (1985) "Basics of Computer Conferencing, and Thoughts on Its Applicability to Education," excerpted from "The New School Online," unpublished report, January. Reprinted in Levinson, Paul (1995) "Learning Cyberspace." San Francisco: Anamnesis Press.

————— (1986) "Marshall McLuhan and Computer Conferencing," IEEE Transactions of Professional Communication.

————— (1988) "Mind at Large: Knowing in the Technological Age." Greenwich, Conn: JAI Press.

————— (1992) "Electronic Chronicles: Columns of the Changes in our Time." San Francisco: Anamnesis Press.

————— (1997) "The Soft Edge: A Natural History and Future of the Information Revolution." New York and London: Routledge.

————— (1998) "The Book on the Book," Analog Science Fiction and Fact, June, pp. 24-31.

————— (1999) "Digital McLuhan: A Guide to the Information Millennium." New York and London: Routledge.

————— (1999) "The Silk Code" (novel). New York: Tor.

————— (2003) Interview about Jayson Blair and the New York Times, "World News Now," ABC-TV, May 11.

————— (2003) "Realspace: The Fate of Physical Presence in the Digital Age, On and Off Planet." New York and London: Routledge.

————— (2004) "Cellphone: The Story of the World's Most Mobile Medium." New York: Palgrave/Macmillan.

————— (2004) Interview by Bill O'Reilly, "The O'Reilly Factor," Fox News, television, about journalists having private lives, Jan. 23.   video: http://www.youtube.com/watch?v=uSOytS96YhI

————— (2005) Interview by Joe Scarborough about Dan Rather and "Docu-Gate," "Scarborough Country," MSNBC, Feb. 16.   transcript: http://www.sff.net/people/paullevinson/scar021605.html and   videoclip: http://www.youtube.com/watch?v=VmvzYfY_gJA

———— (2005) "The Flouting of the First Amendment," Keynote Address, Sixth Annual Media Ecology Conference, Fordham University, New York City, June 23. Reprinted in Explorations in Media Ecology, vol 5, no 3, 2006, pp. 199-210, and in Paul Levinson's Infinite Regress blog, July 12, 2007.   http://paullevinson. blogspot.com/2007/07/flouting-of-first-amendment-transcript.html

———— (2006) "Every Eye's a Camera, Every Ear's a Mike," Light On Light Through podcast, Nov. 25.   http://paullev.libsyn.com/index.php?post_id=155207

———— (2006) Interview on "Squawk Box" about violence and videogames, CNBC-TV, June 22.   videoclip: http://www.youtube.com/watch?v=-XtWV-tIeVg

———— (2006) "The Plot to Save Socrates" (novel). New York: Tor.

———— (2006) "'The Wire' and 'The Wealth of Nations,'" Twice Upon a Rhyme MySpace blog, Aug. 13.   http://blogs.myspace.com/index.cfm?fuseaction=blog .view&friendID=17346415&blogID=155375148

———— (2006) "'The Wire' Without Stringer," Light On Light Through podcast, Nov. 4.   http://paullev.libsyn.com/index.php?post_id=148095

———— (2007) "First YouTube/CNN Presidential Debate," Paul Levinson's Infinite Regress blog, July 23.   http://paullevinson.blogspot.com/2007/07/ first-youtubecnn-presidential-debate.html

———— (2007) "Four Imus Fallacies," Light On Light Through podcast, April 15. http://paullev.libsyn.com/index.php?post_id=203730

———— (2007) "Free Josh Wolf," Light On Light Through podcast, March 10. http://paullev.libsyn.com/index.php?post_id=190952

———— (2007) "Good for Dan Rather: CBS Deserves To Be Sued," Paul Levinson's Infinite Regress blog, Sept. 19.   http://paullevinson.blogspot.com/2007/09/ good-for-dan-rather-cbs-deserves-to-be.html

———— (2007) "Hannity & Colmes Split Over Ron Paul's 1st Place in Fox's Latest Post-Debate Poll," Paul Levinson's Infinite Regress blog, Oct. 22.   http://paullevinson. blogspot.com/2007/10/hannity-colmes-split-over-ron-pauls-1st.html

———— (2007) "How to Research Ancient History for Science Fiction," Light On Light Through podcast, Feb. 11.   http://paullev.libsyn.com/ index.php?post_id=180692

———— (2007) Interview by Ken Hudson (Kenny Hubble), "Media Ecology Seminar in Second Life," Nov. 5.   video: http://blip.tv/file/475397

———— (2007) Interview by Mark Molaro, The Alcove, Nov. 27. http://www.youtube.com/watch?v=aqZNGYit3kY

———— (2007) Interview with Rich Sommer, Light On Light Through podcast, Oct. 28.   http://paullev.libsyn.com/index.php?post_id=271587

———— (2007) Interview with Stanley Schmidt," Light On Light Through podcast, Dec. 1.   http://paullev.libsyn.com/index.php?post_id=283468

—— (2007) "Marshall McLuhan as Micro Blogger," Paul Levinson's Infinite Regress blog, Oct. 9.   http://paullevinson.blogspot.com/2007/10/marshall-mcluhan-as-micro-blogger.html

—— (2007) "My Four Rules: The Best You Can Do to Make It as a Writer," Light On Light Through blog, Aug. 26.   http://paullev.libsyn.com/index.php?post_id=249175

—— (2007) "Now Obama's Poll Results are Denigrated by a Professional Pollster," Paul Levinson's Infinite Regress blog, Nov. 1.   http://paullevinson.blogspot.com/2007/11/now-obamas-poll-results-are-denigrated.html

—— (2007) "Obama Girl Applauded in My Class at Fordham This Afternoon," Paul Levinson's Infinite Regress blog, Sept. 21.   http://paullevinson.blogspot.com/2007/09/obama-girl-applauded-in-my-class-at.html

—— (2007) "Open Letter to CNBC about Taking Down Post-Debate Poll Won by Ron Paul," Paul Levinson's Infinite Regress blog, Oct. 12.   http://paullevinson.blogspot.com/2007/10/open-letter-to-cnbc-about-taking-down.html

—— (2007) Phone-in guest on Shaun OMac's BlogTalkRadio show, "TV Talk", episode about "Journeyman," with special guest Kevin Falls, Oct. 23.   http://www.blogtalkradio.com/stations/bc/SHAUNOMACRADIO/blog/2007/10/24/Journeyman-rocks-Shaun-OMac-Radio

—— (2007) "Rating the News Networks in their Campaign Coverage," Paul Levinson's Infinite Regress blog, Sept. 21.   http://paullevinson.blogspot.com/2007/09/rating-news-networks-in-their-election.html

—— (2007) Reading from "The Plot to Save Socrates" at "Meet the Author," with interview by Adele Ward, Second Life, SLCN.tv (Second Life Cable Network), Dec. 9. video of complete interview and reading: http://slcn.tv/meet-author-paul-levinson   and   excerpt: http://www.youtube.com/watch?v=VhGqdCQCATs

—— (2007) "Republican YouTube/CNN Debate in Florida," Paul Levinson's Infinite Regress blog, Nov. 28.   http://paullevinson.blogspot.com/2007/11/republican-youtubecnn-debate-in-florida.html

—— (2007) "Republicans Now Thumb Their Noses at YouTube as well as Evolution," Paul Levinson's Infinite Regress blog, July 27.   http://paullevinson.blogspot.com/2007/07/republicans-now-thumb-noses-at-youtube.html

—— (2007) Review of "Brotherhood," Season 1 Finale, Paul Levinson's Infinite Regress blog, Dec. 3.   http://paullevinson.blogspot.com/2007/12/brotherhood-season-2-finale.html

—— (2007) Review of "Lost," Season 3 Finale, Paul Levinson's Infinite Regress blog, May 23.   http://paullevinson.blogspot.com/2007/05/lost-season-3-finale-flashforwards.html

—— (2007) Review of "Mad Men" 1.12, Paul Levinson's Infinite Regress blog, Oct. 12.   http://paullevinson.blogspot.com/2007/10/mad-men-11-admirable-don.html

———— (2007) "RIAA's Monstrous Legacy," Paul Levinson's Infinite Regress blog, July 13.   http://paullevinson.blogspot.com/2007/07/riaas-monstrous-legacy.html

———— (2007) "The KNX Sunday Morning Interviews," Paul Levinson's Infinite Regress blog, June 30.   http://paullevinson.blogspot.com/2007/06/knx1070-sunday-morning-interviews.html

———— (2007) "The Secret Riches of the Panda," Light On Light Through blog, July 30.   http://paullev.libsyn.com/index.php?post_id=240416

———— (2007) "YouTube Video of My Aug 28 Talk in New York: Ron Paul and the Mass Media," Light On Light Through podcast, Sept. 8.   http://paullev.libsyn.com/index.php?post_id=253883

———— (2008) "Announcing Obama's Choice Through Email Not Good Idea," Daily Kos, Aug. 11.   http://www.dailykos.com/storyonly/2008/8/11/154117/227/164/566307

———— (2008) "Cyberbullying Mom on MySpace Got Just What She Deserved," Twice Upon a Rhyme MySpace blog, Nov. 27.   http://blog.myspace.com/index.cfm?fuseaction=blog.view&friendID=17346415&blogID=452143917

———— (2008) "George's Guitar Gently Weeps Through the Ages," Paul Levinson's Infinite Regress blog, June 15.   http://paullevinson.blogspot.com/2008/06/harrisons-my-guitar-gently-weeps-ala.html

———— (2008) "I'm a Progressive Libertarian," Paul Levinson's Infinite Regress blog, Aug. 16.   http://paullevinson.blogspot.com/2008/08/im-progressive-libertarian.html

———— (2008) Interview by KnitWitch (Máia Whitaker) about promoting your writing on the web, KnitWitch Zone, Feb. 26.   http://www.talkshoe.com/talkshoe/web/talkCast.jsp?masterId=28497&cmd=tc

———— (2008) "Katie Couric, Hero of the Revolution," Paul Levinson's Infinite Regress blog, Nov. 13; cross-posted on Open Salon, Nov. 13.   http://paullevinson.blogspot.com/2008/11/katie-couric-hero-of-revolution.html *and* http://open.salon.com/content.php?cid=43629

———— (2008) "Keeping Obama with His Email," Paul Levinson's Infinite Regress blog, Nov. 16.   http://paullevinson.blogspot.com/2008/11/keeping-president-obama-with-his-email.html

———— (2008) "MSNBC Runs Canned Doc Bloc as Mumbai Burns," Paul Levinson's Infinite Regress blog, Nov. 28.   http://paullevinson.blogspot.com/2008/11/inane-msnbc-programming-on-friday-eve.html

———— (2008) "Obama and FDR: Not Just New New Deal, New New Media," Paul Levinson's Infinite Regress blog, Nov. 15.   http://paullevinson.blogspot.com/2008/11/obama-on-youtube-and-fdr-on-radio-not.html

———— (2008) "Obama Should Reject McCain's Call to Postpone Friday Debate," Paul Levinson's Infinite Regress blog, Sept. 24; cross-posted on Open Salon,

Sept. 24. http://paullevinson.blogspot.com/2008/09/mccains-to-postpone-fridays-debate-i.html *and* http://open.salon.com/content.php?cid=21963

———— (2008) Review of "Mad Men," 2.4, Paul Levinson's Infinite Regress blog, Aug. 18. http://paullevinson.blogspot.com/2008/08/mad-men-24-betty-and-dons-son.html

———— (2008) "Superb Speeches by Bill Clinton and John Kerry," Paul Levinson's Infinite Regress blog, Aug. 27; cross-posted on Open Salon and Daily Kos. http://paullevinson.blogspot.com/2008/08/superb-speeches-by-bill-clinton-and.html *and* http://open.salon.com/blog/paul_levinson/2008/08/27/superb_speeches_by_b_clintonkerry_-_tv_shows_just_bills *and* http://www.dailykos.com/storyonly/2008/8/28/577065/-The-Cable-All-News-Networks-Diss-John-Kerry

———— (2008) "Take It from a College Prof: Obama's 'Missing' Paper Is Another Conservative Red Herring," Daily Kos, July 25. http://www.dailykos.com/storyonly/2008/7/25/16275/4548/308/557010

———— (2008) "The Shame of Joe Lieberman," Paul Levinson's Infinite Regress blog, Nov. 6. http://paullevinson.blogspot.com/2008/11/shame-of-joe-lieberman.html

———— (2008) "Unburning Alexandria" (novelette). Analog Science Fiction and Fact, Nov., pp. 116-133.

———— (2008) "Where Have Olbermann and Maddow Disappeared To?" Paul Levinson's Infinite Regress blog, Nov. 19. http://paullevinson.blogspot.com/2008/11/where-have-olbermann-and-maddow.html

———— (2009) Interview by The Gypsy Poet, BlogTalkRadio, May 17. http://www.blogtalkradio.com/Gypsypoet/2009/05/17/Gypsy-Poet-Radio-Presents-Paul-Levinson

———— (2009) "New New Media vs. the Mullahs in Iran," Paul Levinson's Infinite Regress blog, June 16. http://paullevinson.blogspot.com/2009/06/new-new-media-vs-mullahs-in-iran.html

———— (2009) Response to "What Is [a] Podcast," Podcast Alley, Jan. 8. http://podcastalley.com/forum/showthread.php?t=145349

Levinson, Paul and Fox, Ed (1971) "Merri-Goes-'Round," music recording, single; HappySad Records.

Levinson, Paul and Krondes, Jim (1969) "Snow Flurries," Lady Mac Music, demo by Louis Caraballo, Paul Levinson and Peter Rosenthal. Played on Kane and Brandt (2007).

Lewin, James (2006) "Podcast Goes From Zero to One Million Downloads in Four Months," Podcasting News, Nov. 28. http://www.podcastingnews.com/2006/11/28/podcast-goes-from-zero-to-one-million-downloads-in-four-months/

Liza (2008) "Netroots' Bloggers Boycott of Associated Press Is Working," culturekitchen blog, June 16. http://culturekitchen.com/liza/blog/netroots_bloggers_boycott_of_associated_press_is_w

MacBeach (2008) Comment to Alex Chitu's "The Unlikely Integration Between Google News and Digg," Google Operating System blog, July 23. http://googlesystem.blogspot.com/2008/07/unlikely-integration-between-google.html

MacManus, Richard (2008) "Top 10 YouTube Videos of All Time, 2008 Edition," Read Write Web, Sept. 29.   http://www.readwriteweb.com/archives/top_10_youtube_videos_of_all_time_2008.php

Maeroff, Gene (1979) "Reading Achievement of Children in Indiana Found as Good as in '44," The New York Times, April 15, p. 10.

Malkin, Bonnie (2008) "Pakistan Ban to Blame for YouTube Blackout," The Daily Telegraph, Feb. 25.   http://www.telegraph.co.uk/news/uknews/3356520/Pakistan-ban-to-blame-for-YouTube-blackout.html

Manjoo, Farhad (2008) "Don't Blame YouTube, MySpace for Teen Beating Video," Machinist, April 4.   http://machinist.salon.com/blog/2008/04/08/myspace_beating/

————— (2009) "I Do Solemnly Swear That I Will Blog Regularly," Slate, Jan. 20. http://www.slate.com/?id=2209275

Marder, Rachel (2007) "Two Students Sued for Illegal Downloading," The Justice, July 12.   http://www.thejusticeonline.com/home/index.cfm?event=displayArticle&ustory_id=7461e8a8-4bea-4883-af39-1ee5a8ac8fb2&page=1

Markoff, John (2006) "Entrepreneurs See a Web Guided by Common Sense," The New York Times, Nov. 12.   http://www.nytimes.com/2006/11/12/business/12web.html

Masterson, Michele (2008) "'Cyberbully' Mom Closer to Learning Her Fate," ChannelWeb, Nov. 26.   http://www.crn.com/software/212200723

mavrevMatt (2008) Comment on Alex Chitu's "The Unlikely Integration Between Google News and Digg," Google Operating System blog, July 23.   http://googlesystem.blogspot.com/2008/07/unlikely-integration-between-google.html

Max, Tucker (2006) "I Hope They Serve Beer in Hell." New York: Citadel.

McCain, John (2008) Transcript of speech, as delivered in Louisiana, Politico, June 3.   http://www.politico.com/news/stories/0608/10820.html   and video: http://www.youtube.com/watch?v=A7RuX4pQPLY

McCarthy, Caroline (2008) "Who Will Reign Over Digg: Obama or Jobs?" The Social, CNET News, May 12.   http://news.cnet.com/8301-13577_3-9942496-36.html

McCartney, Paul (2004) Performance of George Harrison's "All Things Must Pass" in Madrid, Spain, 2004. (See also Harrison, George.) video: http://www.youtube.com/watch?v=cYl942_I3W0

McCullagh, Declan (2007) "Ron Paul: The Internet's Favorite Candidate," CNET News, Aug. 6.   http://news.cnet.com/Ron-Paul-The-Internets-favorite-candidate/2100-1028_3-6200893.html

McCullagh, Declan and Broache, Anne (2007) "Blogs Turn 10—Who's the Father?" CNET News, March 20.   http://news.cnet.com/2100-1025_3-6168681.html

McKeever, William A. (1910) "Motion Pictures: A Primary School for Criminals," Good Housekeeping, August, pp. 184-186.

McLuhan, Marshall (1962) "The Gutenberg Galaxy." New York: Mentor.

——— (1964) "Understanding Media." New York: Mentor.

——— (1977) "The Laws of the Media," with a preface by Paul Levinson, Et Cetera journal, 34, 2, pp. 173-179.

McLuhan, Marshall and Fiore, Quentin (1967) "The Medium Is the Massage." New York: Bantam.

Merlot, Miss (2008) "The Caledon Astrotorium Grand Opening Party," March 21. http://merlotzymurgy.blogspot.com/2008/03/caledon-astrotrorium-grand-opening.html

Messerli, Joe (2006) "Why Polls Shouldn't Be Used to Make Decisions," BalancedPolitics.org, Jan. 25.   http://www.balancedpolitics.org/editorial-the_case_against_polls.htm

Milian, Mark (2009) "Digg: Don't Shout, Use Twitter and Facebook Instead," Los Angeles Times, May 26.   http://latimesblogs.latimes.com/technology/2009/05/digg-shout-share.html

Miller, Judith (2005) U.S. Senate Committee on the Judiciary, Hearing on Reporters' Shield Legislation, Oct. 19.   http://judiciary.senate.gov/hearings/testimony.cfm?id=1637&wit_id=4698

——— (2008) Appearance on "Fox News Watch" (TV), Dec. 6.

Milton, John (1644) "Areopagetica."

Mintz, Jessica (2009) "iTunes Price Cut: Apple Announces Tiered System, DRM-Free Tunes," The Huffington Post, Jan. 6.   http://www.huffingtonpost.com/2009/01/06/itunes-price-cut-apple-an_n_155660.html

Moore, Ebony (2006) "Make It Count," recording.   http://www.myspace.com/ebonydmoore

Morris, Tee; Tomasi, Chuck; Terra, Evo (2008) "Podcasting for Dummies," 2nd edition. New York: For Dummies/Wiley.

Mumford, Lewis (1970) "The Pentagon of Power." New York: Harcourt, Brace, Jovanovich.

Musil, Steven (2008) "U.S. Army Warns of Twittering Terrorists," CNET News, Oct. 26. http://news.cnet.com/8301-1009_3-10075487-83.html   and   US Army draft report: http://www.fas.org/irp/eprint/mobile.pdf

"My Box in a Box" (2006) Video featuring Melissa Lamb, written and produced by Leah Kauffman and Ben Relles, song performed by Leah Kauffman, Dec. 26. http://www.youtube.com/watch?v=3xElIikoYso

Nadelman, Stefan (2008) "Food Fight," video written, directed, animated by
        Nadelman, Feb. 27.   http://www.youtube.com/watch?v=e-yldqNkGfo

Nakashima, Ryan (2009) "Facing Stagnant Growth, MySpace Shakes Up Top Exec
        Roles," LinuxInsider, April 23.   http://www.linuxinsider.com/story/66883.html

Nash, Kate (2007) MySpace music page, Feb. 18.   http://www.myspace.com/
        katenashmusic

Nathan, Stephen (2007) "The Glowing Bones in the Old Stone House," "Bones,"
        Season 2, Episode 20, directed by Caleb Deschanel, Fox-TV, May 9.

Nature magazine, editors (2006) "Encyclopaedia Britannica and Nature: A Response,"
        Nature, March 23.   http://www.nature.com/press_releases/Britannica_
        response.pdf

NeoPoiesis Press (2009) MySpace page.   http://www.myspace.com/neopoiesispress

NetLingo (2009) "Cyberstalker."   http://www.netlingo.com/word/cyberstalker.php

Newitz, Analee (2007) "I Bought Votes on Digg," Wired, March 1.   http://www.wired
        .com/techbiz/people/news/2007/03/72832

Nissenson, Marilyn (2007) "The Lady Upstairs: Dorothy Schiff and the New York
        Post." New York: St. Martin's.

Obama, Barack (2008) Interviewed by Barbara Walters, "Barbara Walters Special,"
        ABC-TV, Nov. 26.

———— (2008) Interviewed by John Harwood, CNBC-TV, Jan. 7.

O'Brien, Terrence (2008) "Teen Lands in Jail after Posting Baby-Tossing Video on
        YouTube," Switched, July 3.   http://www.switched.com/2008/07/03/teen-
        lands-in-jail-after-posting-baby-tossing-video-on-youtube/

O'Connor, Mickey (2008) "'Fringe': Our Burning Questions Answered!" Interview
        with Jeff Pinker, Fringe Executive Producer, TV Guide, Nov. 11.
        http://www.tvguide.com/News/Fringe-Burning-Questions-58392.aspx

O'Donnell, Norah (2008) Interview with Daily Kos founder Markos Moulitsas
        about Barack Obama and the 'Liberal Blogosphere,' MSNBC, Nov. 22.

———— (2009) Report about Barack Obama and Blackberry, MSNBC, Jan. 18.

Orlando, Carlos (2009) " 'YouTube for Television' to launch via Sony and
        Nintendo," infopackets, Jan. 27.   http://www.infopackets.com/news/business/
        google/2009/20090127_youtube_for_television_to_launch_via_sony_and_
        nintendo.htm

Orlowski, Andrew (2006) "Nature Mag Cooked Wikipedia Study," March 23.
        http://www.theregister.co.uk/2006/03/23/britannica_wikipedia_nature_study/

Palin, Sarah (2008) Interview by Greta Van Susteren, "Fox News," Nov. 11.
        http://www.foxnews.com/story/0,2933,449884,00.html

———— (2008) Interview by Katie Couric, "CBS Evening News," Sept. 30.
        http://www.youtube.com/watch?v=xRkWebP2QoY

Pash, Adam (2008) "Wikipanion Brings Wikipedia to Your iPhone or iPod Touch," lifehacker, Aug. 20.   http://lifehacker.com/400664/wikipanion-brings-wikipedia-to-your-iphone-or-ipod-touch

———— (2008) "Wikipedia Officially Launches Mobile Version," lifehacker, Dec. 15.   http://lifehacker.com/5110289/wikipedia-officially-launches-mobile-version

Patterson, Ben (2009) "White House Stuck in 'Technological Dark Ages,'" The Gadget Hound, Jan. 22.   http://tech.yahoo.com/blogs/patterson/34463

Perez-Pena, Richard (2008) "Newspaper Circulation Continues to Decline Rapidly," The New York Times, Oct. 27.   http://www.nytimes.com/2008/10/28/business/media/28circ.html

———— (2009) "Keeping News of Kidnapping Off Wikipedia," The New York Times, June 28.   http://www.nytimes.com/2009/06/29/technology/internet/29wiki.html

Pershing, Ben (2009) "Kennedy, Byrd the Latest Victims of Wikipedia Errors," The Washington Post, Jan. 21.   http://voices.washingtonpost.com/capitol-briefing/2009/01/kennedy_the_latest_victim_of_w.html

Petroski, Henry (1999) "The Book on the Bookshelf". New York: Knopf.

Phillips, Rich (2008) "Suspects in Video Beating Could Get Life in Prison," CNN.com, April 11.   http://edition.cnn.com/2008/CRIME/04/10/girl.fights/index.html

Popkin, Helen A. S. (2009) "Activism Evolves for the Digital Age," MSNBC.com June 19.   http://www.msnbc.msn.com/id/31432770/ns/technology_and_science-tech_and_gadgets/

Powell, Colin (2008) Interview by Fareed Zakaria on "GPS," CNN, Dec. 14.   transcript: http://transcripts.cnn.com/TRANSCRIPTS/0812/14/fzgps.01.html

"Quantum of Solace" (2008) Directed by Marc Forster, written by Paul Haggis and Neal Purvis & Robert Wade, MGM.

Rahm Emanuel Facts (2009) Web site with quotes from and about Rahm Emanuel.   http://rahmfacts.com

Raphael, J. P. (2008) "Wikipedia Censorship Sparks Free Speech Debate," PC World, Dec. 10.   http://www.washingtonpost.com/wp-dyn/content/article/2008/12/08/AR2008120803188.html

Reardon, Marguerite (2009) "Smartphones Offer Hope in Declining Cell Phone Biz," CNET News, Feb. 4.   http://news.cnet.com/8301-1035_3-10156897-94.html

Reilly, Cameron (2009) Interview by Mark Hunter about the "death of newspapers," Podcastmatters Social Media podcast, Feb. 6.   http://socialmediapodcast.tumblr.com/post/76150739/edition-2-twestival-swearing-and-cameron-reilly

Reuters, Adam (2006) "Surge in High-End Second Life Business Profits," Reuters, Dec. 5.   http://secondlife.reuters.com/stories/2006/12/05/surge-in-high-end-second-life-business-profits/

Rheingold, Howard (2003) "Smart Mobs: The Next Social Revolution." New York: Basic.

Ribeiro, John (2008) "In Mumbai, Bloggers and Twitter Offer Help to Relatives," IDG News, PC World, Nov. 27.   http://www.pcworld.com/article/154621/ in_mumbai_bloggers_and_twitter_offer_help_to_relatives.html

Richards, I. A. (1929) "Practical Criticism". London: K. Paul.

Riley, Duncan (2007) "CSI: NY Comes to Second Life Wednesday," TechCrunch, Oct. 20. http://www.techcrunch.com/2007/10/20/csiny-comes-to-second-life-wednesday/ *and* videoclip: http://www.youtube.com/watch?v=3-ZmjA7GCzQ

Roark, James L.; Johnson, Michael P.; Cohen, Patricia Cline; Stage, Sarah; Lawson, Alan; and Hartmann, Susan M. (2007) "The American Promise." Boston: Bedford/St. Martin's Press, p. 719.

Rose, Carl (1951) "What's That, Mama?" cartoon, about radio in the attic, The New Yorker, July 28.

Rove, Karl (2009) "Back in Washington…" Twitter, Feb. 14.   http://twitter.com/karlrove

Ryan, Jenny (2008) "The Virtual Campfire: An Ethnography of Online Social Networking," thesis, Master of Arts in Anthropology, Wesleyan University, May.

Saffo, Paul (2008) "Obama's 'Cybergenic' Edge," abcnews.com, June 11. http://abcnews.go.com/Technology/Politics/Story?id=5046275

Sagan, Carl (1978) "The Dragons of Eden." New York: Ballantine.

Saleem, Muhammad (2006) Interview by Tony Hung, "Insights From an Elite Social Bookmarker," BloggerTalks, Nov.   http://www.bloggertalks.com/2006/11/ muhammad-saleem-insights-from-an-elite-social-bookmarker/

———— (2007) "Ron Paul Supporters Need a Lesson in Social Media Marketing," Pronet Advertising, July 6.   http://www.pronetadvertising.com/articles/ron-paul-supporters-need-a-lesson-in-social-media-marketing34389.html

———— (2007) "Ruining the Digg Experience, One Shout at a Time," Social Media Strategy for New Entrepreneurs, Oct. 31.   http://muhammadsaleem.com/ 2007/10/31/ruining-the-digg-experience-one-shout-at-a-time/

———— (2007) "The Bury Brigade Exists, and Here's My Proof," Pronet Advertising, Feb. 27.   http://www.pronetadvertising.com/articles/the-bury-brigade-exists-and-heres-my-proof.html

———— (2007) "The Social Media Manual—Read Before You Play," .docstoc, Nov. 20.   http://www.docstoc.com/docs/265428/The-Social-Media-Manual--by-Muhammad-Saleem

Sansone, Ron (2007) "Digg Dirt: Exposing Ron Paul's Social Media Manipulation," iAOC blog (International Association of Online Communications), July 3. http://www.iaocblog.com/blog/_archives/2007/7/3/3068799.html

Sawyer, Miranda (2006) "Pictures of Lily," The Observer, Guardian, May 21. http://www.guardian.co.uk/music/2006/may/21/popandrock.lilyallen

Schmidt, Eric (2008) Guest on "The Rachel Maddow Show," MSNBC-TV, Nov. 17.

Schonfeld, Eric (2009) "Twitter Surges Past Digg, LinkedIn, And NYTimes.com With 32 Million Global Visitors," Techcrunch, May 20.   http://www.techcrunch.com/2009/05/20/twitter-surges-past-digg-linkedin-and-nytimescom-with-32-million-global-visitors/

Schwartz, Mattathias (2008) "The Trolls Among Us," The New York Times, Aug. 3. http://www.nytimes.com/2008/08/03/magazine/03trolls-t.html

Scorsese, Martin (2005) "No Direction Home," movie documentary about Bob Dylan. Paramount.

Sharma, Dinesh C. (2005) "Podcast Start-Up Creates Music Network," CNET News, Aug. 23.   http://news.cnet.com/Podcast-start-up-creates-music-network/2100-027_3-5841888.html

Sharp, David (2008) "Audio Book Sales Are Booming—What Makes Them So Great?" ezine articles, Dec. 22.   http://ezinearticles.com/?Audio-Book-Sales-Are-Booming—What-Makes-Them-So-Great?&id=1814019

Shawn, Eric (2008) Report about Facebook groups, Fox News television, Dec. 1.

Sierra, Kathy (2007) "My Favorite Graphs … And the Future," Creating Passionate Users blog, April 6.   http://headrush.typepad.com/

Silversmith, David (2009) "Google Losing up to $1.65M a Day on YouTube," Internet Evolution, April 14.   http://www.internetevolution.com/author.asp?section_id=715&doc_id=175123&

Sinderbrand, Rebecca and Wells, Rachel (2008) "Obama Takes Top Billing on U.S. Television," CNN.com, Oct. 29.   http://edition.cnn.com/2008/POLITICS/10/29/campaign.wrap.spending/index.html

Sirota, David (2008) "The Politico's Jayson Blair," Open Salon, Dec. 7. http://open.salon.com/content.php?cid=57773

Sklar, Rachel (2007) "A Crush on Obama, And an Eye on the Prize," The Huffington Post, July 16.   http://www.huffingtonpost.com/2007/07/16/a-crush-on-obama-and-an-e_n_53057.html

Smith, Justin (2008) "Facebook Infrastructure up to 10,000 Web Servers," Inside Facebook blog, April 23.   http://www.insidefacebook.com/2008/04/23/facebook-infrastructure-up-to-10000-web-servers/

Smith, Shepard (2008) "Fox Report with Shepard Smith," Fox News, Dec. 2.

Socialmediatrader (2008) "What Would Happen if the US Elections Were Held on Digg?" Jan. 18.   http://socialmediatrader.com/what-would-happen-if-the-us-elections-were-held-on-digg/

Spiegel, Brendan (2007) "Ron Paul: How a Fringe Politician Took Over the Web," Wired, June 27.   http://www.wired.com/politics/onlinerights/news/2007/06/ron_paul

Stirland, Sarah Lai (2007) "News Recommendation Site Launches 'Digg The Candidates': Ron Paul & Obama End Up on Top," Wired, Nov. 21. http://blog.wired.com/27bstroke6/2007/11/news-recommenda.html

"Stop the 'Doc Bloc' on MSNBC" (2008) Facebook group. http://www.facebook.com/group.php?gid=49254779160

Stranahan, Lee (2008) "Markos, John, & Elizabeth: How Daily Kos Keeps Swallowing The Kool-Aid," The Huffington Post, Aug. 12. http://www.huffingtonpost.com/lee-stranahan/markos-john-elizabeth-how_b_118343.html

Strate, Lance (2007) BlogVersed, Lance Strate's MySpace blog. http://blogs.myspace.com/index.cfm?fuseaction=blog.view&friendID=176504380&blogID=284027048

Stuart, Sarah Clarke ("swampburbia") (2009) "The Infinite Narrative: Intertextuality, New Media and the Digital Communities of 'Lost,'" syllabus, University of North Florida course, Spring. http://lostinlit.wordpress.com

Suellontrop, Chris (2008) "The Kerry Surprise," The New York Times, Aug. 28. http://opinionator.blogs.nytimes.com/2008/08/28/the-kerry-surprise/

Sullivan, Andrew (2008) "The Kerry Speech," The Daily Dish, Aug. 28. http://andrewsullivan.theatlantic.com/the_daily_dish/2008/08/the-kerry-speec.html

Talamasca, Akela (2008) "Second Life on an iPhone," Massively, Feb. 13. http://www.massively.com/2008/02/13/second-life-on-an-iphone/

Talkshoe (2009) "New to Talkshoe?" http://www.talkshoe.com/se/about/TSAbout.html

Teachout, Zephyr and Streeter, Thomas, et al. (2008) "Mousepads, Shoe Leather, and Hope: Lessons from the Howard Dean Campaign for the Future of Internet Politics." Boulder, Co., and London: Paradigm.

Technology Expert (2008) "Texting More Popular than Talking: Report," Tech-Ex, Sept. 29. http://technologyexpert.blogspot.com/2008/09/texting-more-popu-lar-than-calling.html

Techradar (2008) "Facebook, MySpace Statistics," Jan. 11. http://techradar1.wordpress.com/2008/01/11/facebookmyspace-statistics/

Tedford, Thomas (1985) "Freedom of Speech in the United States." New York: Random House.

Terdiman, Daniel (2008) "AMC Decides to Allow Fans' 'Mad Men' Twittering," CNET News, Aug. 27. http://news.cnet.com/8301-13772_3-10027152-52.html

"Terminator: The Sarah Connor Chronicles" (2008) Season 2, Episode 10, Fox TV series, Nov. 24.

"Terminator: The Sarah Connor Chronicles" (2008) Season 2, Episode 13, Fox TV series, Dec. 15.

"The New Millennium: Science, Fiction, Fantasy" (2000) Fox News TV special, Jan. 1.

Themediaisdying (2009). http://www.twitter.com/themediaisdying

Time (2008) Magazine cover, Nov. 24.

TMZ staff (2006) "'Kramer's' Racist Tirade—Caught on Tape," TMZ, Nov. 20. http://www.tmz.com/2006/11/20/kramers-racist-tirade-caught-on-tape/

Todd, Brian (2008) Report on bloggers nixing presidential appointment, CNN, Dec. 26.

Tossell, Ivor (2008) "Teeny-Tiny Twitter was the Year's Big Story," Globe and Mail, Dec. 25. http://www.theglobeandmail.com/servlet/story/RTGAM .20081225.wwebtossell1226/EmailBNStory/Technology/home

Trippi, Joe (2004) "The Revolution Will Not Be Televised: Democracy, the Internet, and the Overthrow of Everything." New York: William Morrow.

Truth on Earth Band (2008) "Shot with a Bulletless Gun," recording. http://www.truthonearthband.com/song_bulletlessgun.html *and* MySpace page: http://www.myspace.com/truthonearthband

Valéry, Paul (1933) "Au Sujet Du Cimetière Marin," reprinted in "Oeuvres de Paul Valéry," Paris: Gallimard, La Pléiade, 1957.

Van Grove, Jennifer (2009) "One Giant Leap for Twitterkind; Mike Massimino Tweets from Space," Mashable, May 12. http://mashable.com/2009/05/12/first-tweet-from-space/

VanDenPlas, Scott (2007) "Ron Paul, Barack Obama, and the Digital Divide," morefishthanman.com, May 21. http://www.morefishthanman.com/ 2007/05/21/ron-paul-barack-obama-and-the-digital-divide/

Vance, Ashlee (2009) "Online Video of Inauguration Sets Records," The New York Times, Jan. 20. http://www.nytimes.com/2009/01/21/us/politics/21video.htm

Vargas, Jose Antonio (2007) "On Wikipedia, Debating 2008 Hopefuls' Every Facet," The Washington Post, Sept. 17. http://www.washingtonpost.com/wp-dyn/ content/article/2007/09/16/AR2007091601699_pf.html

Vedro, Steven (2007) "Digital Dharma." Wheaton, IL: Quest Books.

Wales, Jimmy (2009) Interview by Mark Molaro, The Alcove, May 26. video: http://www.youtube.com/watch?v=e1t88Bul5is

Walsh, Joan (2007) "Men Who Hate Women on the Web," Salon.com, March 31. http://www.salon.com/opinion/feature/2007/03/31/sierra/

——— (2008) Comment on Paul Levinson's "Obama Should Reject McCain's Call to Postpone Friday's Debate," Open Salon, Sept. 24. http://open.salon.com/ content.php?cid=21963

Washington Post (2008) "President-Elect Obama's First YouTube Address," Nov. 15. http://voices.washingtonpost.com/44/2008/11/15/president-elect_obamas_first_y .html *and* video: www.youtube.com/watch?v=uYVRzNkmvfc

Wastler, Allen (2007) "An Open Letter to the Ron Paul Faithful," Political Capital with John Harwood blog, CNBC.com, Oct. 11. http://www.cnbc.com/id/21257762

"Weeds" (2009) Season 5, Episode 1, Showtime TV series, June 8.

Weist, Zena (2009) "Twitterers: How Old Are You?" Nothin' but SocNET, Feb. 21.
http://nothingbutsocnet.blogspot.com/2008/02/twitterers-how-old-are-you.html

Wellman, Barry (2008) "I Was a WikiWarrior for Barack Obama," CITASA, Nov. 8.
http://list.citasa.org/pipermail/citasa_list.citasa.org/2008-November/
000057.html

Wertheimer, Linda (2008) "Age Likely to Be Key Factor in Presidential Campaign,"
National Public Radio, June 24. Also, quoted in full on this page: Liasson, Mara
(2008) "Parsing the Generational Divide for Democrats," National Public Radio,
May 1.   http://www.npr.org/templates/story/story.php?storyId=91853809

White House Blog, The (2009) "Change Has Come to WhiteHouse.gov," Jan. 20.
http://www.whitehouse.gov/blog/change_has_come_to_whitehouse-gov/

Wikipedia (2009) "Blog."   http://en.wikipedia.org/wiki/Blogging

———— (2009) "Category: Wikipedia Behavioral Guidelines."   http://en.wikipedia
.org/wiki/Category:Wikipedia_behavioral_guidelines

———— (2009) "Conflict of Interest."   http://en.wikipedia.org/wiki/Wikipedia:COI

———— (2009) "Kate Nash."   http://en.wikipedia.org/wiki/Kate_Nash

———— (2009) "Lily Allen."   http://en.wikipedia.org/wiki/Lily_Allen

———— (2009) "List of James Bond gadgets."   http://en.wikipedia.org/wiki/
List_of_James_Bond_gadgets

———— (2009) "Mignon Fogarty."   http://en.wikipedia.org/wiki/Mignon_Fogarty

———— (2009) "Sean Kingston."   http://en.wikipedia.org/wiki/Sean_Kingston

———— (2009) "The Traveling Wilburys."   http://en.wikipedia.org/wiki/The_
Traveling_Wilburys

———— (2009) "Virgin Killer" (Scorpions album, with nude girl on cover).
http://en.wikipedia.org/wiki/Virgin_Killer

———— (2009) "Web 3.0."   http://en.wikipedia.org/wiki/Web_3.0

———— (2009) "Wikipedia servers."   http://en.wikipedia.org/wiki/Wikipedia#
Software_and_hardware

Winfield, Nicole (2009) "Vatican 2.0: Pope Gets His Own YouTube Channel,"
Associated Press, Jan. 23.   http://www.twine.com/item/11txv7jzw-ns/vatican-
2-0-pope-gets-his-own-youtube-channel-yahoo-news

Winograd, Morley and Hais, Michael D. (2008) "Millennial Makeover: MySpace,
YouTube, and the Future of American Politics." New Brunswick, NJ, and
London: Rutgers University Press.

Wortham, Jenna (2008) "'Puppy Torture' Video Sparks Outrage, Military
Investigation," Wired, March 4.   http://blog.wired.com/underwire/
2008/03/puppy-torture-v.html

Wright, Benjamin and Winn, Jane K. (1998) "The Law of Electronic Commerce," 3rd ed. Aspen, Co.: Aspen Law & Business.

Young, Neil (2009) "Fork in the Road," song.　http://www.youtube.com/watch?v=m7L7XsHKCVs

Zavis, Alexandra (2009) "Judge Tentatively Dismisses Case in MySpace Hoax That Led to Teenage Girl's Suicide," Los Angeles Times, July 2. http://latimesblogs.latimes.com/lanow/2009/07/myspace-sentencing.html/

Zeleny, Jeff (2008) "Lose the BlackBerry? Yes He Can, Maybe," The New York Times, Nov. 15.　http://www.nytimes.com/2008/11/16/us/politics/16blackberry.html

Zenter, Kim (2008) "Experts Say MySpace Suicide Indictment Sets 'Scary' Legal Precedent," Wired.com, May 15.　http://blog.wired.com/27bstroke6/2008/05/myspace-indictm.html

——— (2008) "Lori Drew Not Guilty of Felonies in Landmark Cyberbullying Trial," Wired.com, Nov. 26.　http://blog.wired.com/27bstroke6/2008/11/lori-drew-pla-5.html

Ziegler, John (2009) "Media Malpractice," film documentary. videoclip: http://www.youtube.com/watch?v=qXnG8rxOdvQ

Zunes, Stephen (2009) "Iran's History of Civil Insurrections," The Huffington Post, June 19.　http://www.huffingtonpost.com/stephen-zunes/irans-history-of-civil-in_b_217998.html

Zurawik, David (2008) "Is Obama the First 'Cybergenic' Candidate?" Baltimore Sun, Aug. 12.　http://www.mediachannel.org/wordpress/2008/08/12/is-obama-the-first-cybergenic-candidate/

about the author

PAUL LEVINSON'S eight nonfiction books—including "The Soft Edge" (1997), "Digital McLuhan" (1999), "Realspace" (2003), and "Cellphone" (2004)—have been the subject of major articles in the New York Times, Wired, the Christian Science Monitor, and have been translated into ten languages. His science fiction novels include "The Silk Code" (1999, winner of the Locus Award for Best First Novel), "Borrowed Tides" (2001), "The Consciousness Plague" (2002), "The Pixel Eye" (2003), and "The Plot To Save Socrates" (2006). His short stories have been nominated for Nebula, Hugo, Edgar, and Sturgeon Awards. Paul Levinson appears on "The O'Reilly Factor" (Fox News), "The CBS Evening News," "NewsHour with Jim Lehrer" (PBS), "Nightline" (ABC), and numerous national and international TV and radio programs. He reviews the best of television in his InfiniteRegress.tv blog, and was listed in The Chronicle of Higher Education's "Top 10 Academic Twitterers" in 2009. Paul Levinson is a Professor of Communication & Media Studies at Fordham University in New York City.